CASE STUDIES IN

CULTURAL ANTHROPOLOGY

GENERAL EDITORS

George and Louise Spindler

STANFORD UNIVERSITY

YĄNOMAMÖ

The Fierce People

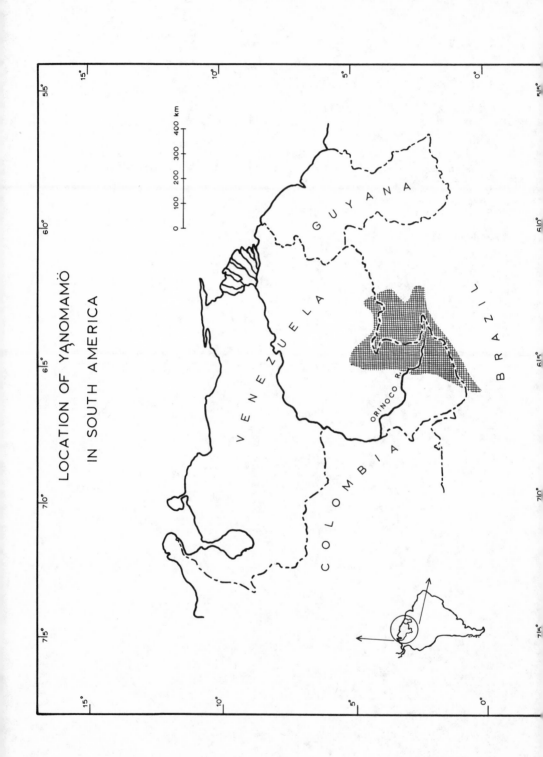

LOCATION OF YĄNOMAMÖ
IN SOUTH AMERICA

YĄNOMAMÖ

The Fierce People
Second Edition

By

NAPOLEON A. CHAGNON

Pennsylvania State University

HOLT, RINEHART AND WINSTON

NEW YORK   CHICAGO   SAN FRANCISCO   ATLANTA

DALLAS   MONTREAL   TORONTO   LONDON

To Kąobawä, Rerebawä and Dedeheiwä, valiant and cherished friends who taught me much about being human.

Cover Photograph: Kąobawä, headman of Bisaasi-teri, trading with his allies in Reyaboböwei-teri.

Library of Congress Cataloging in Publication Data

Chagnon, Napoleon A.   1938–
  Yąnomamö, the fierce people.

  (Case studies in cultural anthropology)
  Bibliography: p. 167
  Includes index.
  1. Yąnomamö Indians. I. Title. II. Series.
F2520.1.Y3C5 1977   301.29′174′98   76-46431
ISBN: 0-03-089978-8

Foreword

About the Series

These case studies in cultural anthropology are designed to bring to students, in beginning and intermediate courses in the social sciences, insights into the richness and complexity of human life as it is lived in different ways and in different places. They are written by men and women who have lived in the societies they write about and who are professionally trained as observers and interpreters of human behavior. The authors are also teachers, and in writing their books they have kept the students who will read them foremost in their minds. It is our belief that when an understanding of ways of life very different from one's own is gained, abstractions and generalizations about social structure, cultural values, subsistence techniques, and the other universal categories of human social behavior become meaningful.

About the Author

Napoleon A. Chagnon was born the second of twelve children in Port Austin, Michigan, in 1938. He is married and has two children. He began his academic training in the Michigan College of Mining and Technology at Sault Ste. Marie (now Lake Superior State College) in the physics curriculum. After one year there, he transferred to the University of Michigan, changed his major to anthropology, and received his B.A. (1961), his M.A. (1963), and Ph.D. (1966) in anthropology at the University of Michigan. After earning his Ph.D., he joined the faculty of the Department of Human Genetics at the University of Michigan's Medical School from which base he participated in an extensive multidisciplinary study of the Yąnomamö Indians. Dr. Chagnon also held a joint appointment in the Department of Anthropology at the University of Michigan until 1972, when he moved to Pennsylvania State University. He is currently Professor of Anthropology at the Pennsylvania State University and continues to study the Yąnomamö with the assistance of his graduate students. To date, Chagnon has made ten field trips to the Yąnomamö and has published dozens of articles about his findings in a wide range of professional and popular scientific journals. He has also produced a large number of documentary films on the Yąnomamö. The twenty-one films currently in distribution have been widely used in anthropology courses as a supplement to the first edition to this case study (see pp. 170–172).

About the Book

This is indeed a book about a fierce people. Yąnomamö culture, in its major focus, reverses the meanings of "good" and "desirable" as phrased in the ideal postulates of the Judaic-Christian tradition. A high capacity for rage, a quick flash point, and a willingness to use violence to obtain one's ends are considered desirable traits. Much of the behavior of the Yąnomamö can be described as brutal, cruel, treacherous, in the value-ladened terms of our own vocabulary. The Yąnomamö themselves, however, as Napoleon Chagnon came to intimately know them in the year and a half he lived with them, do not all appear to be mean and treacherous. As individuals, they seem to be people playing their own cultural game, with internal feelings that at times may be quite divergent from the demands placed upon them by their culture. This case study furnishes valuable data for phrasing questions about the relationship between the individual and his culture.

The Yąnomamö appear to be constantly on the verge of extranormal behavior, as we define it, and their almost daily use of hallucinogenic drugs reinforces these drives to what might seem to the outside observer to be the limits of human capacity. Life in their villages is noisy, punctuated by outbursts of violence, threatened by destruction by enemies. To the ethnographer it is frightening, frustrating, disgusting, exciting, and rewarding, and in this case study the ethnographer lets the reader know how he feels. His honest reactions help us, as interested outsiders, to know the Yąnomamö.

This is a study of a fierce people who engage in chronic warfare. It is also a study of a system of controls that usually hold in check the drive toward annihilation. Conflict among the Yąnomamö is regulated through a series of graded escalations, from chest-pounding and side-slapping duels, through club fighting, spear throwing, to raiding in a state of war, to the ultimate—the *nomohoni*—massacre by treachery. The processes of avoidance, settlement, or escalation of disputes are discussed in detail in this case study. There are implications that range beyond the Yąnomamö, and beyond primitive peoples, to the "civilized" world in which we live, for we too live in a state of chronic warfare and are threatened by annihilation.

The Yąnomamö goad each other, within their own villages, to the brink of an explosion (and they goaded the ethnographer in the same way). This hostility is projected on a larger scale in the negotiating of alliances between villages. Each principal must establish the credibility of his own threats, as well as discover the point at which the opposite party's bluffing will dissolve into action. It is, as the author says, a politics of brinksmanship, all too familiar to us.

The study is, however, not confined to a description of regulated violence. Dr. Chagnon provides us with an unusually clear chapter on social organization, with the genealogical details of kinship. The models he produces in his analysis are cast in sharper relief because he also discusses deviations from these models in actual behavior. He links social organization with the processes of fission that produce new villages and the alliances that are created in response to the threat of annihilation, reinforced and validated by the mutual ceding of women between villages. Social organization is presented not as an abstraction but as a dynamic process interrelated with other significant dimensions of life. The anthropological novice will find the analysis of social organization detailed but, with close attention, entirely understandable. The more experienced anthropological reader will grasp the full theoretical implications of the analysis and will find the author's references to various debates in the anthropological literature stimulating.

This case study is given fuller treatment in respect to both the number of photographs and diagrams and text length than is typical in the case study series, due to the unusual nature of the material.

About the Second Edition

As teachers of the introductory course at Stanford there is no question we have been asked more frequently by our students than "What is happening to the Yąnomamö?" These students know that the twentieth century pace of change and the continuing expansion of Western technology and material culture are unlikely to leave even the most remote tribal people untouched. Many of them express the hope that somehow the Yąnomamö, whom they have come to know rather well through this case study, Chagnon's *Studying the Yąnomamö,* and the films by Timothy Asch and Chagnon, have managed to escape the sad fate of most of the other tribal peoples they have studied. The chapter added to the case study in this new edition is addressed to this question.

Western material culture, first in the form of machetes, pots, axes and knives, then shotguns and outboard motors, and clothing, has become a part of the way of life in some Yąnomamö villages. More important is the social impact of missionaries and, in recent years, tourists. Whether relatively tolerant or rigidly orthodox or evangelistic, the purpose of missionaries is to convert "pagans" to Christianity. This purpose strikes at the heart of any ongoing culture. World view and values, and moral justification for behavior, as well as rituals and even social and economic organization, are interpenetrated and supported by religious belief and related behaviors. Everywhere, where the West has met tribal societies, inevitable technological and material change has been accompanied by pressures to forego native religious belief and practice and accept Christianity. This has complicated the adaptive process, it would seem, unnecessarily. Why should tribal peoples have to become Christian, with all the self-doubt and loss of identity this entails, to use the tools of the West and the concepts behind them? The drive to convert and the drive to colonize seem to be expressions of the underlying ethnocentrism of Western culture. Chagnon's treatment of the missionary–Yąnamamö interaction will challenge many readers.

Tourists and missionaries are not the same in purpose, style of interaction with the Yąnomamö, or in their impact upon them. Tourists have a relatively shallow grasp of Yąnomamö life and are in Yąnomamö territory only for self-gratification. But tourists present models and introduce new images of the outside world to the Yąnomamö and the support activities on their behalf have a significant impact upon both the people and the environment. The consequences of their presence have not been good.

Chagnon points out that the Venezuelan government has a moral responsibility to see that the impact of missionaries, tourists, and other sources of change and potential exploitation is regulated with the interests of the Yąnomamö uppermost. The United States is not in a particularly good position to advocate restraint and humane treatment of tribal peoples, given the tragic history of Anglo-European and Native American relationships in our country. Chagnon speaks to the Venezuelan government with this history in mind.

Chagnon ends the new chapter with some comments on the "fierce" image that tends to dominate our thinking about the Yąnomamö. In reading our own About the Book for the first edition (above) we are struck by the extent to which this characterization dominates our communication. It is useful for Chagnon to argue for a more balanced view and yet hold out for an interpretation that places the Yąnomamö within the range of normal, pre-Western tribal life.

GEORGE AND LOUISE SPINDLER
General Editors

November 1976

Preface to Second Edition

I knew, in 1964, when I began living with the Yąnomamö that I was, as a social scientist, racing against time and the inevitability of the acculturation pressures that would affect and transform their culture, that it was an open question whether I could witness, document, and explain the many subtle and delicate cultural and demographic patterns that were certain to change with increased contact with our kind of culture. It was clear that the Yąnomamö were one of the last sovereign tribes, one of the last opportunities that anthropology would have to understand particular features of a truly primitive cultural adaptation. I found it especially sobering to realize that the twentieth century would witness the end—the extinction—of particular varieties of culture that had endured for thousands of years, that tribal culture was an endangered and vanishing social species, and that I had some sort of professional and personal responsibility to record and document what I could before it was altered or destroyed by our culture. That is why I spent 48 months among them rather than the more common 12-month field trip. I hoped, as a teacher and researcher, that I could convey some sense of reality and dignity about life in such a culture and that my efforts would be somewhat more than a mere catalogue of "cultural traits" and statistical frequencies.

Thus, in 1967, as I wrote the first draft of *Yąnomamö: The Fierce People,* I decided that I would let my own experiences as a student be my guide as an author, for I wanted as much to communicate with students of anthropology as with my professional colleagues. I remember my student days and how much I enjoyed reading monographs that were sprinkled with real people, that described real events, and that had some sweat and tears, some smells and sentiments mingled with the words. I especially enjoyed reading the works of other anthropologists who quoted their informants, for the natives seemed forever to know and communicate more about the nature of the real world, as they perceived it, than their observers . . . or perhaps their observers recognized in the native's summary something that could not be communicated by academic prose. I'll always remember reading Douglas Oliver's enchanting description of Soñgi, a Solomon Island big man, his rise to reknown, how he manipulated his culture's institutions and how he dispensed favors to create obligations among kinsmen in his ascent to prominence (Oliver 1955: chap. 13). Accordingly, when I wrote *Yąnomamö: The Fierce People,* I tried to infuse my descriptions of Yąnomamö culture with the real events and real people that made the general seem more comprehensible because specific people—a sensitive headman, a boisterous youth, an aggressive warrior—were involved in and acted out the events of their culture. I felt then and am convinced by the enthusiastic reception the first edition received that the complexity, dignity, and substance of another culture can be made to come alive in the formal process of anthropological education, and I sincerely thank my many colleagues and students who share that perspective with me.

The most commonly asked questions put to me by students of anthropology have to do with "how did they accept you" and "did you ever try their drugs?" The final chapter of this edition provides a partial answer to these questions, but within the matrix of issues that range far beyond academic curiosity. The reciprocal and generally good-natured mischief with which the Yąnomamö and I treated each other during my first 15-month stay among them gradually evolved into a much warmer and more intimate relationship as I returned to live among them nearly every year since I wrote the first edition of *Yąnomamö: The Fierce People*. On my most recent field trip (1975) I was amused by the candor of one of my long-time friends as he reflected about my early days in his village. "I remember when you first came to live with us," he said as we dozed in our hammocks on some trail between two remote villages, waiting for night to come. "We could really intimidate and trick you then and make you give away vast quantities of valuable goods for almost nothing and convince you that it was a fair bargain." He laughed aloud and sighed: "Those days are gone, for you know the language too well now, and you have become just like us . . . you know how to trade. You have become a Yąnomamö." It has been a great privilege to live among the Yąnomamö and take an intimate glimpse beyond history, whither we came, and to better understand where we presently are.

N. A. C.

November 1976

Acknowledgments

The research on which this monograph is based was supported by the National Institute of Mental Health Predoctoral Fellowship Fl MH–25–052 and attached grant MH 10575–01 BEH RO4 and an Atomic Energy Commission Area Grant AT(11–1)–1552. I am also indebted to the faculty and administration of Instituto Venezolano de Investigaciones Científicas (I.V.I.C.) for their cooperation and support. I wish also to thank the members of the Staff of the Air Force of Venezuela and Brazil for transporting me and my equipment into and out of the Yąnomamö area. I am equally indebted to the Venezuelan Malarialogía personnel who arranged for the purchase and transportation of many of my supplies. My sincere thanks also to the members of the New Tribes Mission and Salesian Mission, whose kindness and cooperation made my field work more pleasant than it might otherwise have been. I am grateful to Professors Eric Wolf, Mervyn Meggitt, James Neel, Elman Service, and Leslie White of my Ph.D. committee for many useful suggestions; this monograph is based in part on my doctoral thesis, and their criticisms have been incorporated into the present work. I wish to thank Professors Marshall Sahlins, Eric Wolf, and Lévi-Strauss for reading earlier drafts of some of the chapters in the present monograph. I thank my wife Carlene for her patience in reading portions of the text and offering her helpful criticisms. Finally, I wish to thank my brother, Verdun P. Chagnon, for his artistic rendition of Figure 2–4.

Contents

Visitors waiting in village circle for hosts to invite them "home" (described in Chapter 4).

Shaman (carrying club) chanting to Hekura (demons) while curing a patient (man sitting in foreground). Patient later died of malaria (described in Chapter 2).

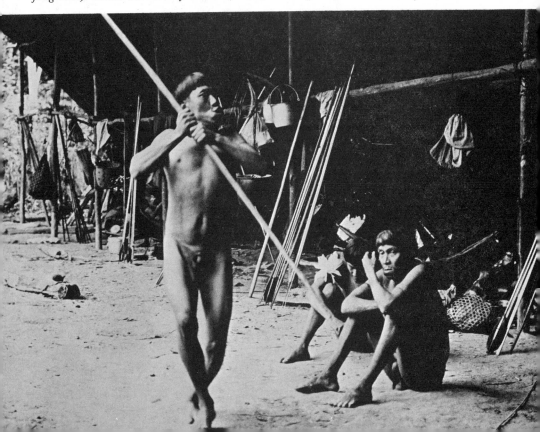

Clay pots and banana (plantain) peelings; preparations for a feast (described in Chapter 4). Note quantities of plantains hanging up and on the ground.

Monou-teri men shooting at a wooden dummy (in hammock) in a mock raid. They left on the actual raid the next day (described in Chapter 5).

1

Doing Fieldwork among the Yąnomamö

THE YĄNOMAMÖ[1] INDIANS live in southern Venezuela and the adjacent portions of northern Brazil (see frontispiece map, p. iv). Some 125 widely scattered villages have populations ranging from 40 to 250 inhabitants, with 75 to 80 people the most usual number. In total numbers their population probably approaches 10,000 people, but this is merely a guess. Many of the villages have not yet been contacted by outsiders, and nobody knows for sure exactly how many uncontacted villages there are, or how many people live in them. By comparison to African or Melanesian tribes, the Yąnomamö population is small. Still, they are one of the largest unacculturated tribes left in all of South America.

But they have a significance apart from tribal size and cultural purity: the Yąnomamö are still actively conducting warfare. It is in the nature of man to fight, according to one of their myths, because the blood of "Moon" spilled on this layer of the cosmos, causing men to become fierce. I describe the Yąnomamö as "the fierce people" because that is the most accurate single phrase that describes them. That is how they conceive themselves to be, and that is how they would like others to think of them.

I spent nineteen months with the Yąnomamö,[2] during which time I acquired some proficiency in their language and, up to a point, submerged myself in their culture and

---

[1]The word Yąnomamö is nasalized through its entire length, indicated by the diacritical mark [ą]. When this mark appears on a word, the entire word is nasalized. The terminal vowel [-ö] represents a sound that does not occur in the English language. It corresponds to the phone [ɨ] of linguistic orthography. In normal conversation, Yąnomamö is pronounced like "Yah-no-mama," except that it is nasalized. Finally, the words having the [-ä] vowel are pronounced at that vowel with the "uh" sound of "duck." Thus, the name Kąobawä would be pronounced "cow-ba-wuh," again nasalized.

[2]I spent a total of twenty-three months in South America of which nineteen were spent among the Yąnomamö on three separate field trips. The first trip, November 1964 through February 1966, was to Venezuela. During this time I spent thirteen months in direct contact with the Yąnomamö, using my periodic trips back to Caracas to visit my family and to collate the genealogical data I had collected up to that point. On my second trip, January through March 1967, I spent two months among Brazilian Yąnomamö and one more month with the Venezuelan Yąnomamö. Finally, I returned to Venezuela for three more months among the Yąnomamö, January through April 1968.

1

Fig. 1-1. Members of allied villages engaged in a chest-pounding duel which followed a feast.

way of life. The thing that impressed me most was the importance of aggression in their culture. I had the opportunity to witness a good many incidents that expressed individual vindictiveness on the one hand and collective bellicosity on the other. These ranged in seriousness from the ordinary incidents of wife beating and chest pounding to dueling and organized raiding by parties that set out with the intention of ambushing and killing men from enemy villages (Fig. 1-1). One of the villages discussed in the chapters that follow was raided approximately twenty-five times while I conducted the fieldwork, six times by the group I lived among.

The fact that the Yąnomamö live in a state of chronic warfare is reflected in their mythology, values, settlement pattern, political behavior, and marriage practices. Accordingly, I have organized this case study in such a way that students can appreciate the effects of warfare on Yąnamamö culture in general and on their social organization and politics in particular (Fig. 1–2).

I collected the data under somewhat trying circumstances, some of which I will describe in order to give the student a rough idea of what is generally meant when anthropologists speak of "culture shock" and "fieldwork." It should be borne in mind, however, that each field situation is in many respects unique, so that the problems I encountered do not necessarily exhaust the range of possible problems other anthropologists have confronted in other areas. There are a few problems, however, that seem to be nearly universal among anthropological fieldworkers, particularly those having to do with eating, bathing, sleeping, lack of privacy and loneliness, or discovering that primitive man is not always as noble as you originally thought.

This is not to state that primitive man everywhere is unpleasant. By way of contrast, I have also done limited fieldwork among the Yąnomamö's northern neighbors, the Carib-speaking Makiritare Indians. This group was very pleasant and charming, all

Fig. 1–2. One way that warfare affects other aspects of Yąnomamö social organization is in the great significance of intervillage alliances. Here members of an allied village dance excitedly in their hosts' village in anticipation of the feast and chest-pounding duel that will follow.

of them anxious to help me and honor bound to show any visitor the numerous courtesies of their system of etiquette. In short, they approached the image of primitive man that I had conjured up, and it was sheer pleasure to work with them. The recent work by Colin Turnbull (1966) brings out dramatically the contrast in personal characteristics of two African peoples he has studied.

Hence, what I say about some of my experiences is probably equally true of the experiences of many other fieldworkers. I write about my own experiences because there is a conspicuous lack of fieldwork descriptions available to potential fieldworkers. I think I could have profited by reading about the private misfortunes of my own teachers; at least I might have been able to avoid some of the more stupid errors I made. In this regard there are a number of recent contributions by fieldworkers describing some of the discomforts and misfortunes they themselves sustained.[3] Students planning to conduct fieldwork are urged to consult them.

My first day in the field illustrated to me what my teachers meant when they spoke of "culture shock." I had traveled in a small, aluminum rowboat propelled by a large outboard motor for two and a half days. This took me from the Territorial capital, a small town on the Orinoco River, deep into Yąnomamö country. On the morning of the third day we reached a small mission settlement, the field "headquarters" of a group of Americans who were working in two Yąnomamö villages. The missionaries had come out of these villages to hold their annual conference on the progress of their mission work, and were conducting their meetings when I arrived. We picked up a passenger at the mission station, James P. Barker, the first non-Yąnomamö to make a sustained, permanent contact with the tribe (in 1950). He had just returned from a year's furlough in the United States, where I had earlier visited him before leaving for Venezuela. He agreed to accompany me to the village I had selected for my base of operations to introduce me to the Indians. This village was also his own home base, but he had not been there for over a year and did not plan to join me for another three months. Mr. Barker had been living with this particular group about five years.

We arrived at the village, Bisaasi-teri, about 2:00 PM and docked the boat along the muddy bank at the terminus of the path used by the Indians to fetch their drinking water. It was hot and muggy, and my clothing was soaked with perspiration. It clung uncomfortably to my body, as it did thereafter for the remainder of the work. The small, biting gnats were out in astronomical numbers, for it was the beginning of the dry season. My face and hands were swollen from the venom of their numerous stings. In just a few moments I was to meet my first Yąnomamö, my first primitive man. What would it be like? I had visions of entering the village and seeing 125 social facts running about calling each other kinship terms and sharing food, each waiting and anxious to have me collect his genealogy. I would wear them out in turn. Would they like me? This was important to me; I wanted them to be so fond of me that they would adopt me into their kinship system and way of life, because I had heard that successful anthropologists always get adopted by their people. I had learned during my seven years of

---

[3]Maybury-Lewis 1967, "Introduction," and 1965b; Turnbull, 1966; L. Bohannan, 1964. Perhaps the most intimate account of the tribulations of a fieldworker is found in the posthumous diary of Bronislaw Malinowski (1967). Since the diary was not written for publication, it contains many intimate, very personal details about the writers' anxieties and hardships.

anthropological training at the University of Michigan that kinship was equivalent to society in primitive tribes and that it was a moral way of life, "moral" being something "good" and "desirable." I was determined to work my way into their moral system of kinship and become a member of their society.

My heart began to pound as we approached the village and heard the buzz of activity within the circular compound. Mr. Barker commented that he was anxious to see if any changes had taken place while he was away and wondered how many of them had died during his absence. I felt into my back pocket to make sure that my notebook was still there and felt personally more secure when I touched it. Otherwise, I would not have known what to do with my hands.

The entrance to the village was covered over with brush and dry palm leaves. We pushed them aside to expose the low opening to the village. The excitement of meeting my first Indians was almost unbearable as I duck-waddled through the low passage into the village clearing.

I looked up and gasped when I saw a dozen burly, naked, filthy, hideous men staring at us down the shafts of their drawn arrows! Immense wads of green tobacco were stuck between their lower teeth and lips making them look even more hideous, and strands of dark-green slime dripped or hung from their noses. We arrived at the village while the men were blowing a hallucinogenic drug up their noses. One of the side effects of the drug is a runny nose. The mucus is always saturated with the green powder and the Indians usually let it run freely from their nostrils. My next discovery was that there were a dozen or so vicious, underfed dogs snapping at my legs, circling me as if I were going to be their next meal. I just stood there holding my notebook, helpless and pathetic. Then the stench of the decaying vegetation and filth struck me and I almost got sick. I was horrified. What sort of a welcome was this for the person who came here to live with you and learn your way of life, to become friends with you? They put their weapons down when they recognized Barker and returned to their chanting, keeping a nervous eye on the village entrances.

We had arrived just after a serious fight. Seven women had been abducted the day before by a neighboring group, and the local men and their guests had just that morning recovered five of them in a brutal club fight that nearly ended in a shooting war. The abductors, angry because they lost five of the seven captives, vowed to raid the Bisaasi-teri. When we arrived and entered the village unexpectedly, the Indians feared that we were the raiders. On several occasions during the next two hours the men in the village jumped to their feet, armed themselves, and waited nervously for the noise outside the village to be identified. My enthusiasm for collecting ethnographic curiosities diminished in proportion to the number of times such an alarm was raised. In fact, I was relieved when Mr. Barker suggested that we sleep across the river for the evening. It would be safer over there.

As we walked down the path to the boat, I pondered the wisdom of having decided to spend a year and a half with this tribe before I had even seen what they were like. I am not ashamed to admit, either, that had there been a diplomatic way out, I would have ended my fieldwork then and there. I did not look forward to the next day when I would be left alone with the Indians; I did not speak a word of their language, and they were decidedly different from what I had imagined them to be. The whole situation was depressing, and I wondered why I ever decided to switch from civil engineering to anthropology in the first place. I had not eaten all day, I was soaking wet from perspiration, the gnats were biting me, and I was covered with red pigment, the result of a dozen or so complete examinations I had been given by as many burly Indians. These examinations capped an otherwise grim day. The Indians would blow their noses into their hands, flick as much of the mucus off that would separate in a snap of the wrist, wipe the residue into their hair, and then carefully examine my face, arms, legs, hair, and the contents of my pockets. I asked Mr. Barker how to say "Your hands are dirty"; my comments were met by the Indians in the following way: They would "clean" their hands by spitting a quantity of slimy tobacco juice into them, rub them together, and then proceed with the examination.

Mr. Barker and I crossed the river and slung our hammocks. When he pulled his hammock out of a rubber bag, a heavy, disagreeable odor of mildewed cotton came with it. "Even the missionaries are filthy," I thought to myself. Within two weeks, everything I owned smelled the same way, and I lived with that odor for the remainder of the fieldwork. My own habits of personal cleanliness reached such levels that I didn't even mind being examined by the Indians, as I was not much cleaner than they were after I had adjusted to the circumstances.

So much for my discovery that primitive man is not the picture of nobility and sanitation I had conceived him to be. I soon discovered that it was an enormously time-consuming task to maintain my own body in the manner to which it had grown accustomed in the relatively antiseptic environment of the northern United States. Either I could be relatively well fed and relatively comfortable in a fresh change of clothes and do very little fieldwork, or, I could do considerably more fieldwork and be less well fed and less comfortable.

It is appalling how complicated it can be to make oatmeal in the jungle. First, I had to make two trips to the river to haul the water. Next, I had to prime my kerosene stove with alcohol and get it burning, a tricky procedure when you are trying to mix powdered milk and fill a coffee pot at the same time: the alcohol prime always burned out before I could turn the kerosene on, and I would have to start all over. Or, I would turn the kerosene on, hoping that the element was still hot enough to vaporize the fuel, and start a small fire in my palm-thatched hut as the liquid kerosene squirted all over the table and walls and ignited. It was safer to start over with the alcohol. Then I had to boil the oatmeal and pick the bugs out of it. All my supplies, of course, were carefully stored in Indian-proof, rat-proof, moisture-proof, and insect-proof containers, not one of which ever served its purpose adequately. Just taking things out of the multiplicity of containers and repacking them afterward was a minor project in itself. By the time I had hauled the water to cook with, unpacked my food, prepared the oatmeal, milk, and coffee, heated water for dishes, washed and dried the dishes, repacked the food in the containers, stored the containers in locked trunks and cleaned up my mess, the ceremony of preparing breakfast had brought me almost up to lunch time!

Eating three meals a day was out of the question. I solved the problem by eating a single meal that could be prepared in a single container, or, at most, in two containers, washed my dishes only when there were no clean ones left, using cold river water, and wore each change of clothing at least a week to cut down on my laundry problem, a courageous undertaking in the tropics. I was also less concerned about sharing my provisions with the rats, insects, Indians, and the elements, thereby eliminating the need for my complicated storage process. I was able to last most of the day on *café con leche,* heavily sugared espresso coffee diluted about five to one with hot milk. I would prepare this in the evening and store it in a thermos. Frequently, my single meal was no more complicated than a can of sardines and a package of crackers. But at least two or three times a week I would do something sophisticated, like make oatmeal or boil rice and add a can of tuna fish or tomato paste to it. I even saved time by devising a water system that obviated the trips to the river. I had a few sheets of zinc roofing brought in and made a rain-water trap; I caught the water on the zinc surface, funneled it into an empty gasoline drum, and then ran a plastic hose from the drum to my hut. When the drum was exhausted in the dry season, I hired the Indians to fill it with water from the river.

I ate much less when I traveled with the Indians to visit other villages. Most of the time my travel diet consisted of roasted or boiled green plantains (see Glossary) that I obtained from the Indians, but I always carried a few cans of sardines with me in case I got lost or stayed away longer than I had planned. I found peanut butter and crackers a very nourishing food, and a simple one to prepare on trips. It was nutritious and portable, and only one tool was required to prepare the meal, a hunting knife that could be cleaned by wiping the blade on a leaf. More importantly, it was one of the few foods the Indians would let me eat in relative peace. It looked too much like animal feces to them to excite their appetites.

I once referred to the peanut butter as the dung of cattle. They found this quite repugnant. They did not know what "cattle" were, but were generally aware that I ate several canned products of such an animal. I perpetrated this myth, if for no other reason than to have some peace of mind while I ate. Fieldworkers develop strange defense mechanisms, and this was one of my own forms of adaptation. On another occasion I was eating a can of frankfurters and growing very weary of the demands of one of my guests for a share in my meal. When he asked me what I was eating, I replied: "Beef." He then asked, "What part of the animal are you eating?" to which I replied, "Guess!" He stopped asking for a share.

Meals were a problem in another way. Food sharing is important to the Yąnomamö in the context of displaying friendship. "I am hungry," is almost a form of greeting with them. I could not possibly have brought enough food with me to feed the entire village, yet they seemed not to understand this. All they could see was that I did not share my food with them at each and every meal. Nor could I enter into their system of reciprocities with respect to food; every time one of them gave me something "freely," he would dog me for months to pay him back, not with food, but with steel tools. Thus, if I accepted a plantain from someone in a different village while I was on a visit, he would most likely visit me in the future and demand a machete as payment for the time that he "fed" me. I usually reacted to these kinds of demands by giving a banana, the customary reciprocity in their culture—food for food—but this would be a disappointment for the individual who had visions of that single plantain growing into a machete over time.

Despite the fact that most of them knew I would not share my food with them at their request, some of them always showed up at my hut during mealtime. I gradually became accustomed to this and learned to ignore their persistent demands while I ate. Some of them would get angry because I failed to give in, but most of them accepted it as just a peculiarity of the subhuman foreigner. When I did give in, my hut quickly filled with Indians, each demanding a sample of the food that I had given one of them. If I did not give all a share, I was that much more despicable in their eyes.

A few of them went out of their way to make my meals unpleasant, to spite me for not sharing; for example, one man arrived and watched me eat a cracker with honey on it. He immediately recognized the honey, a particularly esteemed Yanomamö food. He knew that I would not share my tiny bottle and that it would be futile to ask. Instead, he glared at me and queried icily, "Shaki!⁴ What kind of animal semen are you eating on that cracker?" His question had the desired effect, and my meal ended.

Finally, there was the problem of being lonely and separated from your own kind, especially your family. I tried to overcome this by seeking personal friendships among the Indians. This only complicated the matter because all my friends simply used my confidence to gain privileged access to my cache of steel tools and trade goods, and looted me. I would be bitterly disappointed that my "friend" thought no more of me than to finesse our relationship exclusively with the intention of getting at my locked up possessions, and my depression would hit new lows every time I discovered this. The loss of the possession bothered me much less than the shock that I was, as far as most of them were concerned, nothing more than a source of desirable items; no holds were barred in relieving me of these, since I was considered something subhuman, a non-Yanomamö.

The thing that bothered me most was the incessant, passioned, and aggressive demands the Indians made. It would become so unbearable that I would have to lock myself in my mud hut every once in a while just to escape from it: Privacy is one of Western culture's greatest achievements. But I did not want privacy for its own sake; rather, I simply had to get away from the begging. Day and night for the entire time I lived with the Yanomamö I was plagued by such demands as: "Give me a knife, I am poor!"; "If you don't take me with you on your next trip to Widokaiya-teri I'll chop a hole in your canoe!"; "Don't point your camera at me or I'll hit you!"; "Share your food with me!"; "Take me across the river in your canoe and be quick about it!"; "Give me a cooking pot!"; "Loan me your flashlight so I can go hunting tonight!"; "Give me medicine . . . I itch all over!"; "Take us on a week-long hunting trip with your shotgun!"; and "Give me an axe or I'll break into your hut when you are away visiting and steal one!" And so I was bombarded by such demands day after day, months on end, until I could not bear to see an Indian.

It was not as difficult to become calloused to the incessant begging as it was to ignore the sense of urgency, the impassioned tone of voice, or the intimidation and aggression with which the demands were made. It was likewise difficult to adjust to the fact that the Yanomamö refused to accept "no" for an answer until or unless it seethed with passion and intimidation—which it did after six months. Giving in to a demand always established a new threshold; the next demand would be for a bigger item or favor, and the anger of the Indians even greater if the demand was not met. I soon learned

---

⁴"Shaki," or, rather, "Shakiwä," is the name they gave me because they could not pronounce "Chagnon." They like to name people for some distinctive feature when possible. *Shaki* is the name of a species of noisome bee; they accumulate in large numbers around ripening bananas and make pests of themselves by eating into the fruit, showering the people below with the debris. They probably adopted this name for me because I was also a nuisance, continuously prying into their business, taking pictures of them, and, in general, being where they did not want me.

that I had to become very much like the Yąnomamö to be able to get along with them on their terms: sly, aggressive, and intimidating.

Had I failed to adjust in this fashion I would have lost six months of supplies to them in a single day or would have spent most of my time ferrying them around in my canoe or hunting for them. As it was, I did spend a considerable amount of time doing these things and did succumb to their outrageous demands for axes and machetes, at least at first. More importantly, had I failed to demonstrate that I could not be pushed around beyond a certain point, I would have been the subject of far more ridicule, theft, and practical jokes than was the actual case. In short, I had to acquire a certain proficiency in their kind of interpersonal politics and to learn how to imply subtly that certain potentially undesirable consequences might follow if they did such and such to me. They do this to each other in order to establish precisely the point at which they cannot goad an individual any further without precipitating retaliation. As soon as I caught on to this and realized that much of their aggression was stimulated by their desire to discover my flash point, I got along much better with them and regained some lost ground. It was sort of like a political game that everyone played, but one in which each individual sooner or later had to display some sign that his bluffs and implied threats could be backed up. I suspect that the frequency of wife beating is a component of this syndrome, since men can display their ferocity and show others that they are capable of violence. Beating a wife with a club is considered to be an acceptable way of displaying ferocity and one that does not expose the male to much danger. The important thing is that the man has displayed his potential for violence and the implication is that other men better treat him with respect and caution.

After six months, the level of demand was tolerable in the village I used for my headquarters. The Indians and I adjusted to each other and knew what to expect with regard to demands on their part for goods, favors, and services. Had I confined my fieldwork to just that village alone, the field experience would have been far more enjoyable. But, as I was interested in the demographic pattern and social organization of a much larger area, I made regular trips to some dozen different villages in order to collect genealogies or to recheck those I already had. Hence, the intensity of begging and intimidation was fairly constant for the duration of the fieldwork. I had to establish my position in some sort of pecking order of ferocity at each and every village.

For the most part, my own "fierceness" took the form of shouting back at the Yąnomamö as loudly and as passionately as they shouted at me, especially at first, when I did not know much of their language. As I became more proficient in their language and learned more about their political tactics, I became more sophisticated in the art of bluffing. For example, I paid one young man a machete to cut palm trees and make boards from the wood. I used these to fashion a platform in the bottom of my dugout canoe to keep my possessions dry when I traveled by river. That afternoon I was doing informant work in the village; the long-awaited mission supply boat arrived, and most of the Indians ran out of the village to beg goods from the crew. I continued to work in the village for another hour or so and went down to the river to say "hello" to the men on the supply boat. I was angry when I discovered that the Indians had chopped up all my palm boards and used them to paddle their own canoes[5] across the river. I knew that if

---

[5]The canoes were obtained from missionaries, who, in turn, got them from a different tribe.

I overlooked this incident I would have invited them to take even greater liberties with my goods in the future. I crossed the river, docked amidst their dugouts, and shouted for the Indians to come out and see me. A few of the culprits appeared, mischievous grins on their faces. I gave a spirited lecture about how hard I had worked to put those boards in my canoe, how I had paid a machete for the wood, and how angry I was that they destroyed my work in their haste to cross the river. I then pulled out my hunting knife and, while their grins disappeared, cut each of their canoes loose, set it into the current, and let it float away. I left without further ado and without looking back.

They managed to borrow another canoe and, after some effort, recovered their dugouts. The headman of the village later told me with an approving chuckle that I had done the correct thing. Everyone in the village, except, of course, the culprits, supported and defended my action. This raised my status.

Whenever I took such action and defended my rights, I got along much better with the Yanomamö. A good deal of their behavior toward me was directed with the forethought of establishing the point at which I would react defensively. Many of them later reminisced about the early days of my work when I was "timid" and a little afraid of them, and they could bully me into giving goods away.

Theft was the most persistent situation that required me to take some sort of defensive action. I simply could not keep everything I owned locked in trunks, and the Indians came into my hut and left at will. I developed a very effective means for recovering almost all the stolen items. I would simply ask a child who took the item and then take that person's hammock when he was not around, giving a spirited lecture to the others as I marched away in a faked rage with the thief's hammock. Nobody ever attempted to stop me from doing this, and almost all of them told me that my technique for recovering my possessions was admirable. By nightfall the thief would either appear with the stolen object or send it along with someone else to make an exchange. The others would heckle him for getting caught and being forced to return the item.

With respect to collecting the data I sought, there was a very frustrating problem. Primitive social organization is kinship organization, and to understand the Yanomamö way of life I had to collect extensive genealogies. I could not have deliberately picked a more difficult group to work with in this regard: They have very stringent name taboos. They attempt to name people in such a way that when the person dies and they can no longer use his name, the loss of the word in the language is not inconvenient. Hence, they name people for specific and minute parts of things, such as "toenail of some rodent," thereby being able to retain the words "toenail" and "(specific) rodent," but not being able to refer directly to the toenail of that rodent. The taboo is maintained even for the living: One mark of prestige is the courtesy others show you by not using your name. The sanctions behind the taboo seem to be an unusual combination of fear and respect.

I tried to use kinship terms to collect genealogies at first, but the kinship terms were so ambiguous that I ultimately had to resort to names. They were quick to grasp that I was bound to learn everybody's name and reacted, without my knowing it, by inventing false names for everybody in the village. After having spent several months collecting names and learning them, this came as a disappointment to me: I could not cross-check the genealogies with other informants from distant villages.

They enjoyed watching me learn these names. I assumed, wrongly, that I would get the truth to each question and that I would get the best information by working in public. This set the stage for converting a serious project into a farce. Each informant tried to outdo his peers by inventing a name even more ridiculous than what I had been given earlier, or by asserting that the individual about whom I inquired was married to his mother or daughter, and the like. I would have the informant whisper the name of the individual in my ear, noting that he was the father of such and such a child. Everybody would then insist that I repeat the name aloud, roaring in hysterics as I clumsily pronounced the name. I assumed that the laughter was in response to the violation of the name taboo or to my pronunciation. This was a reasonable interpretation, since the individual whose name I said aloud invariably became angry. After I learned what some of the names meant, I began to understand what the laughter was all about. A few of the more colorful examples are: "hairy vagina," "long penis," "feces of the harpy eagle," and "dirty rectum." No wonder the victims were angry.

I was forced to do my genealogy work in private because of the horseplay and nonsense. Once I did so, my informants began to agree with each other and I managed to learn a few new names, real names. I could then test any new informant by collecting a genealogy from him that I knew to be accurate. I was able to weed out the more mischievous informants this way. Little by little I extended the genealogies and learned the real names. Still, I was unable to get the names of the dead and extend the genealogies back in time, and even my best informants continued to deceive me about their own close relatives. Most of them gave me the name of a living man as the father of some individual in order to avoid mentioning that the actual father was dead.

The quality of a genealogy depends in part on the number of generations it embraces, and the name taboo prevented me from getting any substantial information about deceased ancestors. Without this information, I could not detect marriage patterns through time. I had to rely on older informants for this information, but these were the most reluctant of all. As I became more proficient in the language and more skilled at detecting lies, my informants became better at lying. One of them in particular was so cunning and persuasive that I was shocked to discover that he had been inventing his information. He specialized in making a ceremony out of telling me false names. He would look around to make sure nobody was listening outside my hut, enjoin me to never mention the name again, act very nervous and spooky, and then grab me by the head to whisper the name very softly into my ear. I was always elated after an informant session with him, because I had several generations of dead ancestors for the living people. The others refused to give me this information. To show my gratitude, I paid him quadruple the rate I had given the others. When word got around that I had increased the pay, volunteers began pouring in to give me genealogies.

I discovered that the old man was lying quite by accident. A club fight broke out in the village one day, the result of a dispute over the possession of a woman. She had been promised to Rerebawä, a particularly aggressive young man who had married into the village. Rerebawä had already been given her older sister and was enraged when the younger girl began having an affair with another man in the village, making no attempt to conceal it from him. He challenged the young man to a club fight, but was so abusive in his challenge that the opponent's father took offense and entered the village circle with his son, wielding a long club. Rerebawä swaggered out to the duel and hurled insults at both of them, trying to goad them into striking him on the head with their clubs. This would have given him the opportunity to strike them on the head. His opponents refused to hit him, and the fight ended. Rerebawä had won a moral victory because his opponents were afraid to hit him. Thereafter, he swaggered around and insulted the two men behind their backs. He was genuinely angry with them, to the point of calling the older man by the name of his dead father. I quickly seized on this as an opportunity to collect an accurate genealogy and pumped him about his adversary's ancestors. Rerebawä had been particularly nasty to me up to this point, but we became staunch allies: We were both outsiders in the local village. I then asked about other dead ancestors and got immediate replies. He was angry with the whole group and not afraid to tell me the names of the dead. When I compared his version of the genealogies to that of the old man, it was obvious that one of them was lying. I challenged his information, and he explained that everybody knew that the old man was deceiving me and bragging about it in the village. The names the old man had given me were the dead ancestors of the members of a village so far away that he thought I would never have occasion to inquire about them. As it turned out, Rerebawä knew most of the people in that village and recognized the names.

I then went over the complete genealogical records with Rerebawä, genealogies I had presumed to be in final form. I had to revise them all because of the numerous lies and falsifications they contained. Thus, after five months of almost constant work on the genealogies of just one group, I had to begin almost from scratch!

Discouraging as it was to start over, it was still the first real turning point in my fieldwork. Thereafter, I began taking advantage of local arguments and animosities in selecting my informants, and used more extensively individuals who had married into the group. I began traveling to other villages to check the genealogies, picking villages that were on strained terms with the people about whom I wanted information. I would then return to my base camp and check with local informants the accuracy of the new information. If the informants became angry when I mentioned the new names I acquired from the unfriendly group, I was almost certain that the information was accurate. For this kind of checking I had to use informants whose genealogies I knew rather well: they had to be distantly enough related to the dead person that they would not go into a rage when I mentioned the name, but not so remotely related that they would be uncertain of the accuracy of the information. Thus, I had to make a list of names that I dared not use in the presence of each and every informant. Despite the precautions, I occasionally hit a name that put the informant into a rage, such as that of a dead brother or sister that other informants had not reported. This always terminated the day's work with that informant, for he would be too touchy to continue any further, and I would be reluctant to take a chance on accidentally discovering another dead kinsman so soon after the first.

These were always unpleasant experiences, and occasionally dangerous ones, depending on the temperament of the informant. On one occasion I was planning to visit a village that had been raided about a week earlier. A woman whose name I had on my list had been killed by the raiders. I planned to check each individual on the list one by one to estimate ages, and I wanted to remove her name so that I would not say it aloud in the village. I knew that I would be in considerable difficulty if I said this name aloud so soon after her death. I called on my original informant and asked him to tell me the name of the woman who had been killed. He refused, explaining that she was a close relative of his. I then asked him if he would become angry if I read off all the names on the list. This way he did not have to say her name and could merely nod when I mentioned the right one. He was a fairly good friend of mine, and I thought I could predict his reaction. He assured me that this would be a good way of doing it. We were alone in my hut so that nobody could overhear us. I read the names softly, continuing to the next when he gave a negative reply. When I finally spoke the name of the dead woman he flew out of his chair, raised his arm to strike me, and shouted: "You son-of-a-bitch![6] If you ever say that name again, I'll kill you!" He was shaking with rage, but left my hut quietly. I shudder to think what might have happened if I had said the name unknowingly in the woman's village. I had other, similar experiences in different villages, but luckily the dead person had been dead for some time and was not closely related to the individual into whose ear I whispered the name. I was merely cautioned to desist from saying any more names, lest I get people angry with me.

I had been working on the genealogies for nearly a year when another individual came to my aid. It was Kąobawä, the headman of Upper Bisaasi-teri, the group in which I spent most of my time. He visited me one day after the others had left the hut and volunteered to help me on the genealogies. He was poor, he explained, and needed a machete. He would work only on the condition that I did not ask him about his own parents and other very close kinsmen who were dead. He also added that he would not lie to me as the others had done in the past. This was perhaps the most important single event in my fieldwork, for out of this meeting evolved a very warm friendship and a very profitable informant-fieldworker relationship.

Kąobawä's familiarity with his group's history and his candidness were remarkable. His knowledge of details was almost encyclopedic. More than that, he was enthusiastic and encouraged me to learn details that I might otherwise have ignored. If there were things he did not know intimately, he would advise me to wait until he could check things out with someone in the village. This he would do clandestinely, giving me a report the next day. As I was constrained by my part of the bargain to avoid discussing his close dead kinsmen, I had to rely on Rerebawä for this information. I got Rerebawä's genealogy from Kąobawä.

Once again I went over the genealogies with Kąobawä to recheck them, a considerable task by this time: they included about two thousand names, representing several generations of individuals from four different villages. Rerebawä's information was very accurate, and Kąobawä's contribution enabled me to trace the genealogies further back in time. Thus, after nearly a year of constant work on genealogies, Yąnomamö demography and social organization began to fall into a pattern. Only then could I see how kin groups formed and exchanged women with each other over time, and only then did the fissioning of larger villages into smaller ones show a distinct pattern. At this point I was able to begin formulating more intelligent questions because there was now some sort of pattern to work with. Without the help of Rerebawä and Kąobawä I could not have made very much sense of the plethora of details I had collected from dozens of other informants.

---

[6]This is the closest English translation of his actual statement, the literal translation of which would be nonsensical in our language.

I spent a good deal of time with these two men and their families and got to know them well. They frequently gave their information in a way which related themselves to the topic under discussion. We became very close friends. I will speak of them frequently in the following chapters, using them as "typical" Yąnomamö, if, indeed, one may speak of typical anything. I will briefly comment on what these men are like and their respective statuses in the village.

Kạobawä is about 40 years old (Fig. 1–3). I say "about" because the Yąnomamö numeration system has only three numbers: one, two, and more-than-two. He is the head-man of Upper Bisaasi-teri. He has had five or six wives so far and temporary affairs with as many more women, one of which resulted in a child. At the present time he has just two wives, Bahimi and Koamashima. He has had a daughter and a son by Bahimi, his eldest and favorite wife. Koamashima, about 20 years old, recently had her first child, a boy (Fig. 1–4). Kạobawä may give Koamashima to his youngest brother. Even now the brother shares in her sexual services. Kạobawä recently gave his third wife to another of his brothers because she was beshi: "horny." In fact, this girl had been married to two

14

other men, both of whom discarded her because of her infidelity. Kaobawä had one daughter by her; she is being raised by his brother.

Kaobawä's eldest wife, Bahimi, is about thirty-five years old. She is his first cross-cousin (see Glossary). Bahimi was pregnant when I began my fieldwork, but she killed the new baby, a boy, at birth, explaining tearfully that it would have competed with Ariwari, her nursing son, for milk. Rather than expose Ariwari to the dangers and uncertainty of an early weaning, she killed the new child instead. By Yanomamö standards, she and Kaobawä have a very tranquil household. He only beats her once in a while, and never very hard. She never has affairs with other men.

Kaobawä is quiet, intense, wise, and unobtrusive. He leads more by example than by threats and coercion. He can afford to be this way as he established his reputation

Fig. 1–4. Koamashima, Kaobawä's youngest wife, playing with her son, who is holding a tree frog.

for being fierce long ago, and other men respect him. He also has five mature brothers who support him, and he has given a number of his sisters to other men in the village, thereby putting them under some obligation to him. In short, his "natural" following (kinsmen) is large, and he does not have to constantly display his ferocity. People already respect him and take his suggestions seriously.

Rerebawä is much younger, only about twenty-two years old (See Fig. 1–5). He has just one wife by whom he has had three children. He is from Karohi-teri, one of the villages to which Kąobawä's is allied. Rerebawä left his village to seek a wife in Kąobawä's group because there were no eligible women there for him to marry.

Rerebawä is perhaps more typical than Kąobawä in the sense that he is concerned about his reputation for ferocity and goes out of his way to act tough. He is, however, much braver than the other men his age and backs up his threats with action. Moreover, he is concerned about politics and knows the details of intervillage relationships over a large area. In this respect he shows all the attributes of a headman, although he is still too young and has too many competent older brothers in his own village to expect to move easily into the position of leadership there.

He does not intend to stay in Kąobawä's group and has not made a garden. He feels that he has adequately discharged his obligations to his wife's parents by providing them with fresh game for three years. They should let him take the wife and return to his own village with her, but they refuse and try to entice him to remain permanently in Bisaasi-teri to provide them with game when they are old. They have even promised to give him their second daughter if he will stay permanently.

Although he has displayed his ferocity in many ways, one incident in particular shows what his character is like. Before he left his own village to seek a wife, he had an affair with the wife of an older brother. When he was discovered, his brother attacked him with a club. Rerebawä was infuriated so he grabbed an axe and drove his brother out of the village after soundly beating him with the flat of the blade. The brother was so afraid that he did not return to the village for several days. I recently visited his village with him. He made a point to introduce me to this brother. Rerebawä dragged him out of his hammock by the arm and told me, "This is the brother whose wife I had an affair with," a deadly insult. His brother did nothing and slunk back into his hammock, shamed, but relieved to have Rerebawä release the vise-grip on his arm.

Despite the fact that he admires Kąobawä, he has a low opinion of the others in Bisaasi-teri. He admitted confidentially that he thought Bisaasi-teri was an abominable group: "This is a terrible neighborhood! All the young men are lazy and cowards and everybody is committing incest! I'll be glad to get back home." He also admired Kąobawä's brother, the headman of Monou-teri. This man was killed by raiders while I was doing my fieldwork. Rerebawä was disgusted that the others did not chase the raiders when they discovered the shooting: "He was the only fierce one in the whole group; he was my close friend. The cowardly Monou-teri hid like women in the jungle and didn't even chase the raiders!"

Even though Rerebawä is fierce and capable of being quite nasty, he has a good side as well. He has a very biting sense of humor and can entertain the group for hours on end with jokes and witty comments. And, he is one of few Yąnomamö that I feel I can trust. When I returned to Bisaasi-teri after having been away for a year, Rerebawä was in his own village visiting his kinsmen. Word reached him that I had returned, and he immediately came to see me. He greeted me with an immense bear hug and exclaimed, "Shaki! Why did you stay away so long? Did you know that my will was so cold while you were gone that at times I could not eat for want of seeing you?" I had to admit that I missed him, too.

Of all the Yąnomamö I know, he is the most genuine and the most devoted to his culture's ways and values. I admire him for that, although I can't say that I subscribe to or endorse these same values. By contrast, Kąobawä is older and wiser. He sees his own culture in a different light and criticizes aspects of it he does not like. While many of his peers accept some of the superstitions and explanatory myths as truth and as the way things ought to be, Kąobawä questions them and privately pokes fun at some of them. Probably, more of the Yąnomamö are like Rerebawä, or at least try to be.

Fig. 1–5. Rerebawä during an ebene *session sitting on the sidelines in an hallucinogenic stupor.*

2

Adaptation

THE YANOMAMÖ ADAPTATION to their physical, social, and intellectual environments is dealt with in this chapter.

The Physical Environment

Kaobawä's village[1] is Upper Bisaasi-teri, located at the confluence of the Mavaca and Orinoco Rivers. Like most of the villages in this area, it lies at an altitude of about 450 feet. While some villages in Brazil reach 3000 feet in altitude, most Yanomamö villages are located at much lower elevations (Fig. 2-1).

The general area around Kaobawä's village is a low, flat plain interrupted occasionally by gently rolling hills and, more rarely, by a few low mountain ridges. The land is entirely covered with jungle, even the tops of the mountain ridges.

The jungle is relatively dense and characterized by numerous species of palm and hardwood trees. The forest canopy keeps the sunlight from penetrating to the ground, but scrub brush and vines manage to grow in relatively great abundance in most places, making it difficult to walk along the trails. Thorny brush is especially heavy along the banks of streams, where adequate sunlight and a constant supply of water provide ideal circumstances for its growth.

---

[1]See map, Fig. 2–8. Villages other than Kaobawä's have been included because they are discussed in this and also in a later chapter. Presently occupied villages are indicated in upper-case lettering and by shading. The area shown in this map is unexplored, except for the zone immediately adjacent to the Orinoco River. The map is, therefore, largely calculated guesswork. To establish dates of occupation I estimated ages of individuals and obtained their stated places of birth. Distance and geographical location were determined by compass readings and measured in sleeps required to reach the location from a given point. I also visited many of the locations shown. While I was in Brazil in 1967, I checked the map locations with informants there, being encouraged by the fact that they independently gave approximately the same information. Fig. 2–8 is a simplified version of the more detailed map c in my doctoral thesis (Chagnon 1966). For more information regarding the techniques used in making the map, consult the thesis.

Fig. 2–1. A Yąnomamö village and plantain garden, aerial view (Toototobi River, Brazil).

TRAILS AND TRAVEL Trails lead out from the village in several directions. Some of them terminate in the gardens that surround the village, but a few of them continue on into the jungle and lead eventually to other villages. The unexperienced eye would not recognize them as trails, as they are hardly more than winding paths through brush, over or around logs, through streams and swamps, and up hills. The Yąnomamö take the most direct route to their destination, regardless of the terrain. A foreigner learns how to recognize a trail only after considerable experience. The most telltale signs are the numerous broken twigs at about knee height left by Yąnomamö travelers who compulsively keep their hands occupied snapping off brush and twigs as they walk. Another sign is the occasional log that is worn smooth from the tread of numerous travelers who prefer to walk along a log rather than go around it.

The most commonly used trail from Kąobawä's village leads to the two Shamatari villages, Reyaboböwei-teri and Mömariböwei-teri, southwest of Upper Bisaasi-teri. Hardly a week goes by in the dry season without a few individuals making a trip from one of these villages to Bisaasi-teri or vice versa. A group of young men can make this trip in one day if they walk rapidly and leave early in the morning. Older men, women, and children must plan on a two day journey, as they walk more slowly and rest more frequently. There are a number of temporary shelters along the trail built by previous visitors, so the traveler does not have to spend much time putting one of these into repair should he decide to camp overnight.

The jungle provides a number of hazards to the barefoot traveler in that most species of palm have long, sharp spines protruding from their trunks or leaf stems. The most common and recurrent injury the Yąnomamö sustain is thorns in the feet. A party of ten men can rarely travel an hour without one of them stopping to extract a thorn from his foot. This is always accompanied by hisses and clicks of pain on the part of the victim, who gouges the thorn out with either an arrow point or another thorn. Their feet have thick calluses on them, but because the trails frequently cross streams and swamps, the calluses soften and are easily pierced by thorns.

Another, but rarer, hazard is snakes.[2] There are always a few cases of snake bite in each village every year, although few of them are fatal. Most snake-bite victims recover from the wound with no ill side effects. I treated two cases of snake bite that were like this. But a few bites are severe enough to cause the loss of a limb. One of my better acquaintances, a young man of some thirty years, lost a leg because of a snake bite when he was about fifteen years old, and will spend the rest of his life hopping on one leg, a form of locomotion he has mastered so thoroughly that he almost manages to keep up with the group when they visit other villages.

Most of the intervillage traveling is done from September through April, the dry season. For the remainder of the year the trails, or substantial portions of them, are underwater. At this time the rains are frequent and heavy, and the small streams that can be easily crossed on foot in the dry season become impassable torrents. Small lakes replace the marshy low ground, and communication between villages all but ceases. As the Yąnomamö are an inland people and avoid locating their villages near large streams, all travel is done on foot, and each village becomes an isolated entity at the peak of the wet season (June).[3] If the group must travel, it will make simple vine and pole bridges over the smaller streams. A pair of slender poles is stuck into the river and crossed to form an X-frame. Vines are used to lash the poles together where they intersect, and another pole is laid from the bank to the X-frame, also secured by vines. Then another pair of poles is stuck into the stream and lashed to form another X-frame. The long pole is then extended out further from the bank, and so on, until the stream is bridged. A vine railing is attached to the protruding members of the X-frames. The bridges usually last only a short time. The first heavy rain will swell the stream and the current will wash it away.

TECHNOLOGY Much of Yąnomamö technology is like the pole-and-vine bridge: crude, but very effective, and not destined to last for any great period of time. The only durable artifact produced is a crude, poorly fired clay pot. It is nearly an inch thick at the bottom and tapers to almost nothing at the brim. Consequently, it breaks very easily. For this reason, women, regarded as clumsy, are rarely allowed to touch or handle them. When the clay pots are used, the men do the cooking, as, for example, during feasts. The pot is made by the coil technique: The untempered clay is kneaded to the proper consistency by hand, rolled into long, slender ropes, and these, in turn, placed on top of each other to form a continuous rope of clay. The coils are then scraped flat so that the interior and exterior of the pot are smooth. The conical-shaped pot is allowed to dry in the shade, then fired by placing brush and wood over it. The end product is

---

[2]Two percent of all adult deaths are due to snake bite; 54 percent are due to malaria, and other epidemic diseases (Chagnon 1966) and 24 percent of adult males die in warfare.

[3]The Yąnomamö began moving their villages out to navigable rivers after 1955. Up to that time there was only one village, Mahekodo-teri, located on a navigable portion of the Orinoco River.

black, heavy, and very brittle. It breaks easily, but the pieces are used by the men as grinding surfaces for their drug manufacture, or as baking dishes when the women make cassava bread. As we shall see below, only a few villages make the clay pots and trade them to the members of other groups.

The most distinctive feature of Yąnomamö technology is that it is very direct.[4] No tool or technique is complicated enough to require specialized labor or raw materials. Each village, therefore, can produce every item of material culture it requires from the jungle resources immediately around it. That is, the simplicity of the tools, the processes of manufacture, and the distribution of resources are such that each village can exist independently of its neighbors as far as technological requirements are concerned. Nevertheless, some specialization in trade and manufacturing does occur, but it seems to be more closely related to the development of political alliances and is therefore discussed in a later chapter. I will describe the material culture at this point and relate it to the over-all adaptation later in this and following chapters.

WEAPONS Wood for bows is obtained from two species of palm tree, one that grows wild and one that is cultivated.[5] The bow is very heavy because palm wood is extremely dense. One cannot, for example, drive a nail into palm wood. The fibers that go into the thick bowstring come from the inner bark of a tree; these are twisted into a cord by rolling them with the palm of the hand against the thigh. The cord is so strong when it is new that it can be used as a hammock rope, but it deteriorates with age and must be replaced periodically. The bow itself is shaped with the lower jaw of a large, wild pig. The canine teeth in the pig's lower mandible are worn to razor-sharp edges by chewing and make magnificent cutting tools; the bow stave is held vertically and the mandible is planed up and down the surface, each upward stroke shaving off a fine layer of wood. After much labor and patience, the bow is completed. It has a circular or oval cross section and is very difficult to draw. Most Yąnomamö bows would compare favorably to our best hunting bows in strength.

Palm wood is also used for one type of arrow point. A splinter of palm wood about 15 inches long is smoothed down to a fine point, and several lateral grooves are cut into it along its length. This is done so that the point will break off in the body of the target. This type of point is covered with curare poison, which slowly dissolves in the animal (or man) after the point has broken off. This point is used most frequently for monkey hunting, as monkeys tend to grab hold of branches and tree trunks when they are wounded. The curare relaxes their muscles, and the monkeys sooner or later fall to the ground. Unless the point were coated with curare, the animal might die high in the treetops and could not be easily recovered. The Yąnomamö also carry large supplies of extra palm points in their bamboo quivers since these points break whether or not the arrow strikes the intended target. This type of point is manufactured in large quantities in several villages and is traded to other groups.

The curare vine is also collected wild from the jungle. It is soaked in hot water to leach out the active ingredient. The water containing the poison is then painted onto the palm-wood points over glowing coals; the water evaporates, leaving a brown, sticky

---

[4]For more details on Yąnomamö material culture than are given here, see Becher (1960) and Zerries (1964).

[5]The cultivated palm, *pijiguao,* produces a desirable fruit. It is cultivated for the fruit, but the wood of dead palms is used in bow manufacturing.

layer of poison. Sometimes other ingredients are added to the poison to make it stickier and less soluble. Without these ingredients, the poison would be washed off by the rain. As an extra precaution against this, some men wrap a leaf around the curare point after it has been attached to the arrow.

Arrow-point quivers are made from 2-inch bamboo sections of about 18 inches. The quiver is essentially a tube of wood with a natural joint serving as the bottom of the case. The bamboo grows wild in large stands, and some villages specialize in collecting it, making quivers, and trading them to other groups. A piece of monkey, snake, or jaguar skin, molded to fit over the top prevents water from getting into the tube. It usually contains a dozen or so extra arrow points, fibers for fastening the points to the arrow shaft, a ball of resin used as adhesive, a few splinters of bone used to tip one kind of arrow point, and, occasionally, a magical charm. A fiber or cotton string is tied around the bamboo tube near its top, and a loop is fashioned so that the tube can be worn around the neck. It hangs down the middle of the back.

The Yąnomamö attach their fire drills and a pair of agouti-tooth knives to the outside of the bamboo quiver. The fire drill is made from the wood of the cocoa tree and consists of one or two 20-inch long, slender shafts, circular in cross section, and a 12-inch long lanceolate-shaped piece of cocoa wood into which have been worn several holes. The latter piece of wood is placed on the ground and held firmly in place by the foot. The tip of the slender shaft is placed into one of the holes, and the shaft is twirled rapidly with the palm of the hands; the heat of the friction ignites the wood dust that results from the spinning tip, and this is immediately transferred to some cotton tinder. The men usually work in pairs to start a fire, as the dust cools off by the time a single man can get his hands back up to the top of the slender shaft to begin another downward twirling motion.

The agouti-tooth knives are manufactured from the lower incisor of the agouti rodent. The incisors are long, slender, gently curved, and very sharp. The tip of the incisor is shaped like a wedge and is frequently indented. The exterior part of the tooth is much harder than the pith so that a very sharp edge protrudes slightly above the softer, decayed dentine. The Yąnomamö keep the dentine worn down by periodically "sharpening" the tooth; this is accomplished by cutting into a particular kind of reed, which apparently contains a corrosive ingredient that attacks the dentine but does not affect the enamel of the tooth. The base of the tooth is fastened in a short piece of wood by a resin adhesive and a fiber wrapping. The completed knife is as sharp as any steel chisel, but because of its small size, its usefulness is limited. It is primarily used to whittle lanceolate arrow points from bamboo, a very time-consuming job.

The jungle also provides another kind of poison used by the Yąnomamö to kill fish. The men select a small stream, dam it up, and put the juice of a vine into the water. This stuns the small fish, which then float to the surface where they are scooped up by the women either by handfuls or with loosely woven, shallow baskets (see Fig. 2–2). If the woman is in the middle of the stream, she empties the contents of her basket into her hand and then stores the handful of squirming fish in her mouth until both the basket and her mouth are full. If larger fish are caught, the women bite them behind their heads to kill them and toss them out on the bank. The first one in the stream takes a chance on locating an electric eel; if she is shocked, the others try to locate the eel with sticks and kill it.

"Razor grass"—a reed—also grows wild in the jungle. It is used by the Yạnomamö to cut their hair and to keep their tonsures cleanly shaved. A sliver of this reed is wrapped around the index finger in such a way that the sharp edge is exposed. The practiced hand can shave a head bald in a matter of minutes and with no more pain than would come from using a dull steel razor blade. This grass is also found around some of the villages, but appears not to be cultivated.

HALLUCINOGENIC DRUGS   Another useful plant provided by the jungle is the *ebene* tree. The inner bark of this tree is used in the manufacture of one kind of hallucinogenic drug. The bark is scraped from the trunk after the exterior layer of bark is removed, or is scraped from the inside of the bark surface itself. This material, which is fairly moist, is then mixed with wood ashes and kneaded between the palms of the hands. Additional moisture is provided by spitting periodically into the pliable wad of drug. When the drug has been thoroughly mixed with saliva and ashes, it is placed on a hot piece of broken clay pot and the moisture driven out with heat. It is ground into a

Fig. 2–2. Women fishing in a dammed stream that has been poisoned by the juice of a wild liana. The poison is introduced upstream by the men, and the stunned fish are collected in baskets by the women.

powder as it dries, the flat side of a stone axe[6] serving as the grinding pestle. The dried, green powder, no more than several tablespoons full, is then swept onto a leaf with a stiff feather. The men then gather around the leaf containing the drug, usually in the late afternoon, and take it by blowing the powder into each other's nostrils (see Fig. 2-3). A small quantity of the powder is introduced into the end of a hollow cane tube some 3 feet long. The tube is then flicked with the forefinger to scatter the powder along its length. One end of the tube is put into the nostril of the man taking the drug, and his helper then blows a strong blast of air through the other end, emitting his breath in such a fashion that he climaxes the delivery with a hard burst of air. Both the recipient and the blower squat on their haunches to do this. The man who had the drug blown into his nostrils grimaces, groans, chokes, coughs, holds his head from the pain of the air blast, and duck-waddles off to some leaning post. He usually receives two doses of the drug, one in each nostril. The recipient usually vomits, gets watery eyes, and develops a runny nose. Much of the drug comes back out in the nasal mucus that begins to run freely after the drug has been administered. Within minutes after the drug has been blown into a man's nose, he begins having difficulties focusing his eyes and starts to act intoxicated. The drug allegedly produces colored visions, especially around the periphery of the visual field, and permits the user to enter into contact with his particular *hekura,* miniature demons that dwell under rocks and on mountains. The man begins to chant to the *hekura* when the drug takes effect, inviting them to come and live in his chest.

The Yąnomamö also cultivate a tree, *hisioma,* that produces hallucinogenic seeds. These are prepared in exactly the same manner as the noncultivated drug.

TROUGHS AND CANOES The Yąnomamö use the bark of another kind of tree to make a trough and a crude canoe, both of which are nearly identical in shape, size, and method of construction. The tree is beaten with clubs to loosen the bark. The bark is then removed in one piece and hauled back to the village. The ends are heated in a fire to make them pliable and folded back to make the ends of the container. They are held firm by lashing two sticks together, pinching the folded bark into a flat-nosed basin. The interior bark surface becomes the exterior surface of the soup container. If the container is to be used as a canoe, a crude framework of sticks is added to the inside, giving it more stability. The craft is so crude and heavy that the Yąnomamö generally do not use it for any purpose other than the trip for which it was intended, usually a downstream trip, since it would be almost impossible to move against a current in this rough craft. It is easier to walk than to try to pole the canoe upstream. The canoe, hence, is usually discarded after it makes its maiden voyage. Another will be made when it is needed.

The container is pinioned to the ground with stakes if it is to be used as a soup trough. Each time a feast is held, one or more of these bark containers is made in front of the headman's house, filled with the boiled ripe plantain soup, and frequented by the hungry guests, who dip out the soup with gourd spoons. The trough is thrown on the village rubbage heap after the feast is over.

---

[6]They find the stone axes when they make new gardens, explaining that the spirits left them behind for the Yąnomamö to use. This area was occupied in the distant past by tribes whose relationship to the present Yąnomamö is uncertain.

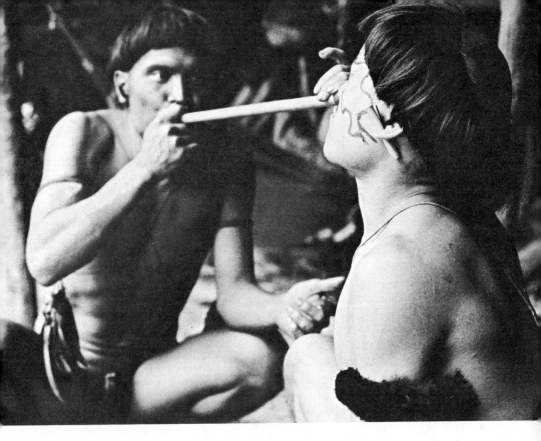

Fig. 2–3. Men blowing ebene, *a hallucinogenic drug, into each other's nostrils by means of a hollow tube.*

SHELTER   All house materials likewise come from the jungle: poles, vines, and leaves. The Yąnomamö permanent house—*shabono*—is probably the most sophisticated manufacture produced by these people. Its construction requires considerable cooperation, planning, labor, and patience. Unfortunately, the *shabono* only lasts one or two years because the leaves begin to leak, or the entire village is burned to the ground in order to destroy the cockroaches, scorpions, spiders, and other vermin that infest the house. These can become such a nuisance that the roof is literally alive with bugs. Kąobawä's house was so badly infested at one point that the noise of thousands of scurrying roaches produced a constant, noticeable din in the village. Whenever someone got out of his hammock, the roof just above his head would suddenly come alive with roaches, disturbed by the movement below. As they scurried to safety, many of them would fall off, producing a shower of bugs on the occupants below. There were so many bugs that the increased activity above the moving person also increased the din, as if a sudden gust of wind had disturbed the dried leaves.

Each individual builds his own section of the *shabono*. The man usually does all the heavy work of locating and fetching poles for the frame, placing them into the ground or tying them overhead, and weaving the numerous leaves into the roof thatch. The wife helps by gathering the leaves and vines used in the construction.

The first step in building a new *shabono* is the selection of the site. This is usually some well-drained portion of the garden, such as a slight rise or hump. The four main posts of the individual house are then sunk into the ground, two short ones about 5 feet high at the back, and two longer ones about 10 feet high at the front (see Fig. 2-4, a and c). The rear posts are placed about 8 or 9 feet away from the front posts, and both pairs are approximately the same distance from each other as well. After these have been tamped securely into the holes, cross poles are lashed to the tops of them, and then long, slender saplings some 20 to 30 feet long are laid about a foot apart from each other on top of the cross poles and secured with vine lashings. Since the two rear posts are only about half as high as those at the front, the long roof poles protrude upward at an angle of 25 to 30 degrees toward the village clearing. A vine is then strung along the bottom of the long, protruding saplings, looped around each pole, and run the entire length of the house. The leaves used in the thatch have a long stem; the individual leaves are bent over the vine where the stem joins the leaf, and the first row of thatching goes on. When this row is completed, another vine, about 8 inches above the first one, is again strung along the entire length of the house and secured to each of the long saplings where it crosses them. The next row of thatch is then put in place; the leaf is inserted into the thatch of the first row of leaves and bent over the second vine. It overlaps the first row of leaves when it is bent down (see Fig. 2-5). The leaves are placed about an inch apart, resulting in a thoroughly impermeable roof. When the rows of leaves reach the two front main posts, a scaffolding is erected, and the roofing is extended to completely cover the entire length of the 30 foot saplings. A fringe of palm leaves is then hung from the top of the roof, adding a little decoration to the structure. An upright pole from the scaffolding is left to support the overhang, since the weight of the leaves might break the slender poles. These uprights, some 20 feet high, are spaced every 15 feet or so around the village.

At this point the village looks like a series of individual houses arranged in a more or less neat circle, a gap of about 3 feet separating the individual houses from each other. These gaps are roofed over by the men whose houses are adjacent to them, and the village then looks like a continuous roof surrounding an open plaza. Some of the gaps are not completely roofed over in order to leave additional exits; the roofing is started at the lower crossbeams, giving an exit about 3 to 5 feet high.

Small houses in some areas are simply round structures with a smoke hole at the top, such as the first house shown in Fig. 2-4a. The Yanomamö *shabono* appears to have developed from such a structure by simply pulling the roof away from the center until the smoke hole grew so large that it, in effect, became a center plaza. Fig. 2-4a shows three house types that are found in Yanomamö country. They are not so much distinct types as different sizes of a single type, the size being a function of the number of people the house shelters.

Where the village is located at a relatively high elevation, palm fronds or banana leaves are placed in front of the house to keep the smoke, and, hence, the heat, in the house. At lower elevations these palm fronds are usually found only at the east end of the *shabono;* they are used to keep the bright rays of the afternoon sun out of the house.

A new *shabono* is very attractive; it smells of freshly cut leaves, looks clean and tidy, and is cooled by the breeze as it drops down into this tiny hole in the otherwise uninterrupted canopy of the forest.

a

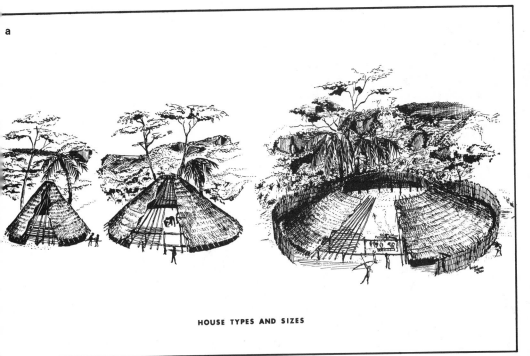

HOUSE TYPES AND SIZES

b

THE COSMOS

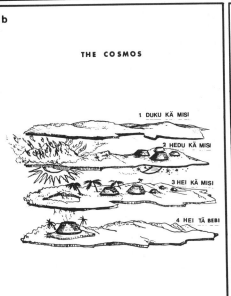

1 DUKU KÄ MISI

2 HEDU KÄ MISI

3 HEI KÄ MISI

4 HEI TÄ BEBI

c

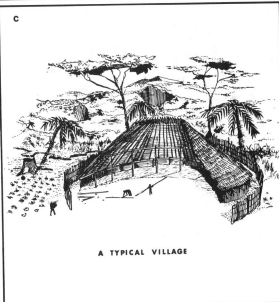

A TYPICAL VILLAGE

Fig. 2–4.

Fig. 2-5. Thatching a new roof with leaves.

The Indians do not like the wind because it blows the leaves off the roof. They do not tie the leaves down, depending on age and the rain to pack them into a homogeneous layer. They sometimes throw long sticks and brush on the roof to keep the wind from blowing the leaves away, but their major defense is magic: when a strong breeze comes up, the shamans rush to the center of the village, wave their arms frantically, and shout incantations to Wadoriwä, the spirit of the wind, enjoining him to stop blowing the leaves off the roof.

The Yąnomamö make another kind of shelter when they travel. It can be erected in less than a half-hour. A long front pole is selected and joined to two shorter back poles with two sticks. The roof structure thus fashioned is triangular in shape, about

4 feet off the ground at the rear and 6 feet off the ground at the front. Shorter sticks are then laid crossways on the major roof poles and these, in turn, covered with several layers of long, broad, wild "banana" leaves (see Glossary, under "Banana, wild"). It is quite small, but can sleep three individuals. Frequently, the traveler finds the remains of one of these houses and has merely to put a new layer of leaves on the roof to make it waterproof; occasionally, he takes a chance that it won't rain that night and does not improve the hut at all.

When the Yąnomamö settle a new area, they erect temporary villages of these crude huts and live in them until they can build a *shabono*. They also live in huts like these while they are re-roofing the old *shabono*.

The permanent village is complete when the palisade of logs is erected around its circumference. This is placed some 3 or 4 feet behind the roof, allowing space for a path around the village inside the palisade. The palisade itself is about 10 feet high and usually made of a mixture of palm and hardwood logs. It is kept in repair only when there is some reason to suspect raiders. Otherwise, people pilfer logs from it for use as firewood. The entrance to the village, as well as the palisade entrance, is covered with brush and logs at night to keep out intruders. Anyone trying to enter will inevitably make the brush move and alarm the village dogs.

FOOD AND ITS GATHERING   The jungle provides numerous varieties of food, both animal and vegetable. The most commonly taken game includes several species of monkeys, two varieties of wild "turkey," two species of wild pig, armadillos, anteaters, tapir, deer, a small alligator, small rodents, and several species of smaller birds. Wild vegetable foods commonly exploited by the Yąnomamö are: palm fruits of several species, hardwood fruits, brazil nuts, tubers, and the seed pods of the feral banana. Of these, the palm fruits are by far the most significant.

These occur seasonally and, for brief periods of time, produce large quantities of fruits. Unfortunately, there is very little edible substance in each fruit, so that in order to get filled, one must eat the edible portion of enormous quantities of fruit. The Yąnomamö extensively exploit two closely related palms, *yei* and *kareshi*. The *yei* fruits are about the size of small hen's eggs and occur in large clusters, weighing 80 pounds and more, near the tops of the palm trees. The *kareshi* fruits are about half that size. The exterior portion of the fruit is a leathery shell which is peeled with the teeth. Inside there is a thin layer of very bitter, white flesh. This is chewed and sucked off. The taste resembles that of a poor grade of bath soap. Of the two, I found *kareshi* the more repugnant. My throat burned when I ate them.

Another commonly exploited palm is the *ediweshi*. It is tangerine red in color and covered with a leather-like skin that consists of hundreds of small scales. They are about the size of large hen's eggs and resemble small hand grenades. When the fruit is dry, as, for example, when it is first cut from the tree, it is almost impossible to get the leathery scales off. The Yąnomamö overcome this difficulty by throwing the fruit bunches into water and letting them soak for several days, after which the scales can be easily scraped off with the fingernails, exposing a thin layer of yellowish, soft flesh that tastes very much like cheese. The fruits begin to ferment after they have soaked, producing a slightly pungent taste. I enjoyed eating *ediweshi* with the Yąnomamö; the fruit was good, and the technique of eating it was very sociable. We would wade into the swamp where the fruit had been submerged and grope around in the murky water to locate it. After we had each accumulated a half bushel or so, we would then proceed to eat them. In general, it takes a lot of work to get filled up on palm fruits.

The Yąnomamö also collect wild honey in considerable quantities. Nothing excites them more than locating a dead tree in which a swarm of bees has built a nest. They will halt everything and, if need be, spend the entire day chopping the tree down to get at the honey. When I began my fieldwork I hired about a dozen men to cut trees for me so that I could build a mud hut. They would be gone all day and return with just a few poles, demanding a full day's pay for their efforts. I decided to accompany them one day to see what they were up to. We spent the entire day wandering through the jungle, eyes glued to the tree tops above. Each time I spotted a suitable tree, they talked me out of cutting it down because "it would rot" or "it is too far away from the river." By mid-afternoon we had not cut a single tree, but had walked over a large area of jungle. Finally, one of the men shouted for the rest of us to come. All the men descended on the large, dead tree he had located, and set about chopping it down with the axes I had provided. It took about an hour to get it down. They then spent another hour chopping holes along the length of the tree trunk to get at the honey inside. When it was exposed, they gleefully tore the combs out, dunked them into the amber liquid, and gorged themselves on the larvae-filled combs. After they had eaten their fill of this, they collected a large pile of leaves and made a crude bowl. Then they stuck handfuls of leaves into the honey and squeezed them out into the leaf bowl. When they had gotten all the honey they could reach, they scoured the nest with leaves and licked them off after each plunge of the hand into the bowels of the trunk. They borrowed the aluminum kettle I had brought along and used to cook our lunch in. As we were some distance from the river and they were impatient, one of them filled the kettle with muddy water he found in a swamp a short distance away. Some of the honey from the bowl was poured into the kettle, along with dead adult bees, twigs, leaves, dirt, and several dozen larvae. They passed this around among themselves, each man drinking about a quart or so of the mead after blowing the debris off the surface in order to expose the water. The remainder of the honey was wrapped up in its leaf bowl, tightly bound with vines, and carried back to the village. On the way back to the canoe we cut a few light trees for my mud hut. They had gotten what they were looking for all day, and I managed to get a few logs. They demanded a full day's pay when we reached home. Thereafter, I paid them by the log rather than by the day.

Finally, several varieties of insects are collected. Perhaps the most desirable food in this category is the grub of an insect that lays its eggs in the decaying pith of dead palm trees. The Yąnomamö come very close to practicing "animal domestication" in their techniques of exploiting this food. They deliberately cut the palm tree down in order to provide fodder for the insect. When they cut the tree, they also eat the heart of the palm, a very delicious, crunchy vegetable that slightly resembles the taste of celery hearts. One palm we cut yielded an edible heart of about 50 pounds. After the pith has been allowed to decay for several months, it contains numerous large, fat, white grubs. The pith is dug out of the tree with sticks, broken open by hand, and the grubs extracted. Each grub is bitten behind his squirming head, and the head and intestines removed simply by pulling the body away from the teeth. If a grub gets damaged in the process of extracting it, the parts are eaten raw on the spot. A fair-sized palm tree will yield three or four pounds of grubs, some of them as large as a mouse. The grubs

Fig. 2-6. Rerebawä climbing a rasha *tree to collect the palm fruit. The tree has many sharp spines on it, and the Yąnomamö use an ingenious device made of crossed poles to climb the tree. The climber stands on one pair of poles and lifts the other pair up the tree. Then he climbs to the upper pair and lifts the bottom pair up. In this way the tree is slowly ascended, and no thorns get stuck in the body.*

are wrapped in small packages of leaves and placed in the hot coals to roast. They render down in the heat, yielding some liquid fat, which is licked off the leaves, and a soft, white body. I could never bring myself around to eat one, but an experienced missionary told me they tasted very much like bacon. But then I suppose that anything cooked in a smoky fire tastes like bacon.

The discarded seeds of palm fruits also get infected with much smaller grubs. The Yąnomamö break the hard seeds open with a rock, extract the grub, and prepare it in the above manner.

Some species of caterpillar are also eaten. They are not cleaned before cooking; the squirming insects are simply wrapped in leaves and thrown into the coals to roast.

They have much less fat on them than grubs, and become dry and crunchy during the cooking, having a texture and form like cheese pone when prepared.

Large spiders are also collected; they are simply placed directly on the hot coals and roasted alive. The legs and thorax are eaten.

Another common insect food is the larvae of a species of large ant. Only the head of the squirming larvae is eaten. It is very crunchy and has a nutty taste, but one must exercise caution in eating them since they are equipped with sharp pincers and can inflict a painful wound on the tongue or lip.

The game animals are all shot with arrows. The curare palm points are usually used for monkey hunting, while the lanceolate bamboo points are used for large game, such as deer, tapir, and wild pigs. A third kind of point is used for birds. It consists of a long, slender stick to the end of which has been bound a splinter of gently curved monkey bone. This serves as the penetrating point and the barb; it is difficult to extract the point once the barb enters the animal.

The Yąnomamö also fashion a fourth kind of arrow point as they need it. It is simply a stick that has numerous twigs branching in a close cluster. The twigs are cut off an inch or so from the main branch, and the stem is inserted into the end of the arrow shaft that usually contains the curare-tipped point. This fourth type of point is used to kill small birds whose feathers are desired for decoration purposes. On one occasion I saw a young man fashion one of these points in a few seconds. He saw a small bird, located a shrub a few feet away, bit off a branch with his teeth, bit the twigs off, and stuck the point into his arrow shaft—without taking his eyes off the small bird for a second. This type of point is discarded after it serves its temporary purpose.

The Yąnomamö do not employ traps or compounds when hunting. They frequently use dogs to run tapir, pigs, and deer, but most hunting is merely the individual stalking and shooting whatever game is available. As men always carry their weapons with them when they leave the village, they are, in effect, hunting continuously. A communal type of hunting trip invariably precedes a feast; this is described in Chapter 4.

The technique for capturing armadillos is very interesting. Armadillos live in burrows deep underground, and the Yąnomamö are always investigating the entrances of these burrows to see if any signs of recent occupation can be found. If the burrow is occupied, the hunters quickly cover the entrance with combustible materials and start a fire. After the fire is blazing strongly, they find a dried termite nest, which produces large quantities of smoke, and put it onto the fire. When this is ignited, they fan the smoke into the burrow, cover the fire with sand, and look for other openings to the armadillo den. These are quickly spotted when smoke begins to emerge from them and covered with sand to keep the smoke in. Then the men crawl around with their ears held to the ground. The armadillo will sometimes start burrowing in order to escape the smoke; when he does, he is heard and his location immediately established. A stick is used to dig into the ground and find the animal, usually 2 or 3 feet below the surface. On one occasion the men had difficulty locating the animal and dug several holes without hitting the burrow. One of them then uncovered the entrance, obtained a thick vine from a nearby tree, and tied a knot in the end of it. He then introduced the knot into the burrow by spinning the vine rapidly between his hands, pushing it in gently as it twirled. When he could not get the vine to go any further, the men listened on the ground to locate the spinning knot. When they found it, they marked the spot. The vine was removed and laid along the ground in the direction of the burrow to measure the distance from the entrance. The men began digging at the end of the vine and located the as-phyxiated armadillo on the first attempt.

The jungle provides many other kinds of foods and products too numerous to mention. Some, like vines and lianas, are very useful and commonly employed in basket-making; others, such as edible mushrooms, crabs, pigments, and decorative plant prod-ucts, are less significant, and exploited only sporadically. Despite the amazing variety of food products to be found in the jungle, however, the Yąnomamö could not exist for any substantial period of time on collected foods only: they rely heavily on their cultivated crops. The tropical forest is much less productive and reliable than one would imagine. The most abundant foods, palm fruits, are seasonal—a group of people could only rely on them for a few months of the year, during which time some 80 group mem-bers would have to forage over a wide area to obtain sufficient palm fruits to keep every-body well fed.

Game animals are not abundant, and an area is rapidly hunted out, so that a group must keep constantly on the move. Furthermore, hunting depends as much on luck as it does on skill and is not a very reliable way to supply nourishment. I have gone on five-day hunting trips with the Yąnomamö in areas that had not been hunted for decades, and had we not brought cultivated foods along, we would have been extremely hungry at the end of this time—we did not collect even enough meat to feed ourselves. On other trips, we often managed to collect enough game in one day to feed the entire village.

GARDENING Although the Yąnomamö spend almost as much time hunting as they do gardening, the bulk of their diet comes from foods that are cultivated. Perhaps 85 percent or more of the diet consists of domesticated rather than wild foods—plantains are by far the most important food in the diet.

The Yąnomamö are constantly looking for potential garden sites. When I hunted with them, the topic of conversation that evening would eventually drift over to the merits of the area as a possible site for a new garden. Most new garden sites are, in fact, discovered by hunters.

The land for a new site should not be heavily covered with brush, which is difficult to remove. The larger trees should not be too numerous either, as it takes a good deal of work to chop them down. Ideally, the new site should have very light jungle cover, should be well drained, near a source of drinking water, and relatively free of thorny underbrush. The Yąnomamö call a garden *hikari täka;* jungle that has the potential of being a good garden is likewise called *hikari täka.*

The first operation in making a new garden is to cut the smaller trees and brush; the bigger trees, *kayaba hi,* are left standing until the underbrush is removed. Then the big trees are felled with axes and left lying on the ground to dry out in the sun.

My older informants claimed that they did not have steel tools when they were younger and had to kill the big trees by cutting a ring of bark off around the base of the stump, using a crude stone axe, piling brush around them, and burning them. The trees rarely fell, but the fire usually killed them, and their leaves dropped off, permitting the sunlight to reach the ground.

They also claimed that making a garden was more arduous in those days because a large area would have to be searched for the necessary quantities of kindling used to kill the big trees. Today, however, steel tools are quite common, being provided by the several missionaries who have recently located posts at a number of locations in Yąno-mamö territory. The tools that they give to their local people are eventually traded inland to more remote villages so that all the Yąnomamö, even those who have not yet had any direct contact with outsiders, now have steel tools.[7] Before the missionaries arrived, the Yąnomamö occasionally obtained steel tools from the Carib-speaking Makiritare Indians, who have long been in contact with civilization. Some of the Makiritare made periodic canoe trips in the last century as far east as Georgetown in order to obtain these tools. Kąobawä told me that when he was a young man, his village had a single piece of steel, a portion of a broken machete that came ultimately from the Makiritare Indians by way of several intermediate Yąnomamö villages. Everybody in the village used this tool when they made their gardens. It was hafted on a split stick and used as an axe. I have seen broken machetes used in this fashion in the more remote, steel-poor villages.

The Yąnomamö usually fell the big trees toward the end of the wet season, although I have seen them do it at all times of the year. In general, the clearing of the land tends to be an activity of the wet season while the burning is done during the dry season, but this schedule is by no means rigorous. An adequate burning can be achieved at the peak of the rainy season, provided that there are two days of sunshine in succession. The dead brush and the leaves of the large trees dry out rather quickly in the sun, provided that they have been lying on the ground for a sufficiently long period of time. The trunks of the large trees are never burned, so that a newly cleared garden is strewn with logs lying helter-skelter all over the cleared patch. These serve as boundaries between individual gardens, as the crops belong to the person who plants them.

Each man clears his own land. Brothers will usually clear adjacent portions of land and, if their father is still living, his garden will be among theirs. The headman of the village generally has the largest garden, as he must produce larger quantities of food; he is obliged to give food away at feasts. He can frequently enlist the aid of other men to help him make a large garden. Kąobawä, for example, is helped by a younger brother, a brother-in-law, and the latter's son. Once in a while one of his sisters who lives in a different village visits for a long stretch of time, and her son-in-law also helps Kąobawä work in the garden during these visits.

After the brush has dried out and the larger trees felled, the portable timber and brush is gathered up into piles and burned, each man having several fires going in his own patch, to which he hauls the brush as he gathers it up. Usually, the fires are built under or next to one of the larger logs. In this way the logs dry out even more completely and can be easily chopped up by the women for firewood. The ashes are not scattered to improve soil fertility.

If the new site is a great distance from the previous garden, the men will have to make numerous trips between the two sites in order to transport the plantain cuttings. If an ally's village is closer to the new garden site, some cuttings can be borrowed from his gardens, thereby reducing the transportation labor. Each mature plantain or banana plant sends out suckers which sprout a few feet away from the adult stalk. When the Yąnomamö cut the bunch of plantains or bananas from the producing plant, they also cut the entire plant down to permit the younger suckers to receive the sunlight. The larger

---

[7]One missionary told me that he has given the residents of his village approximately 3000 machetes over the past eight years! These are traded inland to more remote Yąnomamö.

a newly planted sucker, the more quickly it will bear fruit. Hence, if the Yąnomamö wish to establish a garden that will produce a crop in the shortest period of time, they must plant large cuttings. These can weigh up to 10 pounds each, and transportation of the cuttings becomes a tremendous task.

As will be made clear later, most long moves are usually stimulated by warfare, and the group is under some pressure to establish a new garden as quickly as possible. The Yąnomamö can speed up their schedule of abandoning an area by taking temporary refuge in the village of an ally, by planting crops other than plantains that mature quickly and produce high yields, or by anticipating a serious war and getting an early start on their new garden. When Kąobawä's group was forced to abandon one of its locations because of a war, the group took refuge with an ally and established its new garden near the ally's village. One of the consequences of these factors is that newly established gardens produce their crops in cycles so that there will be periods of plenty interrupted by periods of hunger. After a few years, the garden will mature and produce constantly. The periods of hunger are eased by planting rapidly developing crops such as maize and by working constantly at transplanting the secondary plantain shoots as they appear. Thus, gardening activities vary largely with the relative maturity of the garden and the length of time the people have been living at that site. Once the plantains are producing constantly, other crops are not cultivated as intensively as before. But whatever the Yąnomamö are eating in a given village, they are striving to get their gardens to produce a constant supply of plantains. The fact that a given village may be relying very heavily on maize at some point in time may reflect no more than the fact that the garden is relatively new and the plantains have not yet begun producing constantly.

After a site has been occupied a few years, gardening activities take on a more regular pattern. The "rectum" (bei kä bosi) of the garden is gradually abandoned, and a new "nose" (bei kä hushibö) is added by clearing adjacent land and transplanting crops. Thus, a garden has a direction—it moves, little by little. Sometimes there will be as many as three or four discrete gardens around a village, all of them producing more or less continuously. The older ones are gradually abandoned because it is simply easier to clear new land than to attempt to weed the thorny underbrush out of the old site. If you have ever attempted to clear prickly brush without wearing protective clothing, you should immediately see the wisdom of the Yąnomamö choice.

In an established garden site, labor follows a more regular pattern. The dry season is usually the time for feasting, visiting, trading, and warfare. Gardening activities are at a minimum at this time of year, but the ambitious will try to work a few hours each day at weeding, transplanting, and burning brush. Most of the heavy labor of felling large trees is restricted to the wet season, when it is cloudy and generally cooler, and the demands of feasting and dancing do not interfere with the work. Still, practical considerations are more important than a fixed schedule of work, and if the gardens are producing insufficient quantities of food, the Yąnomamö will expand their gardens at any time of the year.

GARDEN PRODUCTS Each man's garden contains three or four varieties of both plantains and bananas. The larger portion of the cultivated land will contain plantains, as they produce a higher yield than bananas. The garden will also have a sizeable patch of sweet manioc, a root crop that is boiled or refined into a rough flour by grinding it on a rock and then converting the flour into thick, round cakes of baked cassava bread.

Many of the Yąnomamö villages have recently obtained bitter manioc, a poisonous variety that must be leached of its toxic ingredient before it can be eaten. This variety is grown in large quantities by the Carib-speaking Makiritare Indians–and by rural Venezuelans–and most of it has been introduced to the Yąnomamö recently by missionaries. Where the Yąnomamö are in direct contact with the Makiritare, they have, of course, adopted the crop without the intervention of the missionaries.

Next in importance are three other root crops: taro, sweet potatoes, and mapuey. All of these resemble potatoes; they are usually boiled, but occasionally they are roasted directly over the coals.

The Yąnomamö also cultivate a species of palm tree that produces a large crop of fruit each February and a much smaller crop in June. Each tree is owned by the individual who planted it, and his rights to the fruit continue even after the garden has been abandoned. It takes about six or seven years for a newly planted tree to produce its first crop, so the Yąnomamö are quite reluctant to move very far away from sites where they possess producing groves of these trees. When they do move, they return each year to collect the peach-palm fruit. They try, as well, to move to an abandoned garden that still has producing peach palms. If thieves have been raiding the unguarded crop, the Yąnomamö may cut the trees down, keeping the wood to make bows. They would sooner destroy an item of personal property than permit others to exploit it without permission.

Maize is probably next in importance, but in a special sense. It appears to be cultivated as an emergency crop because its seeds are light and easily transported. A group that must move its garden a long distance can carry large quantities of maize seed and produce a substantial crop in a relatively short period of time. Maize does not, however, under normal circumstances, figure prominently in the daily diet of the Yąnomamö.

Cane for arrow manufacturing is also grown. The mature plant consists of a long, slender, pithy cane that has no joints or branches and is ideally suited for arrow shafts. The Yąnomamö use the cane just as they harvest it. Their arrows are over 6 feet long. Wing feathers from the larger species of wild turkey are used to fletch the arrow. On each side of the shaft, one feather is tied with finely spun cotton fibers, being attached in such a way that the arrow will spin when it is released; its accuracy is thus improved in the way a bullet's accuracy is improved by rifling in a gun barrel. A nock is carved from wood with an agouti-tooth knife; it looks very much like a golf-ball tee when finished, except that it is grooved at the large end where it will be fitted to the bowstring. The nock is inserted in the narrow end of the cane and held fast with pitch adhesive and a tight wrapping of fine cotton thread. The large end of the cane is not altered if it is to take a curare tip, since it tapers to a fine point and, therefore, blends into the thin curare point. If the point to be mounted is of the lanceolate type, the tip of the cane is cut off at its maximum diameter, wrapped with heavy cord, and the point jammed into the cane pith with considerable force. The fiber wrapping prevents the cane from splitting while the point is being mounted. The finished product is a very handsome piece of work, and the Yąnomamö are proud of their arrows. They decorate the bamboo points by painting them red and adding black designs, and they attach a few colorful feathers to the fletched end. A seasoned arrow is a prized possession, in high demand in the trading network.

Another important cultivated plant is tobacco. Since men, women, and children all chew tobacco, the patch of ground devoted to its cultivation is quite large. Each family grows its own supply and jealously guards it. It is one of the most commonly stolen crops and, therefore, frequently has a conspicuous stick fence around it to draw the thief's attention to the fact that its owner shows a strong concern for its welfare. A man will even put a fence between his own tobacco and that of his father, should the two crops be planted side by side, and neither man can take a plant belonging to the other without permission. I also saw a young man place a number of sharpened bones in the ground near his tobacco patch so that a thief might suffer a serious foot wound should he trespass.

Cotton is the last plant to which major significance can be attached. The fibers are separated by hand from the seeds and spun into thread with a stick whorl, then several threads are twisted into a thick yarn. The yarn is rolled into balls about the size of a grapefruit and stored until enough has been accumulated to make a hammock. Frequently the balls of yarn are traded to the members of other villages.

The hammocks are manufactured on a crude frame consisting of two upright poles located about 6 feet from each other. The yarn is wrapped around and around the two poles until the desired width of the hammock is reached, usually about a yard, perhaps a little more. About a dozen vertical seams are braided into the horizontal strands of yarn; the poles are removed after the ends of the hammock have been tied with a few strands of cotton string, and the new hammock is completed (see Fig. 2-7). The women also use the yarn to make a short waistband, armband, and halter, and the men use it to make fat, round belts. All ages and sexes use it as a wrist, ankle, knee, and chest cord, and the men make a waist cord of the string, to which they tie their penis foreskins.

Numerous other plants are cultivated in the gardens, but are not as significant in everyday life as those discussed. They include leaf fibers, *bixa* pigment, avocados, drugs, water gourds and gourds for making spoons and ladles, a kind of squash whose seeds are eaten and whose yellow flowers are used by the young girls as decorations, sugar cane, cashew trees, papaya fruit, hot peppers, and a host of magical plants.

Most of the magical plants are associated with benevolent or at least nonmischievous functions. "Female charms" (*sua härö*), for example, are used by men to make women more receptive to sexual advances. The dried leaves of the magical plant are mixed with a fragrant wood, and the resulting powder is said to be able to make a reluctant female hunger for sex. Most men carry a small packet of this at all times. The powder is held in the palm of the hand, which is then held firmly against the nose of the female: She is forced to breathe it into her lungs. After she has done this, she becomes very receptive, and can thereafter be easily seduced by the man who charmed her. Another magical plant is cultivated by the women. Its leaves are thrown on the men when they have club fights because it allegedly keeps their tempers under control and prevents the fight from escalating to shooting. Still other plants are cultivated to insure that male or female children grow up to be healthy adults, a different plant being associated with each sex.

Some of the plants are cultivated for malevolent purposes, such as causing the women in enemy villages to have miscarriages or pains in the back when they are preg-

Fig. 2–7. Örasimi, Kạobawä's brother's daughter, making a hammock for trade with allies.

nant, while other plants allegedly cure the same evils. Kạobawä's followers do not cultivate many of these malevolent magical plants; they claim, however, that the "Waikas"[8] use them extensively and blow harmful charms at their enemies through hollow tubes. The failure of Kạobawä's group to use magical plants in this fashion is cited as a distin-

---

[8]The Yạnomamö are sometimes referred to in the literature by such designations as Shiriana, Xiriana, Guaharinbo, and Waika. The first three terms are foreign words meaning "howler monkey" and have been applied to the Yạnomamö by their northern neighbors, the Carib-speaking Makiritare Indians. A good deal of the early information came from the quite unreliable accounts travelers obtained from the Makiritare. The term *"Waika,"* however, from the verb *waikaö,* is a Yạnomamö word meaning "to kill an animal (or man) that is already dying from a wound." Zerries (1964) used the term *"Waika"* in much the same sense that I am using the term *"Yạnomamö."* *Waika,* however, is very ambiguous and imprecise. For example, members of village "A" will assert that members of village "B" are "Waikas." If you ask members of village "B" if they are Waikas, however, they will deny it and say they are Yạnomamö, adding that the members of village "C" are Waikas. When you question members of village "C," you will get the same answer: The Waikas live in the next village, only Yạnomamö live here. Nevertheless, the term does have currency in the villages near the headwaters of the Orinoco River. One of my informants claimed that the blood of "Moon" (see the third section of this chapter) changed into Waikas, but they became extinct because they were so fierce. He also asserted that the Waikas were Yạnomamö.

guishing feature that sets it aside from other groups of Yąnomamö. Many wild plants are also said to have magical properties.

CONCLUSION   The Yąnomamö have adapted to their jungle environment with a very simple technology. Exploiting both the naturally occurring foods and domesticated crops is relatively easy with this technology, and the resources of both the jungle and the garden provide the people with the two basic necessities of life: food and shelter. Although the resources are extremely varied and numerous, the diet is largely dominated by one food item: plantains. Techniques of manufacturing are so simple and direct that each individual can produce any item he needs from the resources immediately around him. The material aspect of the culture is decidedly rudimentary by comparison with other tropical forest tribes; the Yąnomamö appear to deliberately limit their possessions to an amount that can be easily transported in case the group is obliged to abandon its site on short notice.

Adaptation to the Sociopolitical Environment

The adaptation of the Yąnomamö to their environment can be only partially expressed in terms of how they make a living in the tropical forest with specific kinds of tools, plants, and techniques, for the forest is only one aspect of the external world to which they must adjust. Their adaptation also takes place in a social and political environment. This likewise affects the way in which the Yąnomamö are distributed over the land, how their villages are moved from one location to another, and the kinds of relationships each village has with its neighbors. In short, the Yąnomamö must relate themselves to each other as well as to nature.

ALLIANCES AND VILLAGE SIZE   I spoke of the considerations that must be met when a new garden site is selected. However, the area within which the new site is selected is determined almost exclusively by political factors. A Yąnomamö group would remain indefinitely in the area it settled were it not for the threat of raids from warring neighbors. To be sure, the group would move its garden little by little each year, but the general area would be abandoned only if the people were driven out by stronger groups around them. Again, dissident factions of the village might leave the area if a particularly serious fight developed within the group, but because a garden is necessary for the group to survive as a group, the Yąnomamö abandon them only when faced with disaster. To establish a new garden at a great distance from the old one, a Herculean effort is required just to transport the necessary plantain cuttings and seed, not to mention carrying provisions for eating while the work of clearing the garden and planting the crops progresses. Then, since a new garden produces sporadically for the first year, the people are frequently faced with food shortage. They are, therefore, reluctant to sacrifice the predictability of subsistence at the established garden for insecurity, periods of hunger, and hard work at some distant location.

Instead, they develop political alliances with neighboring villages, thereby adjusting to their social environment. The nature of these alliances is discussed in detail in Chapter 4, but at this point I will make some general statements about the relationships between villages to show why, on the one hand, the social environment calls forth the alliances, and why on the other hand, when alliances fail, a group must abandon its area.

Village size is an important factor in determining the degree to which a Yąnomamö group must depend on its neighbors for military support in the face of raids. Small villages must make alliances to survive. Village size, as I mentioned in Chapter 1, ranges from 40 to 250 inhabitants. Approximately one-third of the village consists of males who are able to participate in the raiding, that is, men who are between 17 and 40 years old. The tactics of warfare are such that a village must be able to field a raiding party of approximately 10 men in order to be able to raid effectively. In addition, when the raiders are away, there must always be a few men at home to protect the women and children. Thus, the military requirements alone seem to demand that a village have at least 15 able-bodied men. As these represent about a third of the group, the minimum village size required by the raiding techniques is 40 to 50 people. I have never seen a village fall below this size in an area where raiding is intense, and virtually every village split I investigated took place only when each of the resulting groups contained 40 or more people.

The upper limit to village size is also determined in large measure by the intensity of warfare. The village of Patanowä-teri, for example, has over 200 people. It was being raided actively by about a dozen different groups while I conducted my fieldwork, groups that raided it about twenty-five times in a period of fifteen months. The Patanowä-teri at one time had split into three groups of about equal size, but raids from their enemies forced them to reunite for common defense. In general, a village will fission after it reaches a population of about 150 because internal feuds and fights are so frequent that peace can only be maintained with great difficulty. A village of 100 individuals, for example, can fission to produce two militarily viable groups of about 50 people each. Only the threat of raids from powerful neighbors will, as in the case of the Patanowä-teri, inhibit the fissioning, and frequently the fission groups will reunite in a single village to fend off the raids of their enemies.

But a small group of 40 to 50 people is not as viable as a group twice that size. Consequently, it enters into alliances with its neighbors.

FISSION AND SETTLEMENT There is a tendency for the group to attempt to maximize its size after it becomes an independent entity. This is done by trying to keep all marriages within the group so that there is very little migration of young men and women to other villages after marriage. A small group also welcomes the addition of families from other villages, families that have gotten into fights in their own group and who prefer to leave rather than attempt to patch up their grievances with their kinsmen. Finally, the group tries to attract young men and women from other villages, encouraging them to settle permanently in the group. Rerebawä, for example, is under considerable pressure to remain permanently in Kąobawä's group.

As the village grows in size and varies in composition, it becomes increasingly difficult to keep order and peace. Extramarital sexual liaisons are more frequent in larger villages, because the probability is lower that the affairs will be discovered. When the Monou-teri rejoined Kąobawä's group to avoid the raids of their enemies, a bloody club fight developed between two men of that village over an affair one of them had with the other's wife. The culprit waited until the group joined Kąobawä's village before approaching the woman, thinking that with so many people in one village he would not be caught.

By the time a village approaches 100 to 150 people, such fights over women are so frequent that the group elects to fission rather than attempt to keep an uneasy internal peace. Although a larger village has an advantage in terms of its capacity to raid other groups and is better able to defend itself from raids, the internal fights often lead to killings within the group. Then, there is no alternative but for one of the factions to leave. Its members may anticipate a situation like this and begin making a new garden long before the fighting becomes violent enough to lead to deaths, or a fight can develop unexpectedly and result immediately in bloodshed. The guilty faction must then seek refuge in the village of an ally until it can establish its own garden. Usually, however, the larger group fissions while its members are on relatively peaceable terms, and the two resulting villages remain in the same general area so that they can reunite when raids threaten them. This is the situation that prevails between Upper and Lower Bisaasi-teri and Monou-teri; all three have a common history as a single village, but the members of each live in separate villages because of the numerous fights that took place within the group while they were still a single village. They continue, however, to rely on each other for protection when raids threaten. The Monou-teri (see Fig. 2-8), in fact, spent about a third of their time in either Lower Bisaasi-teri or in Kąobawä's group while I conducted my fieldwork. They were being raided by the Patanowä-teri and had not completed the new garden they were making. The Patanowä-teri forced them to abandon their producing site and move west.

The Patanowä-teri themselves were forced to establish a new garden because of the incessant raids by a number of villages. In addition to keeping always on the move between their two gardens, they also sought periodic refuge in the village of one of their own allies, a village two days travel to the south of their primary garden.

The raids against the Patanowä-teri by about a dozen villages illustrate a cardinal strategy of Yąnomamö warfare: attack a group when it is beleaguered and weakened by other enemies. When I first arrived, the Patanowä-teri were fighting only three groups. The Monou-teri then entered into the conflict by abducting a number of women from them, an act that ultimately led to raiding and killing. When the Monou-teri entered the conflict, they also persuaded their own allies to participate, bringing four other villages into the war. These, in turn, were joined by some of their allies so that the total number of belligerent villages rapidly grew to about a dozen. Many of them joined the hostilities because they knew that the Patanowä-teri could not defend themselves against a host of enemies. The new belligerents, therefore, stood a good chance of abducting women while being relatively immune to punitive raids. They could also discharge obligations to their allies by supporting their raids against the Patanowä-teri without exposing themselves to great danger.

In Fig. 2-8 the movements of Kąobawä's village over the past seventy-five years are summarized. The village originated at the site of Konata, occupied prior to 1900 by Kąobawä's grandfather. This site was abandoned because several villages (not indicated on the map) began raiding the people with such frequency that they were forced to flee south, cross the Orinoco River, and take refuge with allies at a place called Wareta. Similarly, Wareta was abandoned because of new wars, so the group again crossed the Orinoco River and settled at Namowei. Here, their old enemies again drove them out of the area, so the group migrated to Hąhoyaoba. Kąobawä was born at this location, some forty years ago. This site was abandoned because the soil in that area was very poor; even to this day, there are no Yąnomamö villages located in that general area.

The group then crossed the Orinoco for the third time and settled, sometime around 1925 or 1930, at Patanowä. By this time their numbers had increased to such a level that internal feuds were frequent. As the result of many fights, the group split into two villages in about 1940, and eventually entered into hostilities. The part of the village that remained behind took the name Patanowä-teri and has remained to the present at that site. Kąobawä's group fled to Shįhota, but was driven from there to Kreiböwei by the Patanowä-teri. They occupied this site in 1950–1951, when they were massacred during a feast by the members of two Shamatari villages to their south. This led them to take temporary refuge in the village of Mahekodo-teri on the Orinoco River, as they had not had time to make a new garden. Their site at Kobou was established while they lived with the Mahekodo-teri. It was only a vantage point from which they could establish gardens in more suitable areas, areas that were too far removed from Mahekodo-teri to permit the establishment of the gardens in a single move. Thus, Kobou was abandoned after only a few years' occupation there.

Kąobawä's group split in the process of abandoning the Kobou garden in 1954, a part of them taking the name Monou-teri. The Monou-teri still live at the site they established in 1954, but they were in the process of abandoning it in 1966 because of renewed raids from the Patanowä-teri. Kąobawä's group moved to the Orinoco again, to the site called Barauwä. By 1959 foreigners had finally reached this area, so Kąobawä and his followers moved down the Orinoco to the mouth of the Mavaca River to establish contact there with a government malaria post. They hoped to obtain steel tools from the family of foreigners at the post. They split into two factions after settling, half of them moving to the opposite bank of the Mavaca River. Thus, Bisaasi-teri has an upstream and a downstream settlement, and the members of these two groups refer to themselves as the Upper and Lower Bisaasi-teri, respectively, Bisaasi being the name of a grass commonly found around gardens.

Similarly, the Shamatari villages, indicated as circles in Fig. 2–8, have a settlement pattern characterized by internal village disputes leading to fissioning, gardens being abandoned because of warfare, and a general movement to the south and west away from the Orinoco headwaters. The history of the Shamatari villages is a little more complicated than the history of Kąobawä's group, since village fissioning began much earlier in their moves and produced many more villages. This was probably due to the fact that their original location had more inhabitants. The history of the villages marked as hexagons on the map, Fig. 2–8, is nearly identical in its over-all pattern to the above two groups of villages.

Kąobawä's group and the two Shamatari villages of Mǫmariböwei-teri and Reyaboböwei-teri (see Fig. 2–8) have, together, made some sixteen major moves during the past seventy-five years (Chagnon 1966, Chap. V). Only one of them was stimulated by poor soil conditions; one additional move was the result of the coming of foreigners. The remaining fourteen major moves resulted from either raids emanating from hostile neighbors, or internal village feuds that led to bloodshed and caused a split in the local group.[9] This should suffice to demonstrate that the political and military relationships between

---

[9]This figure does not include the moves that took place while I lived with the Yąnomamö. See Chapter 5 for a discussion of these.

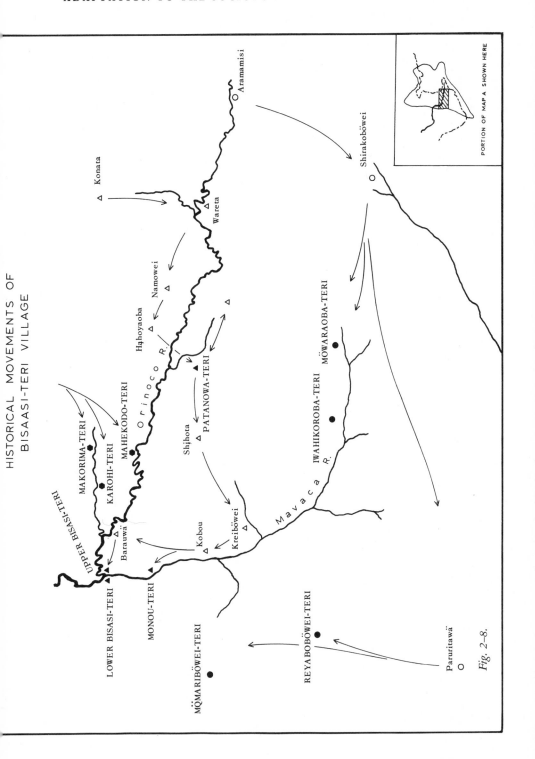

HISTORICAL MOVEMENTS OF
BISAASI-TERI VILLAGE

Fig. 2–8.

villages have a profound effect on the nature of the settlement pattern of Yąnomamö villages, and that this same milieu influences the rate at which larger villages fission into smaller, vulnerable groups.

Finally, I emphasize the importance of cultivation in this pattern of village movement and relocation, particularly in the context of relying on allies. Twice during the history of Kąobawä's group they were obliged to take refuge in the village of an ally. All during my fieldwork the Monou-teri also relied on hospitality of this sort from Kąobawä's group, as they were beleaguered by raids from the Patanowä-teri and had not yet completed their new garden. In short, the fact that the Yąnomamö rely heavily on cultivated food has led to specific obligations between members of allied villages: a good ally is one who will take you in when you are driven from your gardens by enemy raids. The essence of political life, therefore, is to develop stable alliances with neighboring villages so as to create a social network that potentially allows a local group to rely for long periods of time on the gardens of neighboring villages. I will describe the politics of alliance formation in Chapter 4, as it intimately bound up with feasting, trading, and marriage.

Intellectual Environment

The comparative poverty of Yąnomamö material culture is more than compensated for by the richness and complexity of their theological concepts, myths, and legends.

One of the distinctive features of Yąnomamö cosmology and theology is the opportunity it provides for inventiveness. Individuals can and do modify concepts, embellish them, improve on them and, in general, use their imaginations when trafficking in myths or concepts of the soul and afterlife. In short, there is room for thinkers in Yąnomamö culture.

The result of this is that many variants of the same basic myth can be found over a relatively small area. Indeed, each village will contain people who tell the myth a slightly different way; the basic elements remain the same each time, but personal views are interjected and reflect the idiosyncrasies of the narrator. The Yąnomamö appear to enjoy these intellectual exercises, for in myth and cosmology they are able to demonstrate their personal abilities as users of their language, the true language of man.

THE COSMOS   The Yąnomamö conceive of the external world as having an origin, boundaries, supernatural beings, and a specific nature.

The cosmos is comprised of four parallel layers, lying horizontally and located one on top of the other (see Fig. 2–4b). They are like inverted platters: gently curved, thin, circular, rigid, and having two surfaces, top and bottom.

The uppermost layer is the "tender" plane: *duku kä misi*. At the present time, it is "empty" or "void" (*broke*), but some things had their origins there in the distant past. These moved down to other layers. Today, the uppermost layer is sometimes described as being "an old woman" (*sua pata*), a phrase used to describe an abandoned garden or a female who is no longer capable of producing offspring. This layer does not figure prominently in the everyday life of the Yąnomamö; it is merely something that is there and once had a function.

The next layer is called *hedu kä misi:* sky layer. It is made of earth on the top surface and provides the eternal home for the souls of the departed. A complete replica of life on earth is to be found on top of *hedu,* except that the inhabitants are spirits of men, not real men. They garden, make witchcraft, hunt, eat, and in general do what living man does. Everything that exists on earth has a counterpart on *hedu,* a sort of mirror image, although the activities of the two groups of objects and beings are independent of each other.

The bottom surface of *hedu* is the visible portion of the sky. The celestial beings are attached to this surface and move across it. It is not thought to be very far above the earth, since many of my informants asked me if I had crashed into it when I flew in an airplane.

Man dwells below the sky on "this layer": *hei kä misi.* It originated when a piece of *hedu* broke off and fell to a lower level. This layer is a vast jungle, sprinkled with innumerable Yąnomamö villages. These are conceived to be located on earth, as shown in Fig. 2–4c. Even foreigners are thought to live in a type of house that resembles the Yąnomamö dwelling; after all, foreigners derived from the Yąnomamö by a process of degeneration.

Finally, the plane underneath this layer is almost barren. A single village of spirit-men is found here, the Amahiri-teri. A long time ago, after the earth layer was formed by a piece of *hedu,* another chunk of *hedu* fell down and crashed through earth. It hit earth at a place where the Amahiri-teri lived, carrying their village down to the bottom layer. Unfortunately, only their *shabono* and gardens were carried with the piece of *hedu.* Hence, the Amahiri-teri have no neighborhood (*urihi*) in which to hunt for game, and so they send their spirits up to earth to capture the souls of living children and eat them. There is a constant struggle between the evil spirits of Amahiri-teri shamans and the evil spirits of shamans on this layer, earth: They send malevolent demons against each other and preoccupy themselves with defending their respective villages from evil spirits.

The Amahiri-teri people lived at the time of the *no badabö,* the first men. These original Yąnomamö were distinct from living man in that they were part spirit (*yai*) and part human. When they died, they became *yai,* spirits. *No badabö* means, literally, "those who are now dead"; in a cosmological context, it refers to the time of the first beings.

THE FIRST BEINGS The first beings cannot be accounted for. The Yąnomamö simply presume that the cosmos originated with these people. Most of them, and there were many, had a specific function, such as creating a useful plant or object. They figure prominently in mythology. Many of them bear the names of plants and animals that are important in the Yąnomamö economy, and the first beings are considered to be the spirits of these. I will relate a few specific tales about some of these first beings, retaining where possible the Yąnomamö narrative style.

One of the first beings was called Boreawä, or simply Bore. He was the first to acquire plantains, the staple of the Yąnomamö diet. Because he had plantains first, he was the headman (*pata dodihiwä*) of the first beings. Boreawä did not tell the others that he had plantains, as he did not want to share them. At that time, the first beings ate only dirt and animals, as there was no domesticated food. One day another of the first beings, Horonama, got caught in a rain so he took refuge in a sheltered place in the jungle. He was lost and did not know whose neighborhood he was in. By luck, he took refuge in the very place where Boreawä had hidden his cultivated plantains. Horonama, a dirt eater, wondered what kind of strange vegetable food this was, so he stole some. At first he just peeled them and examined them, afraid to eat one. Horonama then sought out Boreawä and asked him how to produce these strange plants and what to do with them after they grew. Boreawä then instructed him in their use, the techniques of cutting jungle with stone axes, burning the fallen logs and brush, and planting the shoots of the young plants. Thus, because Horonama stole the plant from Boreawä, the others learned how to make gardens and no longer had to eat dirt.

Boreawä had a monopoly on many other cultivated crops, but one by one these were taken over by the others until all of the first beings were familiar with their use. Today, when the Yąnomamö find stone axes in the jungle, as they usually do when they clear a new site for cultivation, they explain the axes as something that the first beings, Boreawä in particular, left behind for present man to discover and use.

Another of the first beings was Iwä (alligator). He and his wife, Bruwaheiyoma, were accustomed to go hunting together in the jungle. This was in the days before fire was known to Yąnomamö. Iwä, however, knew about fire and kept some hidden in his mouth. He refused to give fire to the others, so they had to eat their meat and insects raw. Only Iwä and his wife cooked their food in those days. The others decided to make Iwä laugh so that they could steal the fire when he opened his mouth. They made pranks to get Iwä to laugh, but he would not be amused. Finally, Dohomamoriwä did something funny and caused Iwä to laugh. When he opened his mouth, Kanaboriwä, a bird, flew into his mouth, snatched the fire, and took it up with him into a tree, After that, everybody had fire.

Haya (deer) also lived among the first beings. His daughter was married to Aiyakorari. One day Haya sent Aiyakorari out of the village to fetch him some *manaca* fruit from the jungle. Haya was at that time the only one who ate this fruit. He did not know, however, that Aiyakorari had a grove of peach palm, which he cultivated. Thus, Aiyakorari fetched some of his own fruit instead of the *manaca*. His father-in-law, Haya, was very angry over this, so he inhaled a pinch of snuff and began pulling the flesh from his calves up to his thighs. After this had been accomplished, he pulled the flesh of his forearms up to his shoulders and transformed himself into a deer. His wife did the same thing, as this was a propitious moment. Haya's daughter started to do the same thing, but Aiyakorari grabbed her by the hair and prevented her from doing so. Haya and his wife then bounded off into the jungle and became deer.

Omauwä is one of the first beings who figures prominently in a number of Yąnomamö myths. He and his brother Yoawä lived when Öra (jaguar) lived. Öra had a young son who was unable to speak. One day Aiyakorari's mother, Mamokoriyoma, cooked some of her son's peach-palm fruit and fed it to Öra's child. He got sick from eating the fruit and died. After he died, a sister of Omauwä then asked Mamokoriyoma if she could eat the dead child. "Mother-in-law, should I eat the dead child?" she asked. Mamokoriyoma then said, "Eat him." She took the body of the child, pulled a leaf out of the roof of the house, and used it for a dish on which to consume the child's body. When Öra discovered this, he was angry. As he himself was hungry for meat, he in turn ate Moyeinaiyoma, the mother of Omauwä and Yoawä, to get revenge. After he had done so, Yoawä shot him with an arrow and killed him.

Soon after that, the daughter of Raharariyoma went to fetch water at the river where Omauwä and Yoawä were accustomed to catch fish. The two brothers found her there, so they copulated with her. After they quenched their desire for sex, Omauwä caused the girl's vagina to be changed into a mouth with teeth.[10] Howashiriwä, another of the first beings, was sitting on the trail at this time, very hungry for sex. When Raharari-yoma's daughter walked by, he seduced her, but in so doing, lost his penis: her vagina bit it off. It was when this happened that Omauwä's son became very thirsty. Both Omauwä and Yoawä began digging a hole to find water to quench the boy's thirst. They dug the hole so deep that when water did gush forth, it caused a large lake to form and covered the jungle. Then some of the first beings cut down trees, and floated on them to escape the flood. Because this was such a strange thing to do, they changed into foreigners and floated away. Their language also changed into the tongue of foreigners, and gradually became unintelligible to the Yanomamö. This is why foreigners have canoes and cannot be understood.

Many of the first beings were drowned in this flood. Those who managed to escape and remain Yanomamö did so by climbing mountains. They climbed Maiyo, Howashiwä, and Homahewä mountains to escape the flood, Maiyo being a peak near the area where Kaobawä's village had its origin. Then Raharariyoma, the mother of the girl whose vagina was changed into a mouth,[11] took a piece of red pigment and painted dots all over her own body. After she was completely covered with red dots, she plunged into the lake and caused it to recede. Omauwä then caused her to be changed into a *rahara,* a snake-like monster that lives in large rivers. After that, she caused Yanomamö to drown when they tried to cross large rivers, either by eating them or by splashing large waves on them. Omauwä then went downstream and became an enemy to the Yanomamö. Today he sends hiccups, sickness, and epidemics to the Yanomamö.

It is because the foreigners refused to climb the mountains to escape the flood that they became enemies to the Yanomamö. The foreigners tried to make friends with the Yanomamö after the flood, but because their language was so different, the Yanomamö refused to be friends. Today, however, the Yanomamö are becoming friends with foreigners.

After the flood, there were very few original beings left. Periboriwä (Spirit of the Moon) was one of the few who remained. He had a habit of coming down to earth to eat the soul parts of children. On his first descent, he ate one child, placing his soul between two pieces of cassava bread and eating it. He returned a second time to eat another child, also with cassava bread. Finally, on his third trip, Uhudima and Suhirina, two brothers, became angry and decided to shoot him. Uhudima, the poorer shot of the two, began letting his arrows fly. He shot at Periboriwä many times as he ascended to *hedu,* but missed. People say he was a very poor shot. Then Suhirina took one bamboo-tipped arrow (*rahaka*) and shot at Periboriwä when he was directly overhead, hitting him in the abdomen. The tip of the arrow barely penetrated Periboriwä's flesh, but the wound bled profusely. Blood spilled to earth in the vicinity of a village called Höö-teri, near the mountain called Maiyo. The blood changed into men as it hit the earth, causing a large population to be born. All of them were males; the blood of Periboriwä did not change into females. Most of the Yanomamö who are alive today are descended from the

---

[10]In some variants of this myth she put *piranha* fish in her vagina. These fish bit off Howashiriwä's penis.

[11]There are many linguistic parallels between eating and copulating in the Yanomamö language. The verb "to eat" also means "to copulate", the verb "to eat like a pig" also means "to copulate excessively", the adjective meaning "satiated, full" also means "to be pregnant." The context of the statement decides the meaning.

blood of Periboriwä. *Because they have their origin in blood, they are fierce and are continuously making war on each other.* This myth seems to be the "charter" of Yąnomamö society. It is the only one they repeatedly told me without my asking about it.

Where his blood was thickest, in the areas directly underneath the spot where Periboriwä was shot, the wars were so intense that the Yąnomamö in that area exterminated themselves. Where the blood had an opportunity to thin out, the Yąnomamö were less fierce and therefore did not become extinct, although they, too, fought continuously.

After this, there were only men. One of the men, a descendant of the blood of Periboriwä, was called Kanaboroma, not to be confused with Kanabororiwä, the bird who stole fire from Alligator's (Iwä's) mouth. One day his legs became pregnant. Women came out of the left leg, and men out of the right. These Yąnomamö were very *kirii* (docile, afraid) when compared to the ones who were derived from the blood. They rapidly multiplied and also contributed to the present population of Yąnomamö. All the present Yąnomamö came from the blood of Periboriwä or from the leg of Kanaboroma, or from a combination of both. The original beings all changed into *yai:* spirits.

THE SOUL   Yąnomamö concepts of the soul are elaborate and complicated. The true or real portion of living man is his "will" or "self" (*buhii*). At death, this changes into a *no borebö* and travels from this layer to *hedu,* the place above where the souls of the departed continue to exist in an ethereal state, much in the same fashion as do the people on earth: gardening, hunting, and practicing magic.

The trail along which the *no borebö* travel forks after it reaches *hedu.* Sometimes, the Yąnomamö will point to the sky and explain that such and such a cloud is the *no borebö* of a Yąnomamö who is just reaching *hedu.* After the soul reaches the fork in the trail, a spirit, the son of Thunder (Yąru), Wadawadariwä, asks the *no borebö* if it had been generous during its life on earth. If it had been stingy, Wadawadariwä directs the soul along the path that leads to *shobari waka,* a place on *hedu* where souls of stingy Yąnomamö burn eternally. Most of the Yąnomamö I questioned on this asserted that they planned to lie to Wadawadariwä and avoid going to *shobari waka.* In general, they did not fear this place and were convinced that they would not be sent there. They expect Wadawadariwä to direct them to the trail that leads into *hedu* proper.

Another portion of the soul, the *no uhudi* or *bore,* is released at cremation. This part of the soul remains on earth and wanders about in the jungle. The children who die always change into this, as they do not have the *no borebö* portion that goes to *hedu:* it must be acquired. The reason that children do not change into *no borebö* is that their "wills" (*buhii*) are ignorant or innocent (*mohode*). Thus, one has a character only after a certain amount of knowledge and experience are gained; with this, one develops a knowledgeable "will" and can expect to enter *hedu* in the form of a *no borebö.* Apart from this, one is born with an *uhudi* (*bore*), which is invariably released at cremation and wanders eternally in the jungle after death. Some of these wandering *uhudi* are malevolent and attack travelers in the jungle at night. When they do so, they use sticks and clubs. The Yąnomamö usually use the name *bore* when describing the attacks of these malevolent spirits, although this is just an alternate name for the *no uhudi.*

NORESHI   Finally, each individual has a *noreshi.* This is a dual concept: one has a *noreshi* within his being, a sort of spirit or portion of the soul, and, in addition, an animal that lives in the jungle and corresponds to this soul. The *noreshi* animals are inherited patrilineally for men and matrilineally for women.[12] Kạobawä, for example, inherited his *noreshi* animal, the black monkey, from his father and transmitted it to his son. All his male kinsmen have the black monkey as their *noreshi*. Bahimi, Kạobawä's wife, has the dog for her *noreshi* animal, as does her mother and her daughter by Kạobawä. The *noreshi* animal of a woman always travels on the ground below the animal of the husband.

Noreshi animals duplicate the behavior of the person to whom they correspond. When Kạobawä goes hunting, so does his *noreshi* animal. When he is sick, so is his *noreshi* animal. If he takes a journey of two days, the animal likewise travels an equal distance, and so forth.

The *noreshi* animal and the person to whom it corresponds are always in complementary distribution. That is, they never come close to each other, for if they should see each other, they would both die. Their mutual existences are coextensive and coterminous: One lives only as long as the other, and both die at precisely the same instant. If a hunter should shoot Kạobawä's *noreshi* animal and kill it, Kạobawä would also be shot and would die. Similarly, if Kạobawä is shot by raiders and killed, his *noreshi* animal would suffer the same fate.

The soul aspect of the *noreshi*, however, can leave the human body at will and wander. Sickness results when the *noreshi* has left the body; unless it is brought back soon, the person will die. The *noreshi* is the vulnerable portion of the complete being, the part that is the target of witchcraft and harmful magic. The shamans (*shabori*) wage constant war against the evil demons (*hekura*) of enemy groups who have been sent to capture the *noreshi* parts of children. They, in turn, send their own *hekura* to capture the *noreshi* of enemy children; the wars that take place between men who raid to kill are likewise carried over into the domain of the supernatural.

When sickness is deemed to be the result of soul loss, the people who are closely related to the sick person hunt for his *noreshi*. I participated in one of these soul hunts. Kạobawä's group had set up a temporary camp across the river from its main village site, as they suspected raiders would attack them. While they were camped in their temporary village, one of the children became ill, and her malady was thought to be caused by soul loss. When the threat of raiders passed, the temporary camp was abandoned and the group moved back into the main village.

The child's condition worsened, so a group of women and children returned to the temporary camp, suspecting that the *noreshi* had remained there. I went along and, with the others, cut a branch from a shrub and began sweeping the site and calling for the *noreshi* to return. We swept the entire area and converged at one point. Everybody was convinced that the *noreshi* had been herded into this central point. We then lured the *noreshi* back across the river and into the body of the sick child.

The vulnerability of the *noreshi* to magical spells is best examplified by the fact that the shamans of every village spend most of their time chanting to the *hekura* (demons) with the intention of persuading them either to attack the *noreshi* of other (enemy) children or to drive off the *hekura* sent by enemy shamans. Again, the Yạnomamö used two of their concepts of the soul to describe photographs and tape recordings. They were very hostile to me when I attempted to take photographs, especially of children, because

---

[12]The inheritance of these "alter-ego" animals has nothing to do with marriage rules and patrilineage exogamy.

I, in effect, was capturing the *noreshi* of the child: a photograph was called *noreshi*.[13] Tape recordings, in contrast, were not considered to be harmful. If anything, they enjoyed having me record their music and discussions, and always demanded that I play them back for everyone to hear. The word used to describe a recording was *no uhudibö*, the part of the soul that wanders in the jungle after the body is cremated. In short, only the *noreshi* aspect of the soul is vulnerable.

TREATMENT OF THE DEAD   If a person dies in an epidemic, his body, along with those of the others who died, is placed on a tree platform and allowed to decay. After several months, an old man is appointed to strip the remaining decayed flesh from the bones and the bones are then cremated. The Yąnomamö fear the smoke that is produced when a body is cremated, and since epidemics are feared, they do not take a chance on contaminating the houses, implements, and persons with the smoke produced by the burning bodies.

Under normal circumstances, the body of the deceased is placed on a pyre of logs, covered with additional wood, and allowed to burn until nothing but the large bones are left. The burning takes place in the village, usually in the afternoon. The children and women leave, as they are susceptible to contamination by the smoke. They all bathe carefully to wash off any possible contamination. Even the weapons are washed.

After the coals are cool enough to handle, the relatives sift the ashes meticulously with shallow, loosely woven baskets, collecting every bit of bone they can find. The charcoal of the wood is burned, lest a small piece of bone be mixed in with it. The accumulated bones are then ground in a log mortar, hollowed out by means of alternate burning and chopping. These logs are about 4 feet long and 6 to 8 inches in diameter. For grinding the bones of a male, white buzzard down is usually attached around the circumference of the mortar, and curved lines painted on the mortar with red pigment. The mortars used for females are not decorated as elaborately, but usually have decorative fibers of a palm tree, the kind used by women to decorate their perforated ears. Circles and dots are painted on the mortars of females.

The charred bones of the dead are placed, a few at a time, into the mortar and a long, slender pole is used as the pestle. These poles are about 6 feet long, 2 or 3 inches in diameter, and bear painted decorations. The bones are crushed into a black powder by a young man, while the relatives of the deceased sit around the mortar and weep profusely. The ground ashes are then transferred to hollow gourds through a small hole and sealed with wax and buzzard down. A little is left in the mortar and eaten, mixed with boiled plantain soup, on the day of the ceremony. The mortar is always burned after a ceremony.

About a year later, the rest of the ashes are eaten during a feast, again mixed with boiled plantain soup. Occasionally, they will deliberately save some of the ashes, especially ashes of those who were killed in raids, making use of them for a number of ceremonies. Before each attempt at getting revenge, the raiders eat the ashes of their slain kinsman. This puts them into the appropriate state of rage for the business of killing enemies.[14]

---

[13]Many informants gave a more pragmatic explanation of their fear of the camera. They did not want to be reminded of their dead kinsman, and if I had a photograph of the person, this would be an extremely offensive reminder to his relatives that their loved one was dead.

[14]Subsequent field research revealed that only the women eat the ashes of slain kinsmen before a raid.

Fig. 2-9. Three shamans in a drug-induced state chanting to their hekura.

The ashes of the deceased are consumed in order that the living will see their departed friends and relatives in *hedu*. Members of allied villages show their friendship to each other by sharing, in the ashes of particularly important people, in a very intimate act. Endocannibalism, to the Yąnomamö, is the supreme form of displaying friendship and solidarity.

SHAMANS The nature of the relationship between man and spirit is largely one of hostility. The shamans, by and large, spend most of their time casting charms on enemies and enjoining their own personal demons to prevent harm from befalling the local people. Magic and curing are intimately bound up in shamanism, the practitioner devoting his efforts alternatively to causing and curing sickness.

The demons that the shamans contact are *hekura*, very tiny humanoid beings that dwell on rocks and mountains. Particularly successful shamans can control these demons to such an extent that the *hekura* will come and live inside the chest of the shaman. Each shaman solicits the aid of numerous *hekura* and attempts to lure them into his body.

Men who want to become shamans (*shabori*) go through a simple rite of fasting and chastity. They sit before their houses, use only a few trails, eat very little, and spend most of their time in a contemplative stupor brought about by hunger and drugs. After several days of this, the initiate has entered the world of the *shabori*, and can practice his skill. Each village has as many *shabori* as there are men who wish to enter this status: probably half of the men in each village are shamans.

Rerebawä told me that he was going to become a *shabori*, as he enjoyed taking the drugs and making contact with the spirit world. He decided to do this because his wife is still nursing their youngest child so that he cannot have sexual relationships with her anyway; the obligatory chastity associated with becoming a shaman will not be as difficult now as it would be when his wife weans the child. No *hekura* will dwell in the chest of a novice *shabori* who continues to have sexual relationships. After the practitioner has captured the *hekura* and they become acquainted with him, they will stay in his chest after he resumes his sexual activities.

Contact with the *hekura* is achieved by taking drugs. Particularly adept *shabori* can contact their *hekura* with only a pinch of drug, which they inhale directly from their fingers. Most of them, however, take a large dose of the drug by means of the hollow blowing tube. The *shabori* then prances back and forth in front of his house and chants to the demons he attempts to control, enjoining them to descend on enemies and cause them sickness (see Fig. 2-9). If he is curing someone, he chants before the house of the patient, rubs him, massages him, and draws the evil spirit causing the sickness to some extremity, such as an arm or leg. Then he sucks or pulls the spirit out and carries it away from the sick person, either vomiting it out or throwing it away, depending on how he extracted it originally. The Yąnomamö do not employ medicines made from plants or animals. Consequently, they rely exclusively on the cures that the *shabori* effect, fighting supernatural ills with supernatural medicine.

One of the surprises of my field experience was that I had to spend a great deal of time curing the sick, and my medicines were always in demand. The sick people, however, always took their illnesses to the *shabori* after I had treated them—one cannot be too careful.

CONCLUSION In summary, the Yąnomamö have effected an adaptation to their three environments. This is not to say that other means and techniques could not do the job equally well; but the peculiar combination of technology, social organization, and cosmology found among the Yąnomamö distinguishes them as a group from all other tribes. Although their technology is primitive, it permits them to exploit their jungle habitat sufficiently well to provide them with the wherewithal of physical comfort. The nature of their economy—slash-and-burn agriculture—coupled with the fact that they have chronic warfare, results in a distinctive settlement pattern and system of alliances that permits groups of people to exploit a given area over a relatively long period of time. Finally, the Yąnomamö explain the nature of man's ferocity and origin in myth and legend, articulating themselves intellectually with the observable, real world.

Thus, each individual Yąnomamö enters the world with the physical, social, and ideological traditions at his disposal that will permit him to confront and adjust to the jungle, his neighbors, and the demons that cause sickness. The cosmos is ordered and orderly, in *hedu* as it is on earth.

3

Social Organization

THREE ASPECTS of Yąnomamö social organization will be dealt with: the ideal rules about marriage and the logical consequence of these rules—actual cases of Yąnomamö marriage are compared to the pattern of ideal marriage to justify the use of a model to describe Yąnomamö social structure; the demographic and political factors that bring about discrepancies between actual behavior and ideal behavior; the more important aspects of the division of labor and of ordinary daily life in the society.

Social Structure

This section is the most technical portion of the chapter; careful study of the diagrams is required as the text is read. Kinship is the heart of primitive social structure, and it must be understood in detail rather than through generalities. The rules governing marriage, along with the kinship system, together comprise and delineate the structure of Yąnomamö society. There is no simple way to present the data, which itself is frequently boring to even accomplished anthropologists, and students of anthropology must sooner or later come to grips with this important topic. Fortunately, the Yąnomamö kinship system is the type most commonly found among the world's primitives and it is, comparatively speaking, quite easy to grasp once the patterns in the diagram are spotted.

The important features of Yąnomamö social structure are represented in the model shown in Fig. 3-1. This diagram is based on an analysis of Yąnomamö marriage rules, kinship terminology, and other social and ideological features characteristic of their behavior. The symbols given in the legend of Fig. 3-1 will also be used in the diagrams that follow. It should be borne in mind that the model is only an ideal representation of Yąnomamö society; we shall see below how closely actual behavior conforms to this model. One of the objectives of structural anthropology is to attempt comparisons of different kinds of societies by using models of this type. In the discussions that follow I shall present some actual field data to justify the use of this model to represent Yąnomamö social structure.

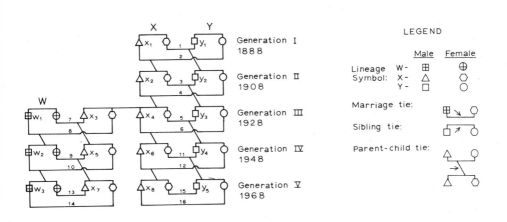

Fig. 3–1. Ideal Yąnomamö marriage pattern.

Fig. 3–1 can be presumed to represent the organization of a particular village over five generations, starting in the year 1888. Let us assume that the village originated in that year when individuals x_1 (and his sister, not numbered) and y_1 (and his sister) broke away from a larger village and established their own garden at some new location. Thus, in the year 1888, the village was comprised of two groups of kinsmen, X and Y. These two kinship groups are called lineages, the distinctive features of which I will discuss later.

In generation I, x_1 married the sister of y_1 and, in exchange, gave his own sister to y_1 as wife. This marriage practice is called *brother-sister* exchange and characterizes Yąnomamö marriage behavior. A man is under considerable obligation to *reciprocate* a woman to the kinship group from which he has taken one. In Fig. 3–1, x_1 married y_1's sister and reciprocated the exchange by giving his own sister to y_1. Because of this obligation of reciprocity, kinship groups become interdependent socially and form pairs of woman-exchanging kin groups. These paired kinship groups are discussed below in the context of village fissioning.

In generation II of Fig. 3–1, the village still contains only two groups of inter-marrying kinsmen. These are the children of the individuals who founded the village. The reciprocal exchanges of women between the two groups of kinsmen (lineages X and Y) continue in the second generation, x_2 getting his wife from lineage Y and vice versa. Like their fathers, x_2 and y_2 exchanged sisters. It will be noted at this point that x_2 has married his mother's brother's daughter, who is simultaneously his father's sister's daughter.[1] This is a logical consequence of the fact that there are only *two* lineages in

---

[1]This is called bilateral cross-cousin marriage. See glossary for definitions. Hereafter the following abbreviations will be used, following Murdock, 1949: Mo—mother; Fa—father; Br—brother; Si—sister; So—son; and Da—daughter. Thus, "mother's brother's daughter" is simply MoBrDa.

the village, the members of which being related to each other as brother and sister, and the fact that individuals must marry outside their own lineages.

The important features of the lineages X and Y are now clearly visible in generation II: The lineages are patrilineal and exogamous. That is, males and females belong to the lineage of their father (patrilineality), and individuals must marry people who belong to a different lineage (exogamy). This can be seen more clearly in the symbols used in Fig. 3–1. All males of lineage X are designated by triangles (x_1, x_2, x_3 . . . x_8), and all females of lineage X are designated by hexagons. Similarly, all males of lineage Y are designated as squares and all females by circles. Males of lineage X marry females of lineage Y. Their children belong to lineage X because their *father* (patrilineality) is of lineage X.

The Yąnomamö kinship system also reflects the rules of lineage exogamy, brother-sister exchange and reciprocity. Their kinship system is called the "bifurcate merging" type with "Iroquois" cousin terms (see Glossary). Within each generation, all the males of one lineage call each other "brother," and all the women call each other "sister." Males of lineage X call males of lineage Y "brother-in-law" and are eligible to marry their sisters. In fact, the males of lineage X call the females of lineage Y "wife" *whether or not they marry them.* This is likewise true for the males of lineage Y with respect to the females of lineage X. This brings us to another important Yąnomamö marriage rule: A male must marry a woman of the category called *suaböya*—"wife." This is called a *prescriptive* marriage rule.[2] To state it more precisely, Yąnomamö society is characterized by a rule that enjoins a man to marry a woman of a specific kinship category; he has no choice with respect to the category.

There is an important controversy over the meaning and implications of the term "prescriptive." I have given the definition held by British anthropologists generally, by Needham (1962a:9) in particular. This definition emphasizes the fact that men have no choice with respect to the category of women from which their wives must come, that men are forbidden to marry women of other categories, and that the society itself is said to be characterized by the prescriptive rule. The opposition to this definition comes largely from certain American anthropologists, who maintain that a society can only be said to have a prescriptive marriage rule when a high percentage (close to 100 percent) of the people marry according to the rule (see Coult and Hammel 1963:291). The issues involved are not quite as simple as this, but a glimmering of the area of contention can be seen in an example provided by Leach (1965). Rephrasing his example, the rule (in our society) "thou shalt not kill" is like the rule (among, say, the Yąnomamö) "thou shalt marry a woman of category A." These rules can be said to exist in the respective societies irrespective of the homocide rate in New York or the frequency of aberrant marriages in a Yąnomamö village. That is, Leach (and Needham) maintain that one cannot discover such a rule by counting examples of murder (or, rather, "non-murder") or marriages of men to women of category A. The more basic issue, however, is the

---

[2]Professor Lévi-Strauss, who read an earlier draft of this chapter, quite correctly pointed out that to say a marriage system is "prescriptive" is to say no more than "a man must marry a marriageable female," which is a tautology. Nevertheless, we must have some way to distinguish a system that permits marriage with only a single category of women from those that permit marriage with women of several categories. By showing what is meant by the Yąnomamö category *suaböya,* as I have attempted to do in Fig. 3–2, the reader will gain some idea of what is meant by that marriage type. I have used the term "prescriptive" because it is the current usage.

meaning of, in this case, "category A." It is customary to represent primitive kinship categories in models (for example, Fig. 3-1) by their closest biological equivalents in *our own kinship system*. Many critics of Needham's definition of prescription fail to appreciate the fact that FaSiDa and MoBrDa in a model like the one given in Fig. 3-1 represent just *two* of several kinds of kinswomen who fall into the prescribed category. That is, they interpret the native's kinship category from the narrow point of view of one of that category's biological meanings in *our own kinship system*. (I have given ten examples of actual Yąnomamö marriages in Fig. 3-2, discussed later, to illustrate what the categories FaSiDa and MoBrDa mean to the Yąnomamö.) The use of Needham's definition of prescription to characterize Yąnomamö marriage rules can be justified, therefore, on several grounds. First, the Yąnomamö assert that a man must marry a woman of the *suaböya* category. Second, of the six primary categories used by men to classify female relatives, five of them embrace women who stand in incestuous relationship to the male speaker, and he is forbidden to marry any woman that falls into any of these five additional categories. Third, we will see below how closely the alternative definition of prescription fits the Yąnomamö, using their own notions of kinship to reckon relationships between males and females.[3]

In Fig. 3-1, marriageable women are related to their husbands as both FaSiDa and MoBrDa; this is an artifact of the way in which the model is drawn. These two kinds of kinswomen are the closest biological equivalents in our kinship system for the Yąnomamö term "*suaböya:*" "wife." It must be emphasized, however, that given the classificatory nature of the Yąnomamö kinship system (for example, men of the same generation and of the same lineage are "brothers"), there are several ways to be related to a woman as "wife."

Something new has happened in generation III. A man (w_1) from a distant village, along with his sister, has joined the group. Both he and his sister have married into lineage X. Thus, there are three lineages represented in the village (W, X, and Y), and the *dual organization* characterizing generations I and II is now lost.[4] A Yąnomamö village can incorporate new lineages into its social life by an extension of marriage ties to its members. As can be seen from Fig. 3-1, the same rules—exogamy, reciprocity, patrilineal descent, and brother-sister exchange—that characterize the behavior of the members of lineages X and Y also hold for the members of the new lineage, W. The incorporation of lineage W takes place this way. W_1 joined the village in 1928 (generation III) because x_3 and x_4 promised him one of their sisters. As shown in Fig. 3-1, he did, in fact, marry one of their sisters and gave, in exchange, one of his sisters to x_3.

This (potentially) brings about an important structural change in the village with

---

[3]For an excellent summary of the various arguments concerning "prescriptive alliance," see Maybury-Lewis 1965*a*.

[4]A society is said to have dual organization when, for example, it is comprised of two intermarrying kinship groups, such as lineages X and Y in generations I and II of Fig. 3-1. In some societies the intermarrying kin groups are named, for example, "Bear Clan (or Moiety)" and "Thunderbird Clan (or Moiety)." The Yąnomamö do not have named kinship groups such as this. Dual organization is, however, implied in their kinship terminology and marriage rules and, as will be seen, villages tend to have two (and only two) politically dominant lineages that intermarry. In short, the Yąnomamö village tends to be comprised *in fact* of two dominant kinship groups but lacks some of the ideology, such as named pairs of intermarrying kin groups, of classical dual organization. See: Maybury-Lewis, 1960 and 1967; Lévi-Strauss, 1963, Chapter VIII; Nimuendajú and Lowie, 1927; and Malinowski, 1926, for further descriptions and analyses of societies having dual organization.

respect to the male members of lineage X. Generation III shows that individuals x_3 and x_4 are full brothers. The individuals x_5 and x_6 of generation IV, however, are not shown as brothers, although in Yąnomamö kinship usage they would be such.

I have not indicated them as being related as brothers in order to draw attention to a fault line that may develop when the members of a single lineage (X in this case) marry into more than one other lineage (W and Y in this case). x_3 and one of his sisters married into lineage W, whereas x_4 and one of his sisters continued to exchange with members of lineage Y. In the following generation the kinship tie of "brother" between x_5 and x_6 is considerably weaker than the same "brother" tie between their fathers (x_3 and x_4). In generation V, the "brother" tie between x_7 and x_8 is weaker still. One of the reasons that *agnatic* ties[5] weaken in this case is that the men in question are drawn into intimate relationship with the kinship groups from which they obtain their wives and assume, because of the principle of reciprocity, obligations to their affinally related (that is, by marriage) kinsmen.

Secondly, because agnates of the same generation are "brothers," they can marry the same women and are, hence, competitors. In other words, the obligations to exchange women (reciprocity) can link the members of affinally related groups to each other more intimately than ties of blood between males of the same lineage. (This can be more readily seen in Figs. 3-5 and 3-6, discussed later, but it can also be partially illustrated here.) If the village shown in Fig. 3-1 were to split in generation V and form two new villages, lineage X would pull apart along the fault line shown. That is, parts of lineage X would end up in each of the two new groups because the affinal (marriage) ties between its members and their wife-givers are stronger than the agnatic ties within the lineage. Individual x_7 and his sister would form a new village with w_3 (and his sister) while x_8, his "brother" (agnate), would remain paired with lineage Y. Lineage X would therefore be represented in both of the two new villages; individuals x_7 and x_8 would "feel" even more remotely related because they now live in different villages, although they would continue to call each other "brother." Finally, the two new villages would again demonstrate the dual organization that characterized generations I and II of the original village of Fig. 3-1. For the sake of simplicity I have shown each married pair with only two children (except in generation III) so that the village remains constant in size, growing only by the addition of new members. In an actual village lineages X and Y might comprise up to 80 percent of the population so that the addition of a few new members such as w_1 would not appreciably alter the dual composition.

In Fig. 3-1, lineage X stands as wife-giver and wife-receiver with respect to the other two lineages. The significance of this relationship cannot be exaggerated in the analysis of Yąnomamö social organization. Its strength derives from the obligations kinship groups have toward each other once they enter into reciprocal marriage exchanges. The wife-giver/wife-receiver relationship is also reflected in the attitudes men have toward their affines, such as brothers-in-law, as opposed to attitudes toward distant agnates. A man is on very intimate terms with his brother-in-law, jokes with him, gives him possessions, and protects him; a man treats an agnate of the same age with great reserve and coolness and tends to be jealous of him. He cannot, for example, directly ask

---

[5]Kinship ties between patrilineally related kinsmen.

him to do a favor, whereas he could ask this of a brother-in-law.[6] As shall presently be seen, the dynamics of Yąnomamö social organization originate in the politics of obtaining a wife. Within this context, agnates are competitors and affines are allies. This has an important effect on the manner in which villages fission and form new groups. The point to remember at this juncture is that ties of marriage are in many cases stronger than ties of blood.

I emphasize this because many anthropologists argue from "first principles" that ties of blood are—by definition—more capable of promoting solidarity and amity than ties by marriage. The controversy over "complementary filiation" between E. R. Leach (1957) and M. Fortes (1959), still not satisfactorily resolved, was essentially a debate about the analytical significance of marriage ties. Focusing on only one of the issues and rephrasing the arguments so as to apply to Fig. 3-2, the debate ran something like this: Both Leach and Fortes seemed to agree that in societies having lineal descent groups (lineages), the descent groups would tend to fall apart unless some kind of tie bound the members to each other. That is, lineages X and Y of Fig. 3-2 would, in short, pull away from each other unless they were held together by some special social tie. Fortes argued that this special tie was the solidarity and amity that grew out of the cognatic (see Glossary) kinship ties between the two lineages which arise when individuals marry blood relatives. Looking at generation V, for example, Fortes would argue that lineages X and Y are bound to each other because x_8 and y_5 married women to whom they are related by blood (as FaSiDa and MoBrDa). He argues from first principles that solidarity emanates from the blood ties. Leach, however, states that in generation V the two lineages are bound to each other by obligations to reciprocate goods, services, and women and that the solidarity of the two lineages derives from the affinal ties themselves (shown as "15" and "16" in Fig. 3-1). If we look only at generation V, the argument cannot be resolved, since the data support both arguments equally well, or at least do not convincingly support one rather than the other. I might add that both arguments can be supported by data not given in Fig. 3-1; Fortes' arguments are supported, for example, by the additional fact that Yąnomamö men do not stringently have to avoid their mothers-in-law when they are related to them in the fashion shown in Fig. 3-1, whereas the avoidance taboo is very onerous when a man's mother-in-law is not a blood relative. If, however, attention is focused on the events of generation III and their consequences examined, it can readily be seen that the affinal (marriage) ties in generation V are stronger than some of the agnatic (blood) ties, and the latter break when the village fissions. (This can be even more readily seen in Fig. 3-4 and 3-5, discussed later.) Thus, it cannot be argued that Yąnomamö lineage solidarity derives exclusively from blood ties and "complementary filiation." There is another issue. Structural analyses depend in large measure on a sharp distinction between marriage (affinal) ties and blood (consanguineal) ties. Fortes seems to deny that affinal ties as such exist independently of blood ties, and he has "subsumed" them into his concept of "complementary filiation." If there is no such thing as affinal ties between lineal descent groups, then structural

---

[6] In addition, it is by no means rare for agnates to get into club fights over women. I even have recorded a number of cases of men shooting and killing a "brother" during raids. This happened on two occasions during my first stay in the field, and I have reports of several additional cases obtained from informants who were describing past raids.

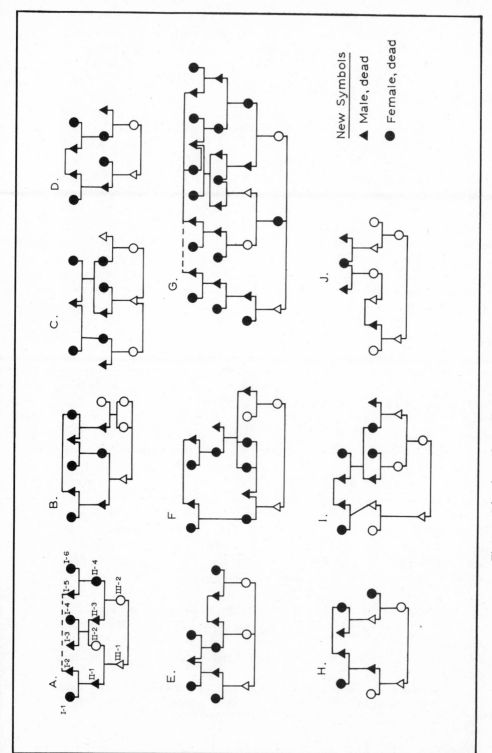

Fig. 3-2. Selected genealogies illustrating actual Yanomamö marriage cases.

analysis of reciprocal marriage exchanges between such groups and the obligations implied in such exchange is seriously hampered. In short, if Yąnomamö marriage exchanges over a number of generations and the kinship basis of village fissioning are examined, the data support Leach's arguments. They do not, however, invalidate Fortes' argument that blood ties create some solidarity, but they do call into question the contention that blood ties by definition, or, rather, on "first principles," account exclusively for the solidarity occurring between lineages.

In summary, Fig. 3–1 represents a number of important features of Yąnomamö social organization. First, people reckon descent through males and are grouped into exogamous, patrilineal lineages. These are called *mashi* by the Yąnomamö, although none of them bear distinctive names.[7] Second, members of these lineages tend to intermarry with the members of a second lineage over a number of generations, being bound to them by obligations to reciprocate women in marriage. This results in a dual organization of kinsmen within the village, whose residents fall into one or the other of the two lineages. Third, new lineages can be incorporated into the village by an extension of marriage ties, potentially bringing about "structural faults" within the lineages of that village. Fourth, men are obliged to marry a woman of a single, specific category, *suaböya*. This category defines a variety of women, two subcategories of which can be translated into the English biological equivalents MoBrDa and FaSiDa. Yąnomamö men prefer to marry women of these subcategories because they are relieved of much of the discomfort of avoiding their mothers-in-law.[8]

The ten partial genealogies shown in Fig. 3–2 show how the Yąnomamö actually marry. The genealogies have been selected with the intention of illustrating how the Yąnomamö reckon relationships between kinsmen in general, and between husband and wife in particular. All ten exemplify prescriptive marriage. They are more or less arranged in decreasing order of correspondence to our own biological concepts of kinship and illustrate the classificatory nature of their kinship system.

The people shown on these genealogies are (or were) real people. Many of the individuals in the examples are related to each other in such ways that all ten of the examples could be drawn as a single, unified genealogy.

The first eight examples are drawn from the village of Patanowä-teri; the last two are from Bisaasi-teri. In case J, for example, the fifth individual of the second generation is Kąobawä. To give a rough idea of the incompleteness of each genealogy, only one of Kąobawä's four marriages is shown and only one of his four children. None of his brothers and sisters are shown either, nor is the fact that he married a MoBrDa indicated.

Case A illustrates the identification procedure to be used in relating the genealogies to the text. There are three generations shown in case A; the first is symbolized by the Roman numeral I, the second, by II, the third, by III. Each individual in each generation is given a number; the number series runs from left to right and begins anew with 1 in each generation. Hence, every individual bears a generation number and a position-within-generation number. Case A illustrates the marriage of individuals III–1 to III–2;

---

[7] *Mashi* means "species," "group," "cluster of similar things," and, in the context of kinship, "that group of people to whom I am related through males;" that is, "patrilineal kinsmen."

[8] I draw attention to the fact that the category is *prescribed,* but within it there are *preferences.* There are very few analyses of societies that have a prescriptive rule within which there are preferences, although Needham has devoted some attention to this interesting phenomenon (1962a, 1962b, and 1963).

Fig. 3–3. *Ariwari, Kąobawä's son, being fondled by his mother's brother. This is a very intimate kinship relationship in Yąnomamö society.*

that is, the marriage of individuals 1 and 2 of the third generation. Although the ten examples are given primarily to illustrate the marriage of individuals of the most recent generation (3 or 4, depending on the number of generations in each example), in some cases additional marriages in ascending generations will be discussed. The point to remember for the time being is that the genealogies should be looked at from the most recent generation; the marriage pattern can be more readily seen in this fashion.

Case A: This exemplifies the *matrilateral cross-cousin* marriage, sometimes called MoBrDa marriage. Here, the Yąnomamö category *suaböya* corresponds exactly with our biological translation to MoBrDa. The man in question (III–1) would have called the woman *suaböya* whether or not he married her. Similarly, she would have addressed him by the term for husband: *hęaroya*.

The marriage of III–1 to III–2 in this case also exemplifies *patrilateral cross-cousin* marriage, for the woman is related to her husband as FaSiDa as well. This is so because individuals II–1 and II–4 are siblings (brother and sister to each other) because their own fathers, in turn, were brothers. (Individual I–2 was an *adopted* brother to I–5, hence the broken sibling line connecting them.) When an individual marries a woman who is simultaneously his FaSiDa and MoBrDa, he is said to marry his *bilateral cross-cousin.* Case A illustrates the preferred form of marriage, for the man does not have to avoid his wife's parents as stringently as he would were they related to him in a different fashion. When a man's father-in-law is his MoBr, he is on extremely intimate terms with him and can even make jokes at his expense. The intimacy of the relationship between a man and his MoBr was brought home to me very indelibly on one occasion. A group of Patanowä-teri men visited Kąobawä, although their two villages were at war. One of the visitors was Kąobawä's wife's brother. After this man rested in a hammock for a few minutes, he got up and found Ariwari, Kąobawä's son. Ariwari was the visitor's sister's son. He played with him in the hammock and hugged him intimately (see Fig. 3–3). Ariwari fell asleep in his arms. This took place in spite of the fact that the visitors were in danger of being killed by other members of Kąobawä's group and narrowly escaped death on their previous visit. (See the section "Division of Labor and Daily Social Life" later in this chapter for a description of the incident.)

Case B: This illustrates the same kind of marriage that took place in Case A, except that the parents of the married people are half-siblings to each other. The Yąnomamö do not distinguish half-siblings from full siblings, so this situation is identical, as far as they are concerned, to the marriage in case A.

Case B also illustrates *sororal polygyny:* III–1 married two women who were related to each other as sisters.

Finally, it should be noted that the father of the man in question married a sister to individual II–3. They stood in wife-giver/wife-receiver relationship to each other and so do their children.

Case C: This illustrates the *patrilateral cross-cousin* marriage, that is, the FaSiDa marriage. Like the MoBrDa marriage, it is preferred because the man does not have to avoid his wife's parents. It is considered to be incestuous for a man to be familiar with his wife's mother if the woman is still sexually active. Hence, he must avoid her. If she is his FaSi, however, incest prohibitions pertaining to that kinswoman would automatically call forth appropriate behavior on his part, and the avoidance taboo is not stringent.

The avoidance taboo prohibits a man from saying his mother-in-law's name. My informants would be extremely embarrassed when I would say the name of their mother-in-law while collecting genealogies. Kạobawä, for example, would grin sheepishly and hide his head. Men must also avoid their mothers-in-law physically and should not look at them. If I took a group of people for a ride in my canoe, there would always be considerable shuffling of bodies so that the men could be situated in the canoe as far away from their mothers-in-law as possible.

Finally, case C illustrates another kind of sororal polygyny: Individuals III–1 and III–3 are sisters to each other because their mothers are sisters. (The equation stating that children of siblings of the same sex are themselves siblings extends indefinitely in the case of males, but breaks down in the case of females after two generations. This is because descent is patrilineal.)

Case D: This also is a case of FaSiDa marriage: I–2 and I–3 were brothers, so one of the parents of each of the third generation individuals were brother and sister to each other. Hence, III–1 married his FaSiDa.

Case E: The marriage of III–1 to III–2 is similar to the marriage in case D, but his marriage to the second wife, III–3, illustrates the use of another kinship equation. She is an actual sister to the first wife, but does not stand in the FaSiDa relationship to her husband. If one of the sisters is FaSiDa, however, then all of them are in Yạnomamö kinship usage.

Case F: This illustrates how affinal ties replace consanguineal ties should the two conflict. III–1 can trace a blood tie to his wife, one that would prevent him from marrying her, but the affinal ties between his own father and the father of his wife permit him to marry according to the prescription. Individual III–1 would call all of his father's wives "mother." Hence, his own wife is, technically, MoBrDa.

Case G: This illustrates a number of marriage rules stated in the preceding examples. I present it as a sort of exercise to reinforce the logic of the Yạnomamö kinship equations given above. Individual II–6 married two brothers, II–5 and II–7, illustrating the *levirate:* the marriage between a man and his brother's widow. Individual II–9 married his FaSiDa (as in case F). Individuals III–3 and III–4 can marry because their fathers were cross-cousins (see case H, below). Individual III–5 married his FaSiDa, as was shown for the similar marriage in case E. Individual IV–1 married two women, each of whom is his FaSiDa. This is so because I–2 and I–4 were adopted brothers, so that their sons (II–2 and II–4) were also siblings. Hence, IV–1 married his FaSiDa (IV–2) and, as in case E, her sister. His second wife is also FaSiDa because her mother (III–6) was a sister to III–2, since their respective fathers (II–9 and II–2) were (adopted) brothers.

Case H: This illustrates a very powerful marriage rule: The children of men who call each other *shoriwä* (brother-in-law) can marry. Practically speaking, in our kinship terms, the rule is that the children of cross-cousins stand in marriageable relationship to each other. II–2 and II–3 stand in wife-giver/wife-receiver relationship to each other and could exchange sisters in marriage. Their sons stand in the same relationship. Another important feature of Yạnomamö kinship and marriage rules is illustrated here. While III–1 married a woman of the prescribed category, he does not reckon his relationship to her patrilaterally or matrilaterally. That is, she is neither FaSiDa nor MoBrDa, but she is both! This emphasizes the fact that they marry primarily in terms of categories rather than by tracing biological ties, as I have done in the above examples. To the Yạnomamö,

FaSiDa is the same as MoBrDa, and both are called by the same term, *suaböya*. Hence, to present the above examples as the Yąnomamö would explain them I would not have had to distinguish MoBrDa from FaSiDa, but rather would have had to use just one term; in every case presented, men married their *suaböya*. (This can be seen in the model shown in Fig. 3–1; each male married a woman who was simultaneously FaSiDa and MoBrDa, that is, *suaböya*, to him.)

Cases I and J: These are a little unusual, but I include them to give some idea of both the potentials of the Yąnomamö kinship system and the people who use it.

In case I, individual II–2 is the headman of Lower Bisaasi-teri, Kąobawä's "father." He has considerable authority in the group. He arbitrarily redefined some of his classificatory daughters as sisters *so that his sons could marry their daughters.* Thus, the marriage of IV-1 to IV-2 is now considered to be legitimate because IV-1 could call his wife's mother his mother-in-law (FaSi), since his father redefined her as sister. Otherwise, it would be incest. Most of the people adjusted their kinship usage to fit the circumstances, but Kąobawä, who gave me the details of the manipulation, refused to adjust his own terms. The redefined women in question are his sisters, and he refused to call them FaSi.

I came upon this, and several identical cases, when I learned that the kinship usage between specific individuals did not reflect the equations implied by genealogies. (After I had collected extensive genealogies on four villages, I spent a considerable amount of time collecting kinship terms from specific individuals for every one of the some two thousand individuals included in the genealogies. This served as a cross-check on the genealogies, but uncovered a large number of incestuous and other interesting marriages that I might not have pinpointed otherwise.)

Case J brings out the full potential of the classificatory nature of Yąnomamö kinship. The man (III-1) married his *suaböya* according to the Yąnomamö, although he was not related to her by any blood ties. The justification for the marriage is the fact that III-1 calls all the women to whom his father and his father's brothers are married by the term for mother. Hence, he married his MoBrDa.

THE LINEAGE   It was shown in Chapter 1 that villages fission to produce new groups. One of the consequences of this pattern is that in a given area there will be a number of villages whose members can trace genealogical ties to each other because they have common male ancestors. Because of the classificatory nature of Yąnomamö kinship, the interrelated members of two different villages will use kinship terms for each other that imply a closeness of relationship. Thus, Kąobawä has "brothers" in all of the villages that have a common history with his own. These men are usually parallel cousins one or two degrees removed, but brothers in terminological categories. (The lineage to which Kąobawä belongs is shown on Fig. 3–5, discussed later as the *Sha* lineage.)

The Yąnomamö do not name their lineages. I have named all the significant lineages after particular male individuals, usually a long-since-dead male whose generation is the last for which I have meaningful genealogies. Thus, the *Sha* lineage is named after a man called *Shamashiadima,* long dead. He and his brothers left many male descendants who today are distributed in several villages. In the history of the movements of Kąobawä's village, the *Sha* lineage has figured prominently in the affairs of the group. Similarly, the *Hor* lineage is named after a man called *Horeboböwä*. The *Sha* and *Hor* lineages have a long history of marriage alliance and the living members of these two lineages constitute the greater fraction of the populations of Patanowä-teri, Monou-teri,

Upper Bisaasi-teri, and Lower Bisaasi-teri (see Table 1). Politically, they are either the two dominant lineages in each of the above-named villages or one of the two dominant lineages. For example, the headmen of Upper and Lower Bisaasi-teri, Kąobawä and Reromauwä, respectively, come from the *Sha* lineage. In Patanowä-teri there are two headmen, one from the *Sha* lineage and one from the *Hor* lineage. Finally, in Monou-teri, the headmanship shifted from the *Sha* lineage to the *Hor* lineage in 1965 because the *Sha* headman was killed in a raid by men from Patanowä-teri. I might add that he was killed by men of his own lineage to whom he was related as "brother." After he died, his brother-in-law, of the *Hor* lineage, assumed the leadership. It is not surprising that the headmanship shifted to this large, important group. In terms of sheer numbers, the *Hor* lineage (see Table 3–1) was stronger than the *Sha* lineage in Monou-teri. The distribution of political power within these two lineages underscores the dual organization of most Yąnomamö villages.

It is apparent from the foregoing example that the ties between agnates who live in different villages are not necessarily amicable. The most bitter fighting, in fact, takes place between members of different villages who are related to each other agnatically. It is not uncommon for men to kill their classificatory brothers in the ensuing raids. As a consequence of the killing of the Monou-teri headman, for example, the raiders from Monou-teri avenged his death by shooting Bosibrei of Patanowä-teri. The two men who actually killed Bosibrei were related to their victim as brothers. Similarly, Kąobawä himself shot Rakoiwä, the present *Sha* headman of Patanowä-teri, wounding him badly. He had shot to kill even though Rakoiwä was his older (classificatory) brother.

Once the lineage splits up and is redistributed in several villages, the ties between the men of that lineage weaken dramatically. And, as we shall see below, the fissioning of a village is frequently the result of a bitter club fight within the village over the possession of women. The result is that many villages that have a common history are at war with each other due to the nature of the feuds that led to their splitting away from the common village. The Patanowa-teri, for example, are at war with all three of the villages from which they originally separated (see Fig. 3–5, discussed later).

The kinship ties between agnates who live in the same village are likewise quite weak. They are strongest between a man and his younger brothers, for the age differences alone call forth a certain amount of respect and amity. An older man can be expected to aid his younger brothers in fights and help them to secure wives. In some cases, the younger man obtains his wife from a polygynous older brother; some men appear to accumulate extra wives with the intention of passing them on to their younger brothers. Kąobawä, for example, gave one of his wives to a younger brother and will probably give another wife to a second younger brother. (He is presently permitting the brother to share her sexual services.) Kąobawä's older wife, Bahimi, is quite jealous of the co-wives because they can command some of the tasty morsels of food that would otherwise be her own prerogative. And, since the younger wives are more attractive physically, Kąobawä does pay considerable attention to them. In Lower Bisaasi-teri, one of Kąobawä's classificatory brothers was forced by his older wife to get rid of his young, attractive second wife. The man gave her to an unmarried younger brother. He himself had acquired the younger wife as part of a political alliance he had made with the members of an allied village, knowing at the time that his first wife would object strenuously to the

TABLE 3–1
VILLAGE COMPOSITION BY LINEAGE MEMBERSHIP*

Lineage	Male	Female	Total
A. Lower Bisaasi-teri			
Sha	9	7	16
Tom	9	3	12
Hor	1	2	3
Kio	2	4	6
Shamatari	3	9	12
Other	1	1	2
	25	26	51
B. Upper Bisaasi-teri (Ką̊obawä's group)			
Sha	11	14	25
Hor	8	5	13
Kio	5	11	16
Kah	5	3	8
Shamatari	3	7	10
Other	5	8	13
	37	48	85
C. Monou-teri			
Sha	11	9	20
Hor	15	8	23
Kio	3	3	6
Shamatari	3	9	12
Other	2	3	5
	34	32	66
D. Patanowä-teri			
Hor	58	33	91
Sha	39	29	68
Kah	17	8	25
Kar	1	3	4
Shamatari	2	6	8
Other	5	11	16
	122	90	212

*Revised version of Appendix A, Chagnon 1966.

transaction. Still, he took the girl. When domestic tranquility could no longer be maintained, he passed her on to his younger brother.

The relationship between a man and his brothers of approximately the same age are generally not amicable. Brothers of the same approximate age tend to be jealous of each other and treat one another with considerable reserve and respect. A man can directly ask an immature younger brother to execute some task for him, but he can only suggest to a brother of the same age that the task should be done. This is equally true should one of them be the village headman. Kąobawä can ask his youngest brothers to perform many menial tasks during the preparations for a feast, but he cannot ask his mature brothers to help out. Thus, when it is time to clean the weeds from the village plaza to prepare the dance site, Kąobawä himself initiates the work, a form of suggestion that the task must be done. After a while his older, politically important brothers will join him, but only on their own initiative. He could not directly ask them to do this work. On one occasion a young man stole my flashlight and gave it to Shiimima, a younger brother to Kąobawä, but already a mature adult. I asked Kąobawä to help me get it back. After a day or so I asked him if he had gotten my flashlight back from Shiimima, whereupon he replied: "I have spoken to him about it. He will return it if he sees fit. I cannot order him to do so because he is already fierce." Adult brothers of the same age are under considerable pressure to establish their prowess and masculinity and do not permit other men, including their mature brothers, to boss them around. By contrast, Kąobawä could have *commanded* his youngest brother to return the flashlight, since the latter was not yet "fierce," that is, politically significant in village affairs, hence, anxious to display personal autonomy.

Finally, people can trace remote genealogical relationships to others under many circumstances. Kąobawä continuously spoke of the headman of a distant village as his brother. When I questioned him about his usage, he explained that he and the other man have a common patrilineal great-grandfather, that is, he *demonstrated* (see Glossary) his genealogical relationship to the man in question. The other headman gave a similar account.

In small villages the male members of the same lineage are usually on fairly intimate terms with each other. As the village grows in size, however, closeness of genealogical relationship becomes an important measure of the amity between brothers. That is, some men who are related as brothers group together and behave as a political unit. They group together because they are closely related genealogically and have common interests with respect to obtaining wives. If the village is very large, there may be two or more such groups of brothers within the same lineage. The larger lineage begins to segment into smaller factions, resulting in groups of agnates who are on more intimate terms with the members of their own group than they are with their genealogically more distant agnates who, in turn, constitute a different group.

THE LOCAL DESCENT GROUP This lineage segmentation was implicit in Generation V of Fig. 3–1 and arose because of the way in which members of lineage X entered into marriage alliances with members of the incorporated lineage W. These groups of brothers—segments—are called local descent groups.[9] Local descent groups have three characteristics. First, membership in them depends on patrilineal descent. Hence, the members all trace relationships to each other through males, and one can only be a member of the group if such a relationship exists. Second, the members of the group live in the same village. If, for example, a young man leaves his village to seek a wife elsewhere, he is no longer a member of the local descent group that includes his brothers and

[9]Leach, 1951. Yąnomamö local descent groups differ slightly from the definition given by Leach; among the Yąnomamö such groups rarely include more than two generations of males, whereas Leach defined them as embracing three generations. Otherwise, Yąnomamö local descent groups closely fit Leach's definition.

father. He can rejoin them later and again become an active member, but while he lives in a different village he does not participate in the political affairs of that group. Third, the group is *corporate* with respect to the functions of arranging the marriages of the female members. This is the most important single feature of the local descent group: its *function*. The first two characteristics of the group dealt only with the manner in which members can be recruited to the group (birth in the group and coresidence of such kinsmen). In anthropological usage, a corporation is a group of people who share some *estate* and have *rights* and *obligations* with respect to each other and to the estate. There are definite rules for recruiting new members into the corporation. Most studies of primitive corporations have dealt with those societies in which *land* is the estate of the corporation. (See, for example, Fried 1957.) Among the Yąnomamö, land has nothing to do with the functions of the corporate group. Women and rights to dispose of women in marriage constitute the estate of the Yąnomamö corporate groups. Leach is the first anthropologist to draw attention to the analytical importance of this kind of corporation (1961, Chapter 5), although Radcliffe-Brown (1953), in one of the first theoretical discussions of primitive corporations, emphasized the importance of rights over *persons* in some kinds of corporations.

Marriages are arranged by the male members of the local descent group. It cannot be supposed, for example, that the marriage rules automatically dictate the manner in which a woman is disposed in marriage; there are always some negotiations brought about by the situation. For example, a small village may require alliances with larger villages for purposes of defense, and the men of the small village may promise to give daughters to men in the larger village; or there may be a number of men within the village that stand in wife-receiving relationship to the girl, and a decision must be made regarding her ultimate disposition. In some cases a woman's daughters are promised to young men even before they are born. Generally, the girls are near puberty age by the time they are definitely given to a specific male, and they begin cohabiting with the man shortly after the puberty ceremony is over. In some situations a woman must be reassigned to an appropriate mate because her first husband died or abandoned her; or she might run away from a cruel husband and seek refuge among her brothers, bringing about a situation in which they must decide what to do with her.

Women abhor the possibility of being given to men in distant villages, since their fate is much less certain. Men in general are cruel to their wives, and the women rely on the protection of their brothers. A woman who is given to a man in a distant village, therefore, will generally have no brothers to protect her.

A man has considerably more say about the disposition of his daughters when he is young and has immature sons. As the sons grow older, they can overrule the father and insist that the girl be given to a man from some lineage that is likely to reciprocate with a sister. Ideally, women like to be given to men within their natal village. In this fashion the women can remain close to their own kinsmen and rely on the support of their brothers should the husband be particularly cruel. The best arrangement for everyone concerned is for the girl to be given to a man to whom she is related as FaSiDa or MoBrDa in the biological sense. Marriages of this kind exempt the husband from the onerous duty of stringently avoiding his parents-in-law, whereas they at the same time bind the wife-giving and wife-receiving groups more closely together in the system of reciprocities. As Kąobawä stated it, "It is good for groups to exchange women back and forth in this fashion. They will be good friends because of it."[10] If the girl marries a man of this category, the probability is high that she will remain in the village with her parents and brothers, since exchanges of this kind keep affinally linked local descent groups bound to each other.

The consequences of the corporate marriage-arranging functions of the local descent group can be most easily seen in the lineage basis for village fissioning, shown in Fig. 3–4. Briefly, the politics of arranging marriages are such that local descent groups of lineage X will pair with similar groups of lineage Y, and largely confine their marriage exchanges to those groups. Putting it more simply, each local descent group of lineage X will pair off with one local descent group of lineage Y, and stand in wife-giver/wife-receiver relationship to that group. When the village fisisons, the paired local descent groups will be more strongly bound to each other by marriage ties than each is to the other local descent groups of its own lineage.

VILLAGE FISSIONING   Fig. 3–4 presents the structural basis of village fissioning in terms of paired local descent groups. Village A contains two lineages, X and Y. Each lineage has four local descent groups. For simplicity of presentation, only the male

[10]I obtained a nearly identical explanation of reciprocal marriage exchanges of this kind from one of the Makiritare Indians, northern neighbors to the Yąnomamö. The Carib-speaking Makiritare have a prescriptive bilateral cross-cousin marriage rule like the Yąnomamö. My informant told me, in Spanish: "It is necessary for a man to marry his *yeitanade* [their equivalent to the Yąnomamö category of *suaböya*]. In this fashion families become good friends because they marry with each other time after time. When you marry this way, you are good friends with your *wänya* [brother-in-law] and can play and joke with him. You are also good friends with your *wodöma* [father-in-law]. If you marry a different way, you must be careful around your *wodöma* and respect him."

Fig. 3–4. Distribution of paired local descent groups in village fissioning.

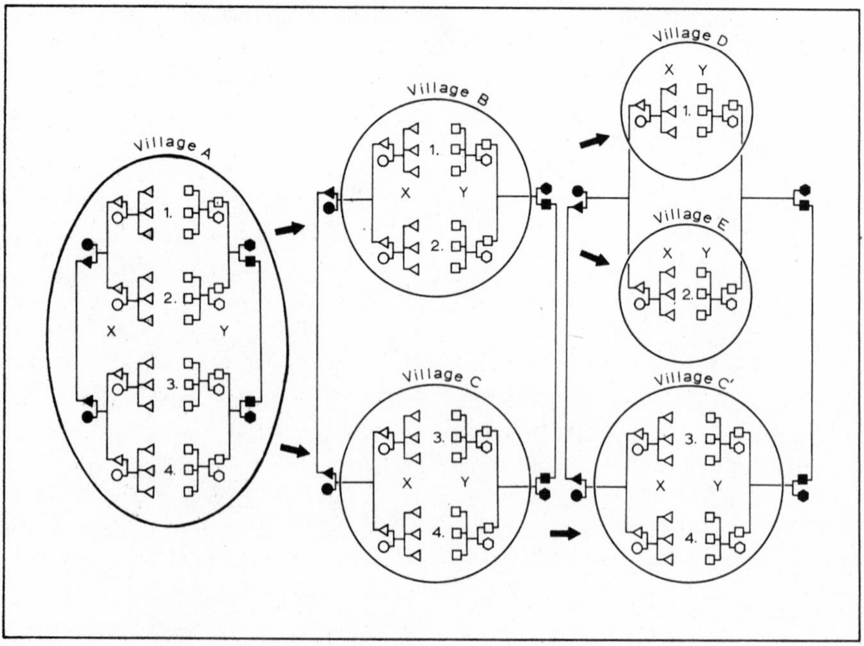

members are shown. Each group is paired off with an equivalent local descent group of the opposite lineage, giving the four numbered pairs. When village A fissions to form villages B and C, lineages X and Y will break at the weakest points, resulting in the formation of two new villages that have an identical composition: Village B is like village C in size and contains two local descent groups of lineages X and Y; the two local descent groups of each lineage in both new villages are paired with the analogous group of the opposite lineage. Fig. 3-4 can be viewed as a diagram of the physical organization of the village. Thus, in village A the male members of lineage X would tend to live on one side of the village, while the males of lineage Y would live on the opposite side. In actual distribution, then, the village has a "diametric dual organization" (Lévi-Strauss, 1961, Chapter 8). The Yąnomamö, however, do not conceive of the village as having discrete halves. That is, they do not have formal rules enjoining the male members of lineage X to live on one side of the village. There are always residential exceptions to the arrangement shown in Fig. 3-4.

Village B fissions again, resulting in the further breakdown of lineages X and Y. The outcome, villages D and E, is essentially like the outcome of the fission in village A; that is, the resulting new villages are alike in composition, size, and structure. Village C has not fissioned and continues to exist as it did after separating from village B. A comparison of the three villages shown in the last step of Fig. 3-4 will reveal that D, E, and C' are interrelated villages because patrilineages X and Y occur in each of them. The members of the patrilineages would still continue to call each other brother and sister, although they would be distributed in three different villages. The genealogical ties connecting villages D, E, and C' have been drawn in to emphasize this relationship.

The reason that lineages break down in this fashion stems from the fact that remote agnatic ties are weaker than the marriage ties that link the paired local descent groups to each other. The strength of the affinal ties between paired local descent groups derives from the obligations of reciprocity in marriage exchanges. Thus, when village B fissioned, local descent group X-1 had stronger ties to Y-1 than it did to X-2. The result was that X-1 and Y-1 separated from X-2 and Y-2 to form their own village, D.[11]

Fig. 3-4 describes the "ideal" pattern of village fissioning. Fig. 3-5 shows the structure and composition of three actual Yąnomamö villages for comparison. As in Fig. 3-4, only the adult males are shown. The incomplete triangles of Upper Bisaasi-teri in Fig. 3-5 signify that the men in question do not live in that village, but they must be included in the diagram to show that their sons live in Upper Bisaasi-teri. The two men actually live in Patanowä-teri, the composition of which is not shown in Fig. 3-5. What has been shown is that the lineages *Hor* and *Sha* extend into Patanowä-teri. In fact, the population of that village is comprised largely of members of these two lineages. See Table 3-1. Only the adult male members of the villages are shown for the three villages in Fig. 3-5, since it is this class of men that dominates the political affairs of the village. For those interested in *all* the genealogical relationships between *all* the members of one of the villages (Lower Bisaasi-teri), see Chagnon, 1966, Figure 2 and Appendix A. As can be seen from Fig. 3-5, each village is characterized by a dual organization of intermarrying lineages. In 1960, Lower Bisaasi-teri and Upper Bisaasi-teri were, in fact, a single village. It can be seen how local descent groups of the *Sha* lineage, for example,

[11]The pair "X-1 and Y-1" is represented on Fig. 3-4 simply by the numeral "1".

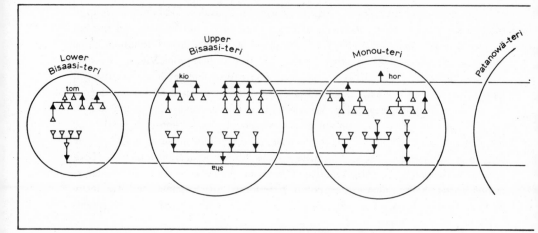

Fig. 3–5. Actual village fissioning.

separated from each other because of the ties each had to affinally linked descent groups of other lineages. Thus, Lower Bisaasi-teri is comprised essentially of two groups: a local descent group of the *Sha* lineage and a local descent group of the *Tom* lineage. Their members have exchanged women with each other for several generations, creating strong bonds of reciprocal obligations to continue to exchange in the future (Chagnon 1966). Similarly, the local descent groups of the *Sha* lineage in the two remaining villages shown in the figure are linked by affinal ties to other lineages.

Further back in history—1954—Monou-teri also constituted a portion of the village that included Upper and Lower Bisaasi-teri (see Fig. 2–8, Chapter 2). Finally the three villages shown on Fig. 3–5 constituted a single village with Patanowä-teri about 1940. The fissioning of the original village (and subsequent village fissioning) resulted in the distribution of local descent groups according to pairs, as shown in Fig. 3–4.[12]

Discrepancies in the Marriage Pattern

I presented in considerable detail the relationship between actual behavior and ideal rules about behavior from a qualitative point of view. This was accomplished by comparing genealogical diagrams describing some actual examples to ideal models of marriage and village fissioning. I will now give some of the quantitative aspects of marriage behavior and the demographic and political bases of the actual marriage pattern.

Table 3–2 shows the distribution of marriage types found in two related villages.

---

[12]In some areas of Brazil the pattern of village fissioning is slightly different. There, a local descent group may even establish its own house, separated from the wife-giving/wife-receiving member of the pair by as much distance as several miles. What I have been calling the "village" in this discussion breaks down, in portions of Brazil, into several "part-villages" that are not capable of carrying on an independent social existence. That is, members of the "part-village," the composition of which is essentially a single local descent group of one lineage, must obtain their wives from some other nonlocal group.

These figures represent a *sample* of marriages in the two villages. The sample consists of all married males who are thirty-five years old or younger. The sample was chosen in this fashion because the analysis of the marriage types depends on genealogical information covering several generations. By selecting only the younger men the analysis can be quite easily undertaken. In Patanowä-teri there were 38 men of this category, many of whom had multiple wives. A man with four wives, therefore, represents four marriages. In Lower Bisaasi-teri only 10 married men were below thirty-five years of age and accounted for the seventeen marriages. If all the men were included, the analysis would be inaccurate because I do not have adequately long genealogies for some of the oldest men. Up to 1940, the villages of Patanowä-teri and Lower Bisaasi-teri were not separate entities; they separated from each other at about that time. Patanowä-teri is a large and powerful village, containing 212 people. Lower Bisaasi-teri, with only 51 people, is militarily dependent on several of its allies.

Four types of marriages are shown in Table 3-2. The term prescriptive refers to the kinds of marriages described in Fig. 3-2. An incestuous marriage is defined as a man marrying a woman of his own patrilineage (or his mother or niece reckoned through his mother's side of the family). Marriages resulting from either alliance or abduction have been lumped into a single category because they represent the recruitment of spouses from outside the group. Finally, a few marriages are unexplainable in terms of Yanomamö kinship and marriage equations; these represent marriages between members of distinct lineages that have recently entered into exchanges with each other.

As can be seen from Table 3-2, there is a major difference between the two villages in the proportion of prescriptive marriages on the one hand and alliance marriages on the other. In short, the Patanowä-teri follow their marriage prescriptions far more rigorously than do the Lower Bisaasi-teri. This is so because Patanowä-teri, a much larger village, does not need to enter into marriage alliances with its neighbors; it is politically and militarily capable of an autonomous existence. Most of the alliance-abduction marriages in Patanowä-teri are, in fact, abductions; in Bisaasi-teri most of them are alliance marriages. Therefore, the relative frequency of alliance-type marriages is much lower for Patanowä-teri than for Lower Bisaasi-teri. This difference in marriage behavior stems from the relative abilities of the two groups to maintain military autonomy in a milieu of chronic warfare, a quality that is largely a function of the size of the group. The members of a militarily vulnerable village will breach the marriage prescriptions in order to establish political alliances with neighboring groups by ceding women to them.

TABLE 3-2

MARRIAGE TYPES IN PATANOWÄ-TERI AND LOWER BISAASI-TERI

		Patanowä-teri	Lower Bisaasi-teri
1.	Prescriptive	37	7
2.	Incestuous	4	1
3.	Alliance and/or abduction	8	9
4.	Unexplained	3	0
	Totals:	52	17

TABLE 3-3
SEX-RATIO DATA ON SELECTED VILLAGES

	Males	Females	Totals
Upper Bisaasi-teri	37	48	85
Lower Bisaasi-teri	25	26	51
Monou-teri	34	32	66
Reyaboböwei-teri	52	46	98
Mǫmariböwei-teri	50	46	96
Patanowä-teri	122	90	212
Aikam-teri and Roko-teri	129	103	232
	449	391	840

Table 3-3 gives sex-ratio data on seven groups of Yąnomamö. The first three villages are not truly representative of the population in general, but are included because
they have been frequently discussed in the text.

They are not representative because some 15 men from these villages were killed in a
single treacherous feast in 1950, a significant fraction of the adult male population. These
feasts are not very frequent. The three groups are allied to each other and have been
extremely successful at coercing two neighboring Shamatari villages out of women; a
surprisingly high proportion of their women come from these allies. As we shall see,
they have been successful because of the geographical and historical relationships that
characterize the alliance network in this area.

DEMOGRAPHIC BASIS As is apparent, there are more males in the Yąnomamö
population than females. This demographic fact results from the practice of selectively
killing female babies: *female infanticide*. The Yąnomamö also practice male infanticide,
but because of the preference to have a male as their first child, they unknowingly kill
more females than males. The Yąnomamö have only three numbers: one, two, and more-
than-two. They are, accordingly, poor statisticians. They are quite unaware of the fact
that they do kill more female babies, and every time I questioned them about it, they
insisted that they killed both kinds—"more-than-two" of both kinds.

A child is killed at birth, irrespective of its sex, if the mother already has a nursing
baby. They rationalize the practice by asserting that the new infant would probably die
anyway, since its older sibling would drink most of the milk. They are most reluctant
to jeopardize the health and safety of a nursing child by weaning it before it is three years
old or so, preferring to kill the competitor instead. Kąobawä's wife, Bahimi, killed a newborn male shortly after I began my fieldwork. She later told me, quite tearfully, that it
would have taken milk away from Ariwari, Kąobawä's favorite child. Ariwari at the
time was over two years old, but Bahimi refused to wean him. Sometimes a child is killed
simply because the mother doesn't feel that she can care for it properly and that it would
be an inconvenience to have to tend a baby. I once saw a plump, well-fed, young mother
eating a large quantity of food that would have been suitable to give to an older infant.
Her emaciated, filthy, and nearly starved child—about two years old—kept reaching out
for the food. The mother explained that the baby had gotten a bad case of diarrhea some
time ago and had stopped eating. As a consequence, her milk dried up. She refused to
attempt to feed it other foods because "it did not know how to eat other foods." When

I insisted that she share her food with the child, he ate it ravenously. In short, she was letting the baby die slowly of starvation. I have similar accounts from missionaries who have also witnessed cases such as this.

Male babies are preferred because they will grow up to be warriors and hunters. Most men make known their wishes to have a son—even to the point of insinuating that the wife ought to deliver a male or suffer the consequences. This is always done in a subtle way, usually by displaying signs of anger or resentment at the thought of having a daughter that constantly eats without being potentially an economic asset or guardian of the village. Many women will kill a female baby just to avoid disappointing their husbands. The Yąnomamö also practice abortion in a very crude but effective way. The pregnant woman will lie on her back and have a friend jump on her belly to rupture the amnion. Sometimes abortions are effected because the woman does not want to kill the baby after it is born. In other cases a man will order his wife to abort if he suspects that somebody else conceived the child.

Several techniques are used to kill a newborn child. The most common method is to strangle it with a vine so as not to touch it physically. Another common method is to place a stick across the child's neck and stand on both ends of it until it chokes. In some cases the child is not given the stimulus to breathe and is simply abandoned. Finally, some women throw the child against a tree or on the ground and just abandon it without checking to see if it was killed by the injuries sustained. One of the New Tribes Missionaries discovered a female baby in 1964 that had been discarded in this fashion and brought her home with him. The baby's face was badly bruised on one side, but she survived. The missionary subsequently adopted her legally and is raising her in England.

The demographic result of the Yąnomamö infanticide practices is that there is a shortage of females.[13] This shortage of females, however slight, assumes greater proportions for a number of culturally determined reasons. That is, the shortage of women is even greater than statistics alone imply because of the practice of polygyny and because of taboos relating to sexual intercourse.

The village of Patanowä-teri, for example, has 122 males and only 90 females (see Table 3-3). But many (about 25 percent) of the politically important men in the village have two or more wives. Hence, many men have no wives. Polygyny, therefore, increases the women shortage because the available women are distributed unequally.

In addition to this, the Yąnomamö have taboos against intercourse when a woman is pregnant or is nursing a child. The taboo is by no means followed to the strict letter, since children are nursed for three years or more—some men sheepishly admit having coitus with a lactating wife. Rerebawä, whose youngest child is about a year old, told me that he recently tried to persuade his wife to make love. He added: "She told me to go take some drugs and chant to my forest spirits; she is still 'stingy' with her vagina." Hence there is considerable concern within the village over the acquisition and possession of

---

[13]The frequency of female infanticide must be considerably higher than the statistics in Table 3-3 imply, since warfare results in the death of more men than women. This shows up in the age and sex distribution: There are more males in the younger age categories than females because of the infanticide preferences. As the males get older, however, they are more liable to death in warfare, resulting in a fairly even distribution of males and females in the thirty- to forty-year age interval. Finally, there are more old women than old men, also reflecting the higher male mortality due to warfare. I have published more substantial data on Yąnomamö demography in Neel and Chagnon, 1968.

sexually active females. Some of the teen-age males have homosexual affairs with each other; the females of their own age are usually married. By the time a young man is twenty years old or so he is anxious to display his masculinity, and at that point becomes a competitor for the sexual favors of the village belles—married belles. This causes considerable friction and results in club fighting. (See Chapter 5.)

Still another factor leads to breaches of the marriage rule: chance. In some villages there are disproportionately more males (or females) of the same lineage because of the way in which the group split from a different village. Again, there may be no eligible females when a young man is old enough to marry. His only choice is to seek a wife in a different village. Rerebawä, for example, was forced into this situation. His own village is quite small (about 50 people), but it is dominated numerically by members of his own lineage. Hence, most of the females in the village are related to him as mother, sister, or daughter. The remaining females are married to his older brothers. He therefore came to Upper Bisaasi-teri—an ally of his village—to seek a wife.

Thus, political necessity, cultural practices relating to population control, unequal distribution of women, and chance combine to produce situations in which people cannot follow their prescriptive marriage rules. The factors dealing with politics are the most meaningful in explanations of the discrepancy between Yąnomamö marriage behavior and ideal models of that behavior.

POLITICAL BASIS   The importance of politics can be demonstrated by citing a few incidents in the history of several villages and explaining how alliances and hostilities develop over time.

In Chapter 1 I briefly described the political milieu within which Kąobawä's village was situated. The relationships that exist at the present time make considerably more sense when they are viewed in the perspective of the historical events that led up to them. The reasons for village fissions and wars and why particular villages have entered into alliances with each other will now be explored briefly.[14]

The more important political ties currently maintained by Kąobawä's group have antecedents that go back to approximately 1940. At that time the present villages of Patanowä-teri, Monou-teri, and Upper and Lower Bisaasi-teri were one large village (see Fig. 2–8). In 1940, they were known collectively as the Patanowä-teri. To their south was a series of villages whose residents are collectively known as the Shamatari people. The Patanowä-teri were on friendly terms with most of the Shamatari and frequently visited them in order to trade. Just prior to 1940, an epidemic, probably malaria, resulted in the deaths of a number of Patanowä-teri. The Shamatari were suspected of causing the epidemic by practicing harmful magic. The first Shamatari man to visit the village after the epidemic, Ruwahiwä, was treacherously killed by a man who presently lives in Monou-teri; he bashed his head open with an axe. This immediately precipitated a war between the Patanowä-teri and several of the Shamatari villages.

A few years after the war started the Patanowä-teri fissioned into two groups: They relocated their gardens, but remained fairly close to each other geographically. This split was caused by constant bickering within the group and club fights over women. The two new villages thus formed were friendly enough to each other to live in the same

---

[14]I discussed these relationships in considerable detail in my doctoral dissertation, Chagnon, 1966. The following account is a simplified version.

general area, but too hostile to remain together in a single village. Largely due to food theft, their mutual political relationships gradually worsened. The two groups returned to the old site in order to harvest the fruits of the cultivated peach-palm tree, as each tree is owned by the person who plants it. Some of the fruit belonging to a man in one of the groups was stolen by a man in the other group. This led to a club fight between the two villages, after which they parted on hostile terms. The group that included Kąobawä decided to abandon their new garden and establish another one further away, anticipating a raid from the other group. Ultimately, the members of the two villages began raiding each other and entered into a prolonged and bloody war that was still raging when I left the field in 1967.

About 1949, to avoid the Patanowä-teri raids, Kąobawä and his group moved to an even more remote location. From here, they began visiting one of the Shamatari villages, Iwahikoroba-teri, located to the south of them. Unfortunately, the people of Iwahikoroba-teri were allied to the Shamatari group (Ruwahiwä's village) with which Kąobawä's group was at war. At the instigation of Kąobawä's enemies, the Iwahikoroba-teri invited his group to a feast during which many of them were treacherously killed, including Kąobawä's father. This incident took place sometime in the period December–January of 1950–1951. The survivors, many of them badly wounded, fled to a newly cleared garden site they had established a day's walk north of their village. They returned to their village only to obtain food, which they carried back to their new but nonproducing garden. After the wounded had removed the arrow points and were on the road to recovery, the group moved back into their producing garden. By this time word of the treachery had spread to all the villages in the area. The headman of Mahekodo-teri, the only village located on the Orinoco River in 1950, visited Kąobawä's group and invited them to take refuge with his people.[15] Kąobawä and his group readily accepted the invitation, and they moved into Mahekodo-teri, knowing that they could prosecute the war with the Shamatari only if they had allies and could raid from a great distance. Their own village was too close to Shamatari territory, and their capacity to raid was greatly reduced after so many of their men had been killed.

Kąobawä knew that the generous offer from the Mahekodo-teri was not entirely stimulated by altruistic motives. In 1910 his group had been forced to take refuge with an ally because of a war; the ally demanded in return many of the guests' women. Similarly, the Mahekodo-teri coerced Kąobawä's group into ceding a number of women, the price a weakened and dependent village must pay for the support of a stronger ally. It was later learned that the Mahekodo-teri planned to kill the rest of the men and abduct all of the women, but an unexpected war delayed their plot. (See Chagnon 1966.) Two of Kąobawä's sisters were among those claimed by the Mahekodo-teri; one of them still lives there, and the other was taken away from her Mahekodo-teri husband by force by Rerebawä's brother.

Kąobawä and his group lived with their protectors off-and-on for about a year, while they worked assiduously at making their new gardens. Because of internal fighting, they decided to make two new gardens and form two separate villages. The year was

---

[15]James P. Barker of the New Tribes Mission had just moved into Mahekodo-teri a few months earlier, marking the beginning of the Yąnomamö's first sustained contact with any outsiders. He witnessed the arrival of Kąobawä's group.

spent according to a schedule of work alternated with periods of rest. They would live in the Mahekodo-teri village for about three weeks at a stretch, resting from their gardening tasks, and return to their new gardens for about three weeks of intensive clearing and cultivation. Their plantings and seeds were provided by the Mahekodo-teri.[16] They carried their provisions from the Mahekodo-teri gardens while they worked at their new gardens, sending men back for more as these ran short. As soon as one of the new gardens was producing, they moved away from the Mahekodo-teri. The second garden was completed after their move, and the Monou-teri separated from Kąobawä's group. This was about 1954. During the time they lived with the Mahekodo-teri, they raided the Shamatari frequently, and were raided in return. The Shamatari ambushed and killed two Mahekodo-teri on one raid, causing the Mahekodo-teri to actively prosecute the war with the Shamatari to avenge these deaths.

Kąobawä's group abondoned the new site and moved to the Orinoco River shortly after the Monou-teri separated from them. They had established a garden on the Orinoco during the time that the Monou-teri were completing their own site. In short, the garden that was made while Kąobawä and his group lived with the Mahekodo-teri was simply a vantage point that permitted the group to take leave of its protectors as soon as possible, while they established gardens in more desirable locations.

Kąobawä's group moved down the Orinoco River in 1959–1960, after having lived at the new site only five years. This move was stimulated by the appearance of a government malaria team that established a small station at the mouth of the Mavaca River. Kąobawä's group moved across the river from them in order to be in a position to obtain steel tools from the newly arrived foreigners. Kąobawä's group fissioned again in the process of this move; the Lower Bisaasi-teri established a separate garden and built their own village just across the Mavaca River from Kąobawä's group. The fission was not complete, however, as both sections of Bisaasi-teri built a common village that they occupied during the dry season, when they conducted their feasts and went on raiding parties.

Kąobawä's group made contacts with a large Shamatari village, Paruritawä-teri, shortly after having moved to the mouth of the Mavaca River in 1959–1960. This village had fissioned from one of the Shamatari groups that participated in the treacherous feast in 1950 and was on semifriendly terms with it. Thus, Kąobawä and his group saw an opportunity to get revenge on their archenemies. They cultivated an alliance with the Paruritawä-teri and succeeded in getting them to participate in a treacherous feast. The Paruritawä-teri themselves were fissioning into two groups, so they made two new gardens southwest of Kąobawä's village in preparation for the treacherous feast. The feast invitation was sent (1960) to the unsuspecting Shamatari by the Paruritawä-teri. But many of them were sick, and only five men and four women ultimately came to the treacherous feast at Paruritawä-teri. Kąobawä and his followers, as well as the Monou-teri, secreted themselves outside the village while the Paruritawä-teri entertained the hapless guests inside. They managed to kill three of the five men and seized all of the women. The Paruritawä-teri abandoned their garden, anticipating the inevitable revenge raids and moved to the two new sites, fissioning into two groups of about 95 people.

This treacherous feast put the Paruritawä-teri in a very poor position. They were (and are) the westernmost Yąnomamö in the area, and their closest neighbors were the

---

[16]James Barker informed me of the schedule followed by Kąobawä and his group.

Monou-teri, Lower Bisaasi-teri, and Kąobawä's group. All their other neighbors, allied to the victims of the treacherous feast, relentlessly raided them. They were, in short, extremely dependent on Kąobawä's group and the two other villages related to Kąobawä's group.

Kąobawä and his followers have astutely finessed this situation in two ways. First, they have managed to coerce the two Shamatari villages into ceding women without reciprocating an equal number of their own in return. The men who have obtained Shamatari wives have, as well, managed to cut short their period of bride service in the Shamatari village. Conversely, Shamatari men who have been promised women of Kąobawä's group are pressed into very lengthy bride service, sometimes up to three years. Secondly, Kąobawä's group has prevented the two Shamatari allies from re-establishing friendly contacts with the other Shamatari to their southeast by chicane, threat, and intimidation. One of the two Shamatari allies, the Reyaboböwei-teri, has attempted a rapprochement with the Shamatari enemies of Kąobawä's group. In 1965, several months after I had been living in Kąobawä's village, Kąobawä's group managed to stage another treacherous feast for the old enemies by taking advantage of the renewed ties between the Reyaboböwei-teri and the enemies. They learned that the Reyaboböwei-teri planned to invite one of the villages to a feast, so they, along with the Monou-teri, Lower Bisaasi-teri, and Mǫmariböwei-teri, went to the feast in order to ambush the guests. The Reyaboböwei-teri, however, were reluctant to go through with the plan and warned the visitors about it. The visitors were en route to the village when word of the treachery reached them. This had the effect of creating even more difficulties for the Reyaboböwei-teri, for it is highly unlikely that they will succeed in gaining the confidence of their neighbors to the southeast. Nevertheless, some visiting between the groups still continues.[17]

The historical relationships between the villages helps account for the reasons behind contemporary alliance patterns. The discrepancy between marriage rules and actual marriage practice in Lower Bisaasi-teri is a result of the political advantages that group enjoys over one of its allies. It has used this advantage to gain a favorable imbalanced marriage exchange pattern, but one that is only temporary. The Shamatari are also shrewd in their alliance practices, and have succeeded in neutralizing their disadvantages by capitalizing on schisms between Kąobawä's group and Lower Bisaasi-teri. This has been done largely by confining their marriage exchanges to important men in the dominant lineages of Upper and Lower Bisaasi-teri. One of the Shamatari villages, Mǫmaribowei-teri, has restricted its exchanges to Lower Bisaasi-teri and Monou-teri, while completely ignoring Upper Bisaasi-teri. The other Shamatari village has given its women only to Upper Bisaasi-teri. This has resulted in the weakening of ties between the three villages of Upper Bisaasi-teri, Lower Bisaasi-teri, and Monou-teri, whose members are

---

[17]I plan to use these visiting ties to establish contact with the Shamatari villages in that area, none of which have had contact with outsiders. These uncontacted Shamatari, however, know who I am because I attempted to reach them in 1965. They subsequently sent a message out urging me to visit them, angry because my guides forced me to turn back on my first attempt. In 1966 they even sent an old man to Kąobawä's village by way of Reyaboböwei-teri with an invitation for me to visit them. I had already left Venezuela by that time. Most of the men in the two contacted Shamatari villages tried to prevent me from going by telling horrible tales of the treachery that awaited my visit, describing how the Shamatari will kill me. The truth of the matter is that they know that I will bring the uncontacted Shamatari machetes and axes that might otherwise be given to them. The headman of one of the uncontacted villages has a brother in Mǫmariböwei-teri. He privately conceded that no harm would befall me and offered to take me to visit in 1967. He was, unfortunately, bitten by a snake just before I arrived in March of 1967, and my plans were deferred until 1968. [In 1968 I succeeded in contacting the remote Shamatari. A detailed account of this can be found in Chagnon 1974:Chap. 1.]

related agnatically to each other, and who share a common history. That is, they have lost solidarity as a network of allied villages and, therefore, some of the advantages they enjoyed as wife receivers with respect to the Shamatari villages. They are less able to behave as a single political entity and force the Shamatari to cede women because the Shamatari have given them women in such a way so as to make them competitors with each other. This has also weakened the ties between the two Shamatari villages, which are also related to each other by agnatic ties and common history because each group has linked its political fate with the affairs of different allies. Nevertheless, the two Shamatari villages have, by exchanging women in this fashion, reduced the solidarity of the group of villages that once stood as a unified political bloc that coerced them out of women.

This can be demonstrated in two ways. During the period 1964–1966, Upper and Lower Bisaasi-teri still maintained a common village and entertained visitors as a group. Near the end of this period, after the marriage exchanges had begun to show their effects, they abandoned the common village and began to entertain allies independently of each other. At that time they had together managed to acquire two dozen or so women from the Shamatari while having given or promised only a half-dozen in return. When I returned in 1967, the situation had changed appreciably. There were many more Shamatari men living in the group because they had been given women; that is, the exchanges were more balanced. Moreover, the relationships between Upper and Lower Bisaasi-teri were not as amicable as they had been the previous year; each group was becoming more involved in the obligations it had acquired by entering into marriage exchanges with one of the two Shamatari villages. Just before I returned, there was a club fight involving all of the villages: The Upper Bisaasi-teri and Reyaboböwei-teri fought, as a group, against the Lower Bisaasi-teri and Mǫmariböwei-teri; that is, the groups that had entered into marriage exchanges with each other behaved as a unit and fought against their close agnates and erstwhile allies. A group of men from Mǫmariböwei-teri forcefully took a woman from the Reyaboböwei-teri, thereby precipitating a challenge to a club fight. The Monou-teri participated in the club fight as well, taking the side of the Mǫmariböwei-teri, from whom they had taken several women and to whom they had promised several.

Finally, the political situation altered somewhat. When the alliance first developed between Kąobawä's group and the two Shamatari villages in 1960, the political milieu was quite serene. The treacherous feast resulted in a bloody war, but the two Shamatari villages sustained most of the losses. Therefore, the Shamatari allies required the assistance of Kąobawä's group more than the latter needed their help, since Kąobawä's group had no active wars at the time. In 1965, however, the Monou-teri renewed their old war with the Patanowä-teri and it subsequently involved Kąobawä's group and Lower Bisaasi-teri. Only then did they require military assistance from the Shamatari, and only then did the marriage exchanges tend to balance. I will discuss the development of this war in Chapter 4.

Marriage in Yąnomamö society is the result, therefore, of many considerations. It is not merely the outcome of a blind subscription to a rule that enjoins males to marry women of a specific category, for in many cases the political affairs of the group oblige people to give their daughters to men in other villages. The Yąnomamö are practical and enterprising in this regard, particularly those in small villages. The capacity to exist as an independent but small group is greatly enhanced by creating alliances with members of other villages—such alliances are stabilized by exchanges of women between the partners, a breach of the prescriptive marriage rules. It is for this reason that such a large discrepancy exists between the ideal behavior and the actual practice, as noted in Table 2.[18]

Division of Labor and Daily Social Life

The daily activities and general social life are not as circumscribed by rules and regulations as would appear from the foregoing discussion. In fact, one first has the impression that chaos rather than order reigns over the daily activities of the village members![19] Thus, while ideal rules about behavior definitely exist, individuals have a great deal of freedom to manipulate their behavior in such a way that they are not unduly encumbered by them. Most of the run-of-the-mill activities of daily life are not characterized by inflexible prescriptions regarding proper behavior.

MALE-FEMALE DIVISION There are a number of distinctions based on status differences that are important in daily life. Perhaps the most conspicuous and most important is the distinction between males and females.

Yąnomamö society is decidedly masculine. As was discussed earlier, there is a definite preference to have male children, resulting in a higher incidence of female infanticide as opposed to male infanticide. Female children assume duties and responsibilities in the household long before their brothers are obliged to participate in useful domestic tasks. For the most part, little girls are obliged to tend their younger brothers and sisters, although they are also expected to help their mothers in other chores such as cooking, hauling water, and collecting firewood. By the time girls have reached puberty they have already learned that their world is decidedly less attractive than that of their brothers.

As members of local descent groups, girls have almost no voice in the decisions reached by their agnates concerning their marriage. They are largely pawns to be disposed of by their kinsmen, and their wishes are given very little consideration. In many cases, the girl has been promised to a man long before she reaches puberty, and in some cases her husband actually raises her for part of her childhood. In short, they do not participate as equals in the political affairs of the corporate kinship group and seem to inherit most of the duties without enjoying many of the privileges.

Marriage does not enhance the status of the girl, for her duties as wife require her to assume difficult and laborious tasks too menial to be executed by the men. For the most part these include the incessant demands for firewood and drinking water, particularly the former. Women spend several hours each day scouring the neighborhood

---

[18]Reducing kinship usage to the logical extremes to which the Yąnomamö take it, there really is no discrepancy between theory and practice, except in the case of incest. When new villages enter into contact for the first time, their respective headmen call each other *shoriwä* (brother-in-law). The first exchanges between the groups usually involve the children of these men. The children, of course, stand in marriageable relationship to each other because the children of brothers-in-law can, by the prescriptive definitions, marry.

[19]Many fieldworkers do not begin to see the patterns of behavior until they have spent months of intensive contact with their subjects. I was convinced, after five or six months, that there were almost no guidelines for behavior. A part of the difficulty resulted from the language barrier. The patterns began to emerge only after about six months, and only then could I begin asking pertinent questions about many features of social organization.

Fig. 3–6. Women hauling firewood from the jungle to the village at dusk.

for suitable wood. There is usually an abundant supply in the garden within a year of the clearing of the land, but this disappears rapidly. Thereafter, the women must forage further afield to collect the daily supply of firewood, sometimes traveling several miles each day to obtain it. It is a lucky woman who owns an axe, for collecting wood is a tedious job without a steel tool. The women can always be seen at dusk, returning to the village in a procession, bearing enormous loads of wood in their pack-baskets (see Fig. 3–6). Good planners will spend a great deal of time collecting wood on some days so that they can take a vacation from this chore on others. If a woman locates a good supply of wood near the village, she will haul as much as she can and store it rather than let it be taken by her covillagers.

Women must respond quickly to the demands of their husbands. In fact, they must respond without waiting for a command. It is interesting to watch the behavior of women when their husbands return from a hunting trip or a visit. The men march slowly across the village and retire silently to their hammocks. The woman, no matter what she is doing, hurries home and quietly but rapidly prepares a meal for the husband. Should the wife be slow in doing this, the husband is within his rights to beat her. Most reprimands meted out by irate husbands take the form of blows with the hand or with a piece of firewood, but a good many husbands are even more brutal. Some of them chop their wives with the sharp edge of a machete or axe, or shoot them with a barbed arrow in some nonvital area, such as the buttocks or leg. Many men are given over to punishing their wives by holding the hot end of a glowing stick against them, resulting in serious burns. The punishment is usually, however, adjusted to the seriousness of the wife's shortcomings, more drastic measures being reserved for infidelity or suspicion of infidelity. Many men, however, show their ferocity by meting out serious punishment to their wives for even minor offenses. It is not uncommon for a man to injure his errant wife seriously; and some men have even killed wives.

Women expect this kind of treatment and many of them measure their husband's concern in terms of the frequency of minor beatings they sustain. I overheard two young women discussing each other's scalp scars. One of them commented that the other's husband must really care for her since he has beaten her on the head so frequently!

A woman usually depends for protection on her brothers, who will defend her against a cruel husband. If a man is too brutal to a wife, her brothers may take the woman away from him and give her to another man. It is largely for this reason that women abhor the possibility of being married off to men in distant villages; they know that their brothers cannot protect them under these circumstances. Women who have married a male cross-cousin have an easier life, for they are related to their husbands by cognatic ties of kinship as well as by marriage. Kạobawä, for example, is related to Bahimi as FaSiSo, and their marital relationship is very tranquil by Yạnomamö standards. He does beat Bahimi on occasion, but never cruelly. It is considered good to beat a wife every once in a while just to show your concern for her.

A young man in Monou-teri shot and killed his wife a few years before I conducted my fieldwork. Even while I was there, a man in one of the villages shot his wife in the stomach with a barbed arrow. Considerable internal injury resulted when the arrow was removed. The missionaries had her sent out by airplane to the Territorial capital for surgery. Her wound had gotten infected, and the girl was near death by the time the incident came to their attention. Another man chopped his wife on the arm with a machete; the missionaries in that village feared that the woman would lose the use of her hand because some of the tendons to her fingers were severed. A fight involving a case of infidelity took place in one of the villages just before I left the field. The male culprit was killed in the club fight, and the recalcitrant wife had both her ears cut off by her enraged husband. A number of other women had their ears badly mutilated by angry husbands. The women wear sticks of cane in their pierced ear lobes; these are easily grabbed by the husband. A few men jerked these so hard that they tore their wives' ear lobes open.

It is not difficult to understand, then, why Yạnomamö women in general have such a vindictive and caustic attitude toward the external world. By the time a woman is thirty years old she has "lost her shape" and has developed a rather unpleasant disposition. Women tend to seek refuge and consolation in each other's company, sharing their misery with their peers.

A woman gains a measure of respect when she becomes old. By then she has adult children who care for her and treat her kindly. Old women also have a unique position in the world of intervillage warfare and politics. They are immune from the incursions of raiders and can go from one village to another with complete disregard for personal danger. In this connection they are employed as messengers and, on some occasions, as the recoverers of bodies. If a man is killed near the village of an enemy, an old woman from the slain man's village is permitted to recover his body.

Still, the women have one method by which they can exercise a measure of influence over village politics. All women fear being abducted by raiders and always leave the village with this anxiety at the back of their minds. Women always bring their children with them, particularly younger children, so that if they are abducted, the child will not starve to death because of the separation of the mother. They are therefore concerned with the political behavior of their men and occasionally goad them into taking action against some possible enemy by caustically accusing the men of cowardice. This has the effect of establishing the village's reputation for ferocity, reducing the possibility of raiders abducting the women while they are out collecting firewood or garden produce. The men cannot stand being chided by the women in this fashion, and are forced to take action if the women unite against them.

CHILD-ADULT DIVISION Despite the fact that children of both sexes spend much of their time with their mothers, the boys alone are treated with considerable indulgence by their fathers from an early age. Thus, the distinction between male and female status develops early in the socialization process, and the boys are quick to learn their favored position with respect to girls. They are encouraged to be "fierce" and are rarely punished by their parents for inflicting blows on them or on the hapless girls in the village. Kạobawä, for example, lets Ariwari beat him on the face and head to express his anger and temper, laughing and commenting on his ferocity. Although Ariwari is only about four years old, he has already learned that the appropriate response to a flash of anger is to strike someone with his hand or with an object, and it is not uncommon for him to give his father a healthy smack in the face whenever something displeases him. He is frequently goaded into hitting his father by teasing, being rewarded by gleeful cheers of assent from his mother and from the other adults in the household.

Fig. 3–7. Ariwari, Kạobawä's favorite son, building a make-believe house while camping with his father. His "sister" (father's brother's daughter) looks on.

When Kąobawä's group travels, Ariwari emulates his father by copying his activities on a child's scale. For example, he erects a temporary hut from small sticks and discarded leaves and plays happily in his own camp (see Fig. 3–7). His sisters, however, are pressed into more practical labor and help their mother do useful tasks. Still, the young girls are given some freedom to play at being adults and have their moments of fun with their mothers.

But a girl's childhood ends sooner than a boy's. The game of playing house fades imperceptibly into a constant responsibility to help mother. By the time a girl is ten years old or so, she has become an economic asset to the mother and spends a great deal of time working. Little boys, by contrast, spend hours playing among themselves and are able to prolong their childhood into their late teens if they so wish. By that time a girl has married, and may even have a child or two.

A girl's transition to womanhood is obvious because of its physiological manifestations. At first menses (yöbönou) Yąnomamö girls are confined to their houses and hidden behind a screen of leaves. Their old cotton garments are discarded and replaced by new ones manufactured by their mothers or by older female friends. During this week of confinement, the girl is fed by her relatives; her food must be eaten by means of a stick, as she is not allowed to come into contact with it in any other fashion. She must also scratch herself with another set of sticks. The Yąnomamö word for menstruation translates literally as "squatting" (roo), and that fairly accurately describes what pubescent females (and adult women) do during menstruation. Yąnomamö women do not employ tampons; they simply remain inactive during menstruation, squatting on their haunches most of the time. After her puberty confinement, a girl is eligible to begin life as a wife and take up residence with her husband.

Males, on the other hand, do not have their transition into manhood marked by a ceremony. Nevertheless, one can usually tell when a boy is attempting to enter the world of men. The most conspicuous sign is his anger when others call him by his name. When the adults in the village cease using his personal name, the young man has achieved some sort of masculine adult status. Young men are always very touchy about their names and they, more than anyone else, take quick offense when hearing their names mentioned. The Yąnomamö constantly employ teknonymy when a kinship usage is ambiguous. Thus, someone may wish to refer to Kąobawä in a conversation, but the kinship term appropriate to the occasion might not distinguish him from his several brothers. Then, Kąobawä will be referred to as "father of Ariwari." However, when Ariwari gets older, he will attempt to put a stop to this in an effort to establish his status as an adult. A young man has been recognized as an adult when people no longer use his name in teknonymous references. Still, the transition is not abrupt, and it is not marked by a recognizable point in time.

Finally, the children differ from adults in their susceptibility to supernatural hazards. A great deal of Yąnomamö sorcery and mythological references to harmful magic focuses on children as the target of malevolence. Yąnomamö shamans are constantly sending evil spirits (Hekura) to enemy villages. There, they secretly attack and devour the vulnerable portion of the childrens' souls (noreshi), bringing about sickness and death. These same shamans spend an equal amount of time warding off the dangerous spirits sent by their enemies. Children are vulnerable because their souls are not firmly established within their physical beings, and can wander out of the body almost at will. The most common way for a child's soul to escape is to leave by way of the mouth when the child cries. Thus, mothers are quick to hush a bawling baby in order to prevent its soul from escaping. The child's soul can be recovered by sweeping the ground in the vicinity where it most probably escaped, calling for it while sweeping the area with a particular kind of branch. I once helped gather up the soul of a sick child in this fashion, luring it back into the sick baby. One of the contributions I made, in addition to helping with the calling and sweeping, was a dose of medicine for the child's diarrhea. A consequence of this set of attitudes about the vulnerability of children is that much of the village's activity with respect to shamanism and curing is directed toward the children.

RELATIVES BY BLOOD AND BY MARRIAGE   Many forms of interpersonal behavior stem largely from the social roles implied in the kinship system. To be sure, some kinship behavior reflects the two distinctions of age and sex discussed above, for the terminology of kinship itself employs discriminations of this kind. For example, there are terms to distinguish older siblings from younger siblings and terms used by members of one sex only in reference to those of the opposite sex.

The relationship between kinship terms and biological parentage is not the same in the Yąnomamö language as it is in our own. As was shown in the first section of this chapter, people may stand in a child relationship to a number of individuals; that is, it is possible to have multiple "mothers" and "fathers" in Yąnomamö society. The term for mother and father conveys as much of a social as a biological relationship between individuals, and in the daily activities of the Yąnomamö it is the social implications of kinship roles that are most important.

What is implied in the kinship roles can best be seen in the way the kinship terms themselves are formed. All primary kinship terms take the ending *"-mou"* when used to describe the relationship between individuals. Thus, *osheya* means "my younger sibling," but *oshemou* means that individual X *behaves* toward individual Y *as a younger sibling.* This ending, *-mou*, also occurs in nonkinship usage to express "a way of behaving," "to execute a particular activity in a specified manner," or "to perform the activity that is implied by the word to which *-mou* is affixed." For example, *oko* means fresh-water crab and *okomou* means "to go hunting for crabs"; *howashi* means "a mischievous white monkey" and *howashimou* means "to act mischievously, to monkey around"; *nowa naba* means "enemy," and *nowa nabamou* means "to become an enemy by behaving objectionably"; *waiteri* means "fierce" and *waiterimou* means "to behave ferociously."

Whenever I would ask the Yąnomamö a question such as, "What do you call Kąobawä?" the answers would always be in the form of a kinship term to which *"-mou"* was affixed, but rarely in the form "I say such-and-such to him." Calling an individual by a specific term is, however, implied in the "way of behaving" toward that individual. But despite the fact that the Yąnomamö can say, literally, "I call him father" (*kama kä iha, haya ya kuu*), they invariably say *"ya hȫmou"*—"I behave toward him as a child."[20] Thus, they express their relationships to others in terms of *ways of behavior.* Each kinship category implies a set of these behavioral norms, and one's social life in the community is established with respect to all other individuals by the kinship terminology employed in each particular case.

---

[20]Although the word *hȫ* translates literally as "father," the expression *ya hȫmou* can best be understood with the translation given above.

New individuals are incorporated into the community by an extension of kinship ties. Unless one is incorporated into the village in this fashion, there is no basis for social behavior vis-à-vis others, for the kinship system defines one's role in society. An orphaned teen-ager joined Kąobawä's group shortly before I began my fieldwork. He was from a distant Shamatari village and had no blood relatives in Kąobawä's group. He established his position in the community by calling Kąobawä "father." This defined his relationship to all of Kąobawä's kinsmen as well. As an exercise in kinship, I had the young man give me his relationship term for everyone in the village. He not only had specific terms for every member of the group, but he had also extended them to all the residents of Lower Bisaasi-teri and Monou-teri as well, since Kąobawä was related to these people. In short, the boy learned how Kąobawä was related to all the members of three different villages and logically extended his own assumed relationship to Kąobawä outward to the others; and he behaved toward them accordingly: He avoided women he called mother-in-law and refrained from sexual activities with women he called sister.

To emphasize the fact that the kinship categories do not always correspond to biological relationships, let me give an example of an incestuous marriage. Kąobawä's younger brother, Shiimima, recently (1966) took a young girl for his wife, outraging most of the community because he "behaved toward her as brother" before the marriage. The girl's mother had been abducted some twenty years earlier from a distant village and was given to a man who stood in a father relationship to Kąobawä and Shiimima. Thus, both Kąobawä and Shiimima called the abducted woman "mother" and called her daughter "sister." The abducted woman's husband died of malaria; after this, she had a number of temporary affairs with other men before being officially taken as a wife by another man in the village. Her daughter is the issue of a temporary affair she had with the headman of Mahekodo-teri, the group that gave Kąobawä refuge after the treacherous feast in 1950. She is, therefore, biologically unrelated to Kąobawä and Shiimima, but since they behaved toward her as brothers, Shiimima's marriage to her is a blatant case of incest. The matter was as disgusting to my informants as it would have been had Shiimima married his own biological sister.

There are many important kinship distinctions in Yąnomamö social life, but the one between relatives by marriage and agnatic relatives should particularly be emphasized. This distinction is at the basis of Yąnomamö political behavior and village fissioning. This point was emphasized in the discussion of village fissioning and marriage rules in the first section of this chapter.

One of the most important characteristics of affinal ties is that they are capable of growing in strength over time because they can be solidified and reinforced by marriage exchanges between the groups. Ties between agnates, on the other hand, tend to weaken over time. For example, Kąobawä's local descent group could renew its friendship to similar affinally related groups in the village of Patanowä-teri by entering into marriage exchanges with them once again. There is no way, however, in which his own descent group could reinforce or strengthen the agnatic ties with the local descent groups of the *Sha* lineage in Patanowä-teri. By marrying into the affinally related Patanowä-teri descent groups, Kąobawä's group would enter into direct competition with agnatic counterparts in that village, further straining the relationships between the two communities.

There is another way of looking at this situation. Men who are related to each other as agnates (for example, brothers and parallel cousins) get along well with each other when they are children and young men. As time passes and these men become old enough to seek wives, members of the groups to which they belong enter into competition with each other. The men themselves are under some pressure to display their personal autonomy, and they treat each other with considerable reserve as they get older. They cannot boss each other around or expect many favors from one another. Kąobawä, for example, cannot ask his adult brothers to perform menial tasks for him. This is because each man—particularly those men who compete for the same women—attempts to convince all others that he is capable of ferocity. The more remote the genealogical distance, the greater is the reserve with which mature agnates treat each other. That is, distant parallel cousins would behave toward each other with considerably more reserve than would actual brothers, although the men in question are all related to each other terminologically as brothers. If such men live in different villages, their mutual relationships are even more reserved when they meet.

The relationship between men who call each other brother-in-law, however, grows more intimate as the men get older. They can play and joke with each other, whereas agnates cannot, for they are not competitors and are not constrained to exhibit their fierceness to each other. They can cement their relationships to each other by merely promising to give their daughters to each other's sons. They can ask favors of each other, expecting them to be done without complaint.

Kąobawä's relationships to two men in his village illustrate the distinction between agnates and affines. Both men joined his group from the village of Patanowä-teri some time after Kąobawä's group separated from the village. One of the men, Nadesiwä, is related to him agnatically: they call each other "brother" because their fathers were half-brothers. Nadesiwä is in Kąobawä's local descent group, but is not quite on a par with the other members in the political affairs of the group. The other men in the group—Kąobawä and his closer brothers—put pressure on Nadesiwä to give his only daughter to a man in a distant Shamatari village for the purpose of stabilizing an alliance. This was a considerable sacrifice for him to make, as his daughter, after the completion of bride service, will have to live in her husband's village—Nadesiwä will have no coresident son-in-law to provide him with meat when he gets old. Kąobawä and Nadesiwä treat each other with respect and great reserve and do not ask each other for favors.

The other man, Kumamawä, is Bahimi's actual brother; Kąobawä is related to him, therefore, as an affine as well as by cognatic kinship ties. That is, they are first cross-cousins by blood and also related to each other by marriage. Kumamawä is a frequent visitor in Kąobawä's house and enthusiastically executes the numerous tasks that Kąobawä asks of him. They are members of different local descent groups, but their groups are related to each other by marriage exchanges that go back several generations. In short, Kąobawä's personal ties to his brother-in-law are warmer and friendlier than his relationship to one of the members of his own local descent group.

Daily Activities

Kąobawä's village is oval-shaped. His house is located among those of his agnatic kinsmen; they occupy a continuous arc along one side of the village. Each of the men built his own section of the village, but in such a way that the roofs coincided and could be attached by simply extending the thatching. When completed, the village looked like a continuous, oval-shaped lean-to because of the way in which the roofs of the discrete houses were attached. Each house, however, is owned by the family that built it. Shararaiwä, Kąobawä's youngest brother, helped build Kąobawä's house and shares it with him. He also shares Koamashima, Kąobawä's younger wife. Kąobawä's older wife, Bahimi, hangs her hammock adjacent to Kąobawä's most of the time, but when there are visitors and the village is crowded, she ties her hammock under his in order to be able to tend the fire during the night. Ariwari still sleeps with his mother, but will get his own hammock soon: He is nearly four years old. His parents are afraid he will fall into the fire at night and get burned, since he is still a little too young to sleep alone.[21]

Daily activities begin early in a Yąnomamö village. One can hear people chatting lazily and children crying long before it is light enough to see. Most people are waked by the cold and build up the fire just before daybreak. They usually go back to sleep, but many of them visit and talk about their plans for the day.

The entrances are all covered with dry brush so that any movement of people through them is heard all over the village. There is always a procession of people leaving the village at dawn to relieve themselves in the nearby garden, and the noise they make going in and out of the village usually awakens the others.

The village is very smoky at this time of day, since the newly stoked campfires smoulder before they leap into flames. The air is usually very still and chilly, and the ground is damp from the dew. The smoke is pleasant and seems to drive away the coolness.

Clandestine sexual liasons usually take place at this time of day, having been arranged on the previous evening. The lovers leave the village on the pretext of going to the bathroom and meet at some predetermined location. They return to the village by opposite routes.

This is also the time of day when raiders strike, so people must be cautious when they leave the village at dawn. If there is some reason to suspect raiders, they do not leave the confines of the upright log palisade that surrounds the village. They wait instead until full light and leave the village in armed groups.

By the time it is light enough to see, everybody has started preparing breakfast. This consists largely of roasted green plantains, easily prepared and steaming hot. If the family has any meat, it is taken down and shared, the children getting the best portions. Leftover meat is hung over the fire by a vine to keep the vermin off it and to preserve it.

If any of the men have made plans to hunt that day, they leave the village before it is light. Wild turkeys can be easily taken at this time of day because they roost in conspicuous places. During the dry season the *hashimo* (a kind of grouse) sing before dark and can be readily located. If any were heard the night before, the men leave at dawn to stalk them.

Tobacco chewing starts as soon as people begin stirring. Those who have fresh

---

[21]A child fell into a fire and burned to death in 1966—the mother had placed her hammock too close to the fire in order to keep warm, and the baby slipped from her arms while she slept. Bahimi's mother also sleeps in Kąobawä's house, but he does not have to avoid her because she is an old woman.

supplies soak the new leaves in water and add ashes from the hearth to the wad. Men, women, and children chew tobacco and all are addicted to it. Once there was a shortage of tobacco in Kạobawä's village and I was plagued for a week by early morning visitors who requested permission to collect my cigarette butts in order to make a wad of chewing tobacco. Normally, if anyone is short of tobacco, he can request a share of someone else's already chewed wad, or simply borrow the entire wad when its owner puts it down somewhere. Tobacco is so important to them that their word for "poverty" translates as "being without tobacco." I frequently justified my reluctance to give away possessions on the basis of my poverty. Many of them responded by spitting their tobacco into their hand and handing it to me.

Work begins as soon as breakfast is completed; the Yạnomamö like to take advantage of the morning coolness. Within an hour after it is light the men are in their gardens clearing brush, felling large trees, transplanting plantain cuttings, burning off dead timber, or planting new crops of cotton, maize, sweet potatoes, yuca, taro, or the like, depending on the season. They work until 10:30 A.M., retiring because it is too humid and hot by that time to continue with their strenuous work. Most of them bathe in the stream before returning to their hammocks for a rest and a meal.

The women usually accompany their husbands to the garden and occupy themselves by collecting firewood or helping with planting and weeding. In this way the men are sure that their families are safe and that the women are not having affairs with other men.

The children spend a great deal of time exploring the wonders of the plant and animal life around them and are accomplished biologists at an early age. Most twelve-year-old boys can, for example, name twenty species of bees and give the anatomical or behavioral reasons for their distinctions—and they know which ones produce the best honey. An eight-year-old girl brought me a tiny egg-like structure on one occasion and asked me to watch it with her. Presently it cracked open and numerous baby cockroaches poured out, while she described the intimate details of the reproductive process to me.

The younger children stay close to their mothers, but the older ones have considerable freedom to wander about the garden at play. Young boys hunt for lizards with miniature bows and featherless arrows. If they can capture one alive, they bring it back to the village and tie a string around it. The string is anchored to a stick in the village clearing and the little boys chase it gleefully, shooting scores of tiny arrows at it (see Fig. 3–8). Since lizards are very quick, and little boys are poor shots, the target practice can last for hours. Usually, however, the fun terminates when an older boy decides to make an end to the unhappy lizard and kills it with his adult-size arrows, showing off his archery skills to the disgruntled small fry.

Little girls learn very quickly that it is a man's world, for they soon must assume much of the responsibility for tending their younger siblings, hauling water and firewood, and in general helping their busy mothers.

Most of the people rest in their hammocks during the heat of midday, although they will collect fruits and other wild foods from the surrounding area, if any are in season. They avoid being in the direct rays of the midday sun.

If the men return to their gardening, they do so about 4:00 P.M., working until sundown. Otherwise, they gather in small groups around the village and take hallucinogenic drugs in the late afternoon shadows, chanting to the mountain demons as the drugs take effect. This usually lasts for an hour or so, after which the men bathe to wash the vomit or nasal mucus off their bodies. Kạobawä does not participate in the drug-taking, as he finds it unpleasant. Most of the men, however, do take drugs and enjoy doing it, despite the associated unpleasantries of vomiting and the pain that follows the blast of air as the powder is blown deeply into the nasal passages.

Whatever the men do for the afternoon, however, the women invariably search for firewood and haul immense, heavy loads of it to their houses just before dark.

Fig. 3–8. Boys shooting tiny arrows into a lizard they have captured. The lizard is tied to a string and allowed to run around the village while the boys gleefully chase it. Here they have wounded it and are about to fill it full of arrows.

The biggest meal of the day is prepared in the evening. The staple is plantains, but frequently other kinds of food are available after the day's activities. Meat is always the most desirable food and is always considered to be in short supply. It is a happy occasion when one of the hunters bags a tapir, for everyone gets a large share of it.

It is good to share meat with others. This attitude is expressed in the sentiment that a hunter should give away most of the game he kills. One of the obligations men take very seriously is providing adequate quantities of meat for their wives and children. They genuinely abhor hearing their children cry for meat; this calls into question their abilities as hunters and marksmen, both of which are associated with prestige. Rerebawä, for example, collected a large supply of game on one trip we took together. He gave it all to his wife and children and to his wife's parents. At the evening meal he refused to take a portion of the meat so that the others could have more. Later in the evening, he appeared at my hut begging for a can of sardines to satisfy his hunger for meat. He preferred to go hungry rather than risk the onus of being accused of poor marksmanship or stinginess.

Both sexes participate in the cooking, although the women do the greater share of it. Food preparation is not elaborate and rarely requires much labor, time, or paraphernalia. Spices are never used, although the salty ashes of a particular kind of tree are sometimes mixed with water to form a condiment of sorts. The food is dunked into the salty liquid and eaten.

Everyone eats in his hammock using his fingers for utensils. Some meals cannot be eaten from a reclining position, so the members of the family squat in a circle around the common dish. For example, large quantities of tiny fish are cooked by wrapping them in leaves and cooking them in the hot coals. When the fish are done, the package is spread open, and everyone shares its contents.

Animals are never skinned before cooking. They are merely put over the fire after their entrails have been removed, and roasted, head, fur, claws, and all. Most of the fur is singed off in the process of cooking. The animal is dismembered by hand. The head, particularly the head of a monkey, is highly prized because the brain is considered a delicacy. The most common meat is monkey, of which there are several varieties, so that this delicacy is enjoyed rather frequently by the Yąnomamö.

By the time supper is over it is nearly dark. The fires are prepared for the evening; if someone has allowed his own fire to go out during the day, he simply borrows two glowing sticks from a neighbor and rekindles his own hearth. The entrances to the village are sealed off with dry brush so that prowlers can not enter without raising an alarm. Before retiring to their hammocks, the Yąnomamö first sit on them and wipe the bottoms of their bare feet together. This rubs off most of the debris that has accumulated on them during the course of the day. Everyone sleeps naked and as close to the fire as possible. Despite the inevitable last-minute visiting, things are usually quiet in the village by the time it is dark.

Things are not always quiet after dark. If anyone in the village is sick, a shaman will chant to the malevolent spirits most of the night to exorcise them. Or, should anyone be mourning a dead kinsman, he or she will sob and wail long after the others have fallen asleep. Occasionally, a fight will break out between a husband and wife, and soon everybody in the village will be screaming, expressing opinions on the dispute. The shouting may continue sporadically for hours, dying down only to break out anew as someone gets a fresh insight into the problem. Once in a while someone gives a long, loud speech voicing his opinion on the world in general. Those who are interested may add their own comments, but the audience usually grumbles about the noise and falls asleep.

Status Differences and Activities

Daily activities, except those concerning gardening and visiting, do not vary much from season to season. Much of the variation that does occur is a function of one's age or sex, as was shown above.

Other status differences do exist and account for some variation in the activities of particular individuals. Rerebawä, for example, is an outsider to Kąobawä's group and has no intention of joining the village as a permanent resident. Consequently, he does not participate in the gardening activities and has considerably more spare time than other married men. He spends this time hunting for his wife and her parents, one of his obligations as a son-in-law. He is quite dependent on them for the bulk of his diet because they provide him with all his plantains. This is perhaps why he takes his hunting obligations so seriously and gives his game away so unflinchingly. He is quick to make reference to his hunting skills and generosity, perhaps to draw attention away from the fact that he does not cultivate food for his wife and children. He has been able to avoid making a garden because of his status as an outsider; he plans to return to his own village as soon as his bride service is over. But his in-laws want him to stay permanently so that he will be able to provide them with meat and garden produce when they are old. They have no sons to do this for them and have even promised Rerebawä their second daughter on the condition that he remain permanently in the village. They prevent Rerebawä from taking his wife and children home by keeping at least one of the children with them when Rerebawä goes to visit his own family. They know that his wife could not bear to be separated permanently from her child, and Rerebawä invariably brings her back home so that she can be with the child.

By Yąnomamö standards he has done enough bride service and deserves to be given his wife. Also, by their standards he has lived in the village so long that he should be obliged to make his own garden. But he can legitimately refuse to do this because he has discharged his obligations well beyond what was expected of him.

Kąobawä, on the other hand, has the special status of being his group's headman. Apart from this, he is also some fifteen years senior to Rerebawä and has a higher sense of obligation and responsibility to his family. Rerebawä, in addition to refusing to make a garden, thinks nothing of taking a week-long trip to visit friends, leaving his wife and children with her parents. His attitude toward the children, compared to Kąobawä's, is rather indifferent. Kąobawä had planned to accompany me to Caracas to see how foreigners live until Ariwari began crying and appealed to his father's paternal sensitivities. Kąobawä stepped out of the canoe, took off the clothing I had loaned him, and picked up Ariwari; "I can't go with you," he explained, "Ariwari will miss me and be sad."

Kąobawä thinks for the others in the village, many of whom are not able to perceive some of the less obvious implications of situations. In political matters he is the most astute man in group, but he so diplomatically exercises his influence that the others are not offended. Should someone be planning to do something that is potentially dangerous, he simply points out the danger and adds parenthetically, "Go ahead and do it if you want to, but don't expect sympathy from me if you get hurt." Shararaiwä, his youngest brother, planned to take a trip to a distant village with me. I knew that the two villages were not on particularly good terms with each other, but they were not actively at war. Kąobawä arrived at my canoe just as we were about to depart and asked me not to take Shararaiwä along, explaining that the Iyawei-teri might possibly molest him and precipitate hostilities between the two groups. Shararaiwä was willing to take a chance that my presence would be sufficient to deter any potential trouble, but Kąobawä would not risk it.

On another occasion a group of men from Patanowä-teri arrived to explore with

Kąobawä the possibility of peace between their two villages. They were brothers-in-law to him and were fairly certain that he would protect them from the village hotheads. One of the ambitious men in Kąobawä's group saw in this an opportunity to enhance his prestige and made plans to murder the three visitors. This man, Paruriwä, was a very cunning, treacherous fellow and quite jealous of Kąobawä's position as headman. He wanted to be the village leader and privately told me to address him as the headman. On this occasion Kąobawä let it be known that he intended to protect the visitors. For the better part of the day the village was in a state of suspense. Paruriwä and his followers were not to be found anywhere; a rumor spread that they had painted themselves black and were well armed. Kąobawä and his supporters, mostly his own brothers and brothers-in-law, remained in the village all day, their weapons close at hand. Late in the afternoon Paruriwä and his men appeared in their black paint and took up strategic posts around the village. He himself held an axe. He strutted arrogantly up to the visitors holding his axe as if he were ready to strike. The village became very quiet, and most of the women and children left. Neither Kąobawä nor the Patanowä-teri visitors batted an eyelash when Paruriwä approached, although the others were visibly nervous and sat up in their hammocks. Instead of striking the visitors with the axe as he appeared to suggest he was going to do, he invited one of them out to chant with him. Within seconds all three of the visitors had paired off with members of Paruriwä's group and were chanting passionately with them, explaining the reasons for their visit and giving their justification for the state of hostilites.

The crisis had been averted because of Kąobawä's implied threat that he would defend the visitors with force. A number of men in Paruriwä's group were visitors from Monou-teri; their headman had been killed a few months earlier by the Patanowä-teri. When Paruriwä failed to go through with his plan, they left the village in a rage, hoping to recruit a raiding party in their own village and ambush the visitors when they left.

Kąobawä realized that the visitors would not be safe until they got back home, since the Monou-teri would attempt to intercept them. He visited me that night and asked me to take the visitors back to their village at dawn in my canoe, knowing that I had already planned a trip there for the immediate future. After I agreed to accelerate my own plans, he proceeded to give me instructions about the trip: I was not to stop at any of the villages along the Orinoco River to visit, for all of them were at war with the Patanowä-teri and would shoot my companions on sight. The Patanowä-teri men lay on the floor of my canoe and covered themselves with a tarp when we passed these villages. The people on the bank shouted curses at me for not stopping to visit and give them trade goods. At this time the Patanowä-teri were being raided by about a dozen different villages. We had to cover part of the distance to their village on foot, proceeding very cautiously because of the danger of raiders. At one point the men showed me the spot where a Hasaböwä-teri raiding party had killed a Patanowä-teri woman a week earlier. Thus, Kąobawä not only protected the visitors while they were in his village but he also arranged a "safe-conduct" for their return.

Kąobawä keeps order in the village when people get out of hand. Paruriwä, for example, is particularly cruel to his four wives and beats them mercilessly for even slight provocations. None of his wives have brothers in the village, and few people are courageous enough to interfere with Paruriwä when he is angry. On one occasion Kąobawä was holding a feast for the members of an allied village. His preparations were being duplicated by an equal effort on the part of Paruriwä, an obvious attempt by the latter to show that he was also a leader. Some of the visitors arrived early and were visiting in Paruriwä's house. He commanded his wife to prepare food for them, but the woman moved a little too slowly to suit him. Paruriwä went into a rage, grabbed an axe, and swung it wildly at her. She ducked and ran screaming from the house. Paruriwä recovered his balance and threw the axe at her as she fled, but missed. By this time Kąobawä had seen the axe go whizzing over the woman's head; he raced across the village in time to take a machete from Paruriwä before he could inflict much damage with it. He did manage, however, to hit her twice before Kąobawä disarmed him, splitting her hand with one of the blows.

On another occasion one of Kąobawä's brothers took too much drug and became violent. He staggered to the center of the village with his bow and arrows, while people ran frantically out of their houses to avoid being shot. Kąobawä managed to disarm him and hid his weapons.

During the several club fights that took place while I was in the field, Kąobawä stood by with his bow and arrows to make sure that the fighting was kept relatively innocuous (see Fig. 3–9). In one of the chest-pounding duels, he managed to keep the fight from escalating into a shooting war by making sure that everybody in his group took a turn in the fighting. (See Chapter 4 for a description of the fight.) On this occasion

Fig. 3–9. Kąobawä (left, holding his bow) attempts to keep a club fight over a woman from escalating to shooting. The man in front of him has just been bashed on the head and blood is streaming down his neck.

his group was being trounced by their opponents, largely because only a few of the men were doing all the fighting for Kąobawä's group. These men were forced to take several turns in rapid succession, while a large number of men stood by and watched. The fighters wanted to escalate the battle to a duel with axes, hoping to intimidate their opponents into conceding. Kąobawä quickly forced the idle men to participate in the chest pounding, thereby distributing the punishment a little more evenly and reducing the possibility of a bloodier confrontation.

After the duel was over, Kąobawä coolly discussed the fight with the leaders in the opponents' group, explaining that he did not intend to raid them unless they raided first. A number of men in the village, notably Paruriwä and some of his followers, shouted threats at the departing opponents that they would shoot them on sight should they meet again. Paruriwä frequently boasted like this, but rarely put himself in a position that was potentially dangerous. He later ran into a party of hunters from the above-mentioned group while he was leading a raid against the Patanowä-teri. Instead of shooting them on sight as he threatened to do (they could have shot back, as they were armed), he traded arrows with them and rapidly retreated. He boasted in the village how he had terrified these men. I later visited their village and learned that Paruriwä was the one who was terrified. They themselves continued to hunt, while Paruriwä fled for home.

Kąobawä's personality differs considerably from Paruriwä's. Where the former is unobtrusive, calm, modest, and perceptive, the latter is belligerent, aggressive, ostentatious, and rash. Kąobawä has an established status in the village and numerous supporters, whose loyalties are in part determined by their kinship ties and in part because he is a wise leader. Paruriwä is attempting to share in the leadership and does not have a well-established position in this respect. It is obvious who the real leader is: When visitors come to Upper Bisaasi-teri, they seek out Kąobawä and deal with him, no matter how ambitiously Paruriwä attempts to emulate his position. Paruriwä does not have as many living brothers in his group as Kąobawä has, so his "natural following" is somewhat limited. In addition, two of his brothers are married to actual sisters of Kąobawä and have some loyalty to him. Paruriwä, therefore, has very little means with which to establish his position, so he is given over to using bluff, threat, chicanery, and treachery. This he does well, and many of the young men in the village admire him for it. He has gained the support of some of these men by promising them his wives' yet unborn daughters. Remarkably enough, some of them cling to these promises and do his bidding.

Finally, one of Kąobawä's most unpleasant tasks is to scout the village neighborhood when signs of raiders have been found. This he does alone, since it is a dangerous task and one that is avoided by the other men. Not even Paruriwä participates in this.

Kąobawä has definite responsibilities as the headman and is occasionally called upon by the nature of the situation to exercise his authority. He is usually distinguishable in the village as a man of some authority only for the duration of the incident that calls forth his leadership capacity. After the incident is over, he goes about his own business like the other men in the group. But even then, he sets an example for the others, particularly in his ambitions to produce large quantities of food for his family and for the guests he must entertain. Most of the time he leads only by example and the others follow if it pleases them to do so. They can ignore his example if they wish, but most of the people turn to him when a difficult situation arises.

4

Political Alliances, Trading and Feasting

Yᴀɴᴏᴍᴀᴍö ꜰᴇᴀꜱᴛꜱ take place only when one sovereign group entertains the members of another, allied group. Feasts, in brief, are political events. To be sure, economic and ceremonial implications are also significant, but these are relatively minor when compared to the functions of the feast in the context of forming alliances. The chief purpose of entertaining allies is to reaffirm and cultivate intervillage solidarity in the intimate, sociable context of food presentations, thereby putting the ally under obligation to reciprocate the feast in his own village at a later date, bringing about another feast and even more solidarity.

I will describe in this chapter some of the relationships between trade, economic specialization, historical ties between groups, warfare, and intervillage marriage exchanges, all of which are intimately connected and interact with each other in the process of developing political alliances.

I described in Chapter 2 how the members of independent villages cultivated friendships with each other in the process of establishing themselves in a loose network of allied villages. I then showed in Chapter 3 how Kạobawä's followers were related to him and how he, in turn, was related to the members of several other villages. Now I will take up some of the political consequences of the historical ties and how they shape and mould the nature of specific contemporary relationships between Kạobawä's group and those which have political dealings with it. To illustrate this, I will describe the details of a particular feast in the context of the political ties, both historical and contemporary, existing between Kạobawä's group and the guests at the feast. First, however, I will comment on Yạnomamö alliances in general.

General Features of Alliances

One of the expectations and implications of alliance is that the partners are under obligation to provide shelter and sustenance to each other whenever one of them is driven from his village and garden by a powerful enemy. The beleaguered partner may be obliged to remain in the village of his host for a year or longer, approximately the length of time required to establish a new plantation and productive base from which an independent existence is possible. Twice in the recent history of Kąobawä's group they were driven from their gardens by more powerful enemies and were forced to take refuge in the village of an ally. In each case the group remained with the ally for a year or so, moving away only after their new garden began producing. In both cases, the hosts demanded and received a number of women from Kąobawä's group without reciprocating in kind, a prerogative they exercised from their temporary position of strength. The longer the group takes advantage of a hosts' protection, the higher is the cost in terms of women, so visitors always make an attempt to establish their gardens as quickly as possible and move into them as soon as they begin producing. Without allies, therefore, the members of a village would either have to remain at their single garden and sustain the attacks of their enemies or disband into several smaller groups and join larger villages on a permanent basis, losing many of their women to their protectors. The jungle simply does not produce enough wild foods to sustain larger groups, and the threat of warfare is such that smaller groups would soon be discovered by their enemies and exterminated.

Because of the ever-present risk of being driven from one's garden, therefore, no Yąnomamö village can continue to exist as a sovereign entity without establishing alliances with other groups. Warfare is attended by a bellicose ideology which asserts that strong villages should take advantage of weaker ones and coerce them out of women; to prevent this, all villages should therefore behave as if they were strong. Thus, the military threat creates a situation in which intervillage alliance is desirable, but at the same time spawns a military ideology that inhibits the formation of such alliances: Allies need but cannot trust each other. They are obliged to behave aggressively in order to display their respective strength.

Alliances between villages are the product of a developmental sequence that involves casual trading, mutual feasting, and finally the exchange of women. The most intimate allies are those who, in addition to trading and feasting, exchange women. Any developing alliance may stabilize at the trading or feasting stage without proceeding to the woman-exchange phase. These are weak alliances, but serve to limit the degree of war that might possibly obtain between the villages so related: The Yąnomamö tend to avoid attacking those villages with which they trade and feast, unless some specific incident, such as the abduction of a woman, provokes them. Allies that are linked by trade and feasting ties, for example, rarely accuse each other of practicing harmful magic. Allies bound to each other by affinal kinship ties, however, are more interdependent because they are under obligation to each other to continue to exchange women. It is, in fact, by the exchange of women that independent villages extend kinship ties to each other.

Members of allied villages are usually reluctant to take the final step in alliance formation and cede women to their partners, for they are always worried that the latter might not reciprocate as promised. This attitude is especially conspicuous in smaller villages, for their larger partners in defense pressure them into demonstrating their solidarity by ceding women; the strong can and do coerce the weak in Yąnomamö politics. The weak, therefore, are compelled to exaggerate their strength by bluff and intimidation and by attempting in general to appear to be stronger, militarily, than they really are, thereby hoping to convince their partners that they are equals, capable of an independent existence. By so doing, they also inform their partners that any attempt to coerce them out of women will be met with the appropriate reaction, such as a chest-pounding duel or club fight. Nevertheless, each ally expects to gain women in the alliance and enters it with this in mind; and each hopes to gain more women than it cedes in return.

Hence, in order for an occasional nervous meeting of groups of men from different villages to evolve into a stable intervillage alliance based on the reciprocal exchange of women, the long and difficult road of feasting and trading must be traversed. Suspicion must give way to relative confidence, and this must develop into reciprocal feasting during the dry season. Only then has the intervillage relationship reached a point where the partners begin ceding women to each other; and even then, it is done reluctantly.

This is, however, only the ideal pattern in the development of an alliance. Rarely does it develop far enough to reach the stage where women change hands, particularly if the two villages concerned are of approximately the same military strength. Fights and arguments over women or food develop, and the principals withdraw temporarily on semihostile terms, perhaps attempting a rapprochement sometime in the future. Or, if the principals are obviously different military potential, the stronger of the two will coerce its weaker partner into ceding women early in the alliance development, taking advantage of its own military strength, thus altering the course of alliance development in the opposite direction.

Whatever the specific developmental sequence leading to the woman-exchange phase, the milieu within which these developments take place is not conducive to the establishment of warm ties of friendship. Each of the principals attempts to demonstrate his own sovereignty in order to convince the other that he does not really require political alliance to keep his enemies in check. This is accomplished by bragging about past military victories and fierceness in past club fights and chest-pounding duels, and by insinuating that one's group is always on the verge of exploding into a force so great that no combination of allies could overcome its terrible might. The smaller the village and more obvious its vulnerability, the greater is the pressure to insinuate or to demonstrate this potential.

Political maneuvering in this milieu is both a tricky and potentially hazardous undertaking. Each principal in the negotiation must establish the credibility of his own threats, while discovering the point at which his partner's bluff will dissolve abruptly into action; he must discover the point beyond which he must not goad his ally, lest he himself is prepared to suffer the possibly violent outcome. It is a politics of brinkmanship, a form of political behavior in which each negotiator is compelled to expose his opposite's threats as bluffs at the risk of inciting him to violence—a club fight, immediately and honorably, or, later and treacherously, a feast in which the hosts descend on their guests to kill their men and abduct their women.

Trading and Feasting in Alliance Formation

Because an ally is not beyond taking advantage of his weaker partner, especially when the alliance is just developing, there is very little in the way of natural attraction to encourage the two groups to visit each other. Considerations of pride and canons of ferocity preclude obvious attempts to develop stable and predictable alliances and military interdependency. The Yạnomamö cannot simply arrive at the village of a potential ally and declare that they need military assistance because of the raids of a superior enemy. Doing so would admit vulnerability and perhaps invite predation from the potential ally. Instead, they conceal and subsume the true motive for the alliance in the vehicles of *trading* and *feasting,* developing these institutions over months and even years. In this manner they retain an apparent modicum of sovereignty and pride, while simultaneously attaining the true objectives: intervillage solidarity and military interdependence.

Three distinct features of Yạnomamö trading practices are important in the context of alliance formation. First, each item must be repaid with a different kind of item: The recipient is under an *obligation* to repay his partner in a type of exchange called *no mraiha.* Secondly, the payment is delayed, a temporal factor in the trading techniques that is likewise implied by the *no mraiha.* The consequence of these two trading features is that one trade always calls forth another and gives the members of different villages both the excuse and the opportunity to visit each other; and once the trading starts, it tends to continue, for one village in an alliance always owes the other trade goods from their last confrontation. The third significant trade feature is the peculiar specialization in the production of trade items. Each village has one or more special products that it provides to its allies. These include such items as dogs, hallucinogenic drugs (both cultivated and collected), arrow points, arrow shafts, bows, cotton yarn, cotton and vine hammocks, baskets of several varieties, clay pots, and, in the case of the several contacted villages, steel tools and aluminum pots.

This specialization in production cannot be explained in terms of the distribution of natural resources. Each village is, economically speaking, capable of self-sufficiency. (The steel tools and other products from civilization constitute the major exceptions.) The explanation of the specialization must be sought, rather, in the sociological aspects of alliance formation. Trade functions as the social catalyst, the "starting mechanism," through which mutually suspicious allies are repeatedly brought together in direct confrontation. Without these frequent contacts with neighbors, alliances would be much slower in formation and would be even more unstable once formed: A prerequisite to stable alliance is repetitive visiting and feasting, and the trading mechanism serves to bring about these visits.

Clay pots are a good example of the specialization in labor that characterizes Yạnomamö production and trade. The Mọmaribowei-teri (see map, Fig. 2–8) are allied to both Kạobawä's group and the people of a distant Shamatari village, the latter being mortal enemies of Kạobawä. When I first began my fieldwork, I visited the Mọmaribowei-teri, specifically asking them if they knew how to make clay pots. They all vigorously denied knowledge of pot-making, explaining that they once knew how to make them but had long since forgotten. They explained that their allies, the Mowaraoba-teri, made them in quantities and provided all they needed, and therefore they did not have to make them anymore. They also added that the clay in the area of their village was not of the proper type for making pots. Later in the year their alliance with the pot makers grew cool because of a war, and their source of pots was shut off. At the same time, Kạobawä's group began asking them for clay pots. The Mọmaribowei-teri promptly responded by "remembering" how pots were made and "discovering" that the clay in their neighborhood was indeed suitable for pot manufacturing. They had merely created a local shortage of the item in order to have to rely on an ally for it, giving sufficient cause to visit them.

Often the specialization is less individualized than in the case of clay pot manufacture. Kąobawä's group, for example, exports cotton yarn to one ally, but imports it from another. The exported cotton frequently is brought back in the form of manufactured hammocks, the importer merely contributing labor to the process. In some cases, the shortages are merely seasonal; Kąobawä's group may import cotton from a particular ally at one time of the year, but export it at another. Most of the trade, however, involves items that are readily manufactured by or raised by any group, underscoring the fact that trade is the stimulus to visit. Food does not enter the trading system, although hospitality dictates that it must be given to friendly groups. Occasionally, a village will run short of plantains because of a particularly long hot spell, and its members may visit an ally to borrow food to last a week or so. This hospitality is usually reciprocated, but it is not a part of the trading network.

Alliances between villages may stabilize at any one of three points: sporadic reciprocal trading, mutual feasting, or reciprocal women exchange. These are cumulative levels in the sense that the third phase implies the first two: Allies that exchange women also feast and trade with each other. Likewise, allies that merely feast together also trade, but do not exchange women. At the lower end of this scale of solidarity lie those villages with which one fights to kill, while at the upper end are those villages from whom one's group has recently separated. Frequently, the scale is circular rather than linear: A village's mortal enemy is the group from which it has recently split. By way of example, Kąobawä's group trades sporadically with the Makorima-teri, Daiyari-teri, Widokaiya-teri, Mahekodo-teri, and Iyawei-teri. These are fairly weak alliances and even permit limited fighting. His group has more intimate ties with the Reyaboböwei-teri and Mǫmariböwei-teri, with whom it feasts regularly. The alliance with the Reyaboböwei-teri has even reached the point at which they are exchanging women with each other. Finally, at the other end of the scale, Kąobawä's group is at war with the Iwahikoroba-teri, Möwaraoba-teri, and Patanowä-teri. The first two of these groups are historically unrelated to Kąobawä's group, although they have a common history with two of his staunchest allies, the Reyaboböwei-teri and Mǫmaribowei-teri, from whom they separated in the past. The Patanowä-teri are related to Kąobawä and his followers, as was shown in Chapter 3. Nevertheless, they are bitter enemies and are at present raiding each other.

Although there is no rigid geographical correlation of the village settlement pattern to the degree of alliance solidarity, neighboring villages usually are at least on trading terms and are not actively conducting war on each other. Should war develop between neighbors, one of the two principals will abandon its site and move to a new location. Whether the ties between neighboring villages will be one of blood, marriage exchange, reciprocal feasting, or casual trading depends on a large number of factors, particularly on village size, current warfare situation with respect to more distant groups, and the precise historical ties between the neighboring villages. Whatever the nature of the ties beween neighbors, each strives to maintain its sovereignty and independence from the others.

The Yąnomamö do not openly regard trade as a mechanism the ulterior function of which is to bring people repeatedly together, thus establishing an amicable basis from which more stable types of alliance can develop. Nor do they overtly acknowledge the relationships between trading and feasting cycles to village interdependency. In this regard they are like the Trobriand Islanders of Melanesia: They have a "functional ignorance" of the more significant adaptive aspects of their trading institutions. To both the Yąnomamö and the Trobrianders, the mechanisms by which peoples from different groups are compelled to visit each other are ends in themselves and are not conceived to be related to the establishment of either economic or political interdependency. For the Yąnomamö participant in a feast, the feast itself has its significance in the marvelous quantities of food, the excitement of the dance, and the satisfaction of having others admire and covet the fine decorations he wears. The enchantment of the dance issues from the dancer's awareness that, for a brief moment, he is a glorious peacock that commands the admiration of his fellows, and it is his responsibility and desire to present a spectacular display of his dance steps and gawdy accouterments. In this brief, ego-building moment, each man has an opportunity to display himself, spinning and prancing about the village periphery, chest puffed out, while all watch, admire, and cheer wildly.

The hosts, too, have an opportunity to display themselves and strut before their guests. Moreover, the very fact that they have given the feast is in itself a display of affluence and surfeit apparently calculated to challenge the guests to reciprocate with an equally grandiose feast at a later date.[1] Each good feast deserves and calls forth another, and in this way allies become better acquainted with each other as they reciprocate feasts during the dry season and over the years.

Historical Background to a Particular Feast

One of the feasts I witnessed exhibited all the features of intervillage politics. Before describing this feast, I will give the historical antecedents to the event, recapitulating a number of points discussed in Chapter 3 in the context of the history of Kąobawä's village. The significance of the events will then become clear, for Kąobawä's prior relationships to the guests at the feast had a great deal to do with the outcome.

In 1950 Kąobawä's group, almost friendless, beleaguered by enemies, and somewhat isolated, began cultivating an alliance with the Iwahikoroba-teri (see map, Fig. 2–8), a Shamatari village, some two days' traveling distance southeast of their own village at Kreibŏwei. The Iwahikoroba-teri were on friendly terms with another Shamatari group, the Möwaraoba-teri, from whom they had separated some years before. Kąobawä's group, on the other hand, was at war with this village because members of his own group murdered a friendly Möwaraoba-teri visitor in 1940, touching off a series of raids between them. Anxious to develop an alliance, Kąobawä's group accepted a feast invitation from the Iwahikoroba-teri and visited that village to participate in the feast. Up to that point they were only on trading terms with them.

The Iwahikoroba-teri, however, had made a prior arrangement with their friends, the Möwaraoba-teri, to help them massacre Kąobawä's men and abduct his group's women. The Möwaraoba-teri were hidden in the jungle outside the village when Kąo-

---

[1]The competitive aspects of feasting in many primitive societies has been dealt with at length by Marcel Mauss, whose essay *The Gift* is now an anthropological classic.

bawä's group arrived. The men of Kąobawä's group danced both singly and en masse and were invited into the homes of their hosts. At this point their hosts fell upon them with axes and staves, killing about a dozen men before the visitors could break through the palisade and escape. Kąobawä's father was among the victims. Once outside, they were shot from ambush by the Möwaraoba-teri, who managed to kill a few more and wound many others with arrows. A number of women and girls were captured by the hosts, though some were later recaptured by Kąobawä's group in revenge raids. It was probably their host's greed for the women that permitted any survivors at all, as my informants asserted that the Iwahikoroba-teri began chasing the women while the men were still vulnerable. A few of the Iwahikoroba-teri refused to participate in the slaughter and even helped some of Kąobawä's group escape.

The survivors fled to Kobou, a site they had begun clearing for a new garden. Here they removed the arrow points and nursed their wounds before reluctantly returning to Kreiböwei, their only producing garden. Kobou was still too new to support the group, and hunger forced them to return to Kreiböwei. As this location was well known to their treacherous allies, they wished to abandon it as soon as possible, knowing that their enemies could easily kill the rest of the men and abduct the remaining women.

Within a week or so of the treacherous feast, the Mahekodo-teri, a visiting ally of Kąobawä's group, learned of the massacre and offered aid. The Mahekodo-teri headman himself visited Kąobawä's village and invited the entire group to his village to take refuge. They accepted the offer, and in January of 1951, after conducting one revenge raid on the enemies, moved to Mahekodo-teri.

The Mahekodo-teri had been allied to Kąobawä's group a generation earlier, but after Kąobawä's group moved away from the Orinoco River, alliance activity had dwindled to just sporadic trading. True to Yąnomamö political behavior, the Mahekodo-teri, being in an obviously stronger bargaining position, offered their protection and aid with gain in mind: they demanded and received a number of their guests' women. Again, the members of Kąobawä's group suspected further treachery from their new protectors and assiduously worked at establishing a new garden. They were forced to stay with the Mahekodo-teri until their new garden could totally support them—about a year. Even during this time, however, they spent weeks on end away from their host's village, carrying their food with them and working on their new plantations. They would return to obtain new food supplies, rest for a few weeks, and leave again. When Mahekodo-teri later split into three factions, Kąobawä and his group learned from one of them the details of a plot in which the Mahekodo-teri were going to kill the men and abduct the women. The only thing that prevented them from doing so was the development of a new war between Mahekodo-teri and another village, one that required the assistance of Kąobawä and his group.

For a few years after the separation from Mahekodo-teri, Kąobawä's group was invited to feast there. Because they suspected that the Mahekodo-teri were plotting against them, however, usually the men alone would attend the feast, thereby reducing the probability of another massacre. The women and children were concealed in the jungle during the time the men were away at the feast. Gradually, the alliance cooled off again and the two groups remained relatively indifferent towards each other, but at peace.

By 1960, Kąobawä's group had regained some of its military strength and had begun cultivating an alliance with a third Shamatari group, one that was related to the two that conducted the massacre in 1950. The new Shamatari group, Paruritawä-teri (see map, Fig. 2–8), was at war with the Iwahikoroba-teri, but on feasting terms with the Möwaraoba-teri. Kạobawä's group persuaded their new Shamatari allies to invite the Möwaraoba-teri to a feast and planned a massacre similar to that of 1950, but with the tables reversed: Kạobawä's group would lie in ambush, while the Paruritawä-teri attacked the guests within the village. The Möwaraoba-teri were being ravished by a malaria epidemic at this time, and only a handful of them actually came to the feast: The others were too sick to travel. With the aid of their newly found allies, Kạobawä's group managed to kill three of the five men and abducted four of their women. The other two visitors escaped to tell of the treachery. This revenge feast was only considered to be partially successful, and Kạobawä's group was not satisfied with the outcome. Their Shamatari allies, Paruritawä-teri, were obliged to abandon their site to avoid the revenge raids, splitting into two groups in the process: Mọmariböwei-teri and Reyaboböwei-teri, both continuing to remain friendly to Kạobawä's group.

In early 1965, just a few months after I began my fieldwork, Kạobawä and his supporters left to visit Reyaboböwei-teri, one of the two Shamatari allies, hoping to conduct another treacherous feast for the Möwaraoba-teri. They left a few men behind to protect the women and children. The men were gone almost two weeks. All during this time, those who remained behind flocked to my mud hut at dawn and remained in it the whole day, not permitting me to leave. Every hour or so they asked to see my shotgun. I soon discovered that they were frightened and suspected that the Widokaiya-teri were going to raid them to abduct women, for they knew of the plot. My hut lay on the path most likely to be taken by Widokaiya-teri raiders, and the few remaining men stood guard next to my door, hoping to intercept the raiders should they attack at night.

I, unknowingly, guarded the women and children by day with my shotgun, while the men did the same at night with their own weapons. This incident indelibly underscores the almost complete lack of trust between allies; the members of Kạobawä's group expected a raid from their friends and allies rather than from their enemies!

About ten days after the men had left, six visitors from another allied village passed through Upper Bisaasi-teri hoping to trade. It was obvious to them that the men were away and that the women were frightened. They carried word of the situation up the Orinoco River to their own allies, one of which was the Mahekodo-teri.

The evening before the men returned from their trip, one of the Salesian Missionaries, Padre Luiz Cocco, visited me, having traveled up the Orinoco River by dark—a dangerous undertaking at that time of the year. Padre Cocco had just received word by short-wave radio from the mission at Mahekodo-teri that a large party of men had left for Bisaasi-teri intent on capturing women. They had learned of the poorly guarded women from the six visitors and were determined to take advantage of the situation.

My house was full of women and children at dawn the following day, and the raiders were probably en route. I was in a difficult situation. On the one hand, if I told the Indians of the rumor, it would have been sufficient cause to start a war between Kạobawä's group and the Mahekodo-teri. This would have been most unfortunate if the story proved to be false. On the other hand, I dared not remain silent. If raiders were indeed coming, they would probably kill the defenders to capture the women. Fortunately, Kạobawä and the men returned early in the afternoon, and I was able to remain neutral. The treacherous feast for their Shamatari enemies proved to be unsuccessful: The intended victims had accepted the invitation, but were informed of the plot just before they arrived. One of the Reyaboböwei-teri who had close kinsmen among them had misgivings about the matter and warned them.

Late in the afternoon it was learned that the Mahekodo-teri were, in fact, in the vicinity of the village, allegedly on a "camping trip." Kąobawä, of course, suspected their story, but to demonstrate his friendship he invited them to be his guests at a feast. As he and his men had been away for nearly two weeks, there was an abundance of food in their gardens and they could easily afford to entertain the Mahekodo-teri and their traveling companions, the Boreta-teri. Together, the guests numbered about 100—after they fetched their women and children.

This sets the stage for the feast in the kind of context that makes it more intelligible: The specific historical relationships between the participants and the nature of their mutual mistrust. Now I will give the details of the events that followed.

The Feast

Perhaps because he suspected the Mahekodo-teri and Boreta-teri of intimidation, Kąobawä also invited the Karohi-teri to attend the feast. They are a small but dependable ally and had themselves separated from the Mahekodo-teri many years ago. This established a balance of power at the projected feast should any trouble arise, for the combination of both Boreta-teri and Mahekodo-teri was of sufficient strength to worry any host. With the aid of the Karohi-teri, Kąobawä's group was more of a match for the visitors.

The feast started out on a sour note. It is the custom of the Yąnomamö visitors to arrive only after an invitation from their hosts, sent by messenger on the day of the feast. The Mahekodo-teri and Boreta-teri, however, arrogantly arrived nearly a week before Kąobawä's group was prepared to receive them and set up a large, temporary camp a short distance from the village. They were guests and could legitimately demand to be fed. Because of this, Kąobawä and his covillagers were under obligation to feed them, some hundred or so people, and took them to the gardens to supply them with enough plantains to last a week. Kąobawä was a little disturbed that they would be so impolite as to arrive uninvited, but took the situation quite philosophically. After all, they had fed his group for the better part of a year.

He and several other men cut a large quantity of plantains, which were hung in his house and allowed to ripen for a week, to be boiled into *date,* a thick, sweet soup, on the day of the feast. That afternoon Kąobawä and a few of the older men commissioned a hunting party comprised of young men, several of whom were Kąobawä's brothers, whose responsibility would be to obtain a large quantity of fresh meat to give to the visitors on the day after the feast. Most of them were reluctant to go, as their feet were still sore from the trip to the Shamatari village. A few of them claimed to be sick and managed to escape recruitment into the hunting party in this way. This hunt, with the hanging of the plantains in the headman's house, initiated the feast. The excitement that usually attends a feast began at this time.

That evening the young men danced and sang in the village, an institution called *amoamo,* thereby insuring themselves with luck on the hunt. (The Yąnomamö also

Fig. 4–1. Kąobawä, headman, unpacking some of the meat his hunters have just collected for the feast.

amoamo on other occasions, but invariably do so on the day the plantains are hung in the village in anticipation of a feast.) Every evening the men are away on their *heniomou,* the week-long hunt, the young women and girls sing and dance in the village to insure them success.

The hunters left at dawn the following morning, carrying a large supply of roasted and green plantains with them to eat while they hunted. They had picked a site some 25 miles up the Mavaca River for their hunt, as game was known to abound there. Their task was to obtain monkeys, armadillos, wild turkeys, wild pig, tapir or sloth, the only meat deemed worthy to give to guests. They would not be permitted to eat any of this game, but could consume any other game they captured, such as deer, small birds, a small species of wild turkey, or insects and fish they happened to come upon. The feast meat, however, was earmarked for the guests and could not be eaten by the hunters. On this particular hunting trip the men miscalculated the amount of food they would need to sustain them during the hunt, and one of them returned after four days to fetch more plantains. He also gave Kąobawä a report on the hunt's success, creating a small sensation in the village: They had already killed a large number of *basho,* a particularly large and very desirable monkey. They had also come upon a quantity of turtle eggs at a sand bar and were eating as many as they could. When they returned later, they cached the remaining eggs in my house, so as not to have to share them with the visitors.

Meanwhile, the visitors were making gluttons of themselves, and the hosts started to grumble about the large number of plantains they had already eaten. The week's supply they originally provided had been consumed in half that time, and the guests had been given permission a second time to harvest more from their hosts' gardens. This was no way for guests to behave, and it soon became apparent that they were intimidating Kąobawä's group. Still, he and his followers continued to supply them with all the food they needed, keeping their complaints to themselves. They did not want it to be known that they were worried about running short of food. Instead, they planned to conduct the feast on a scale that would be difficult to reciprocate.

The hunters returned and presented their catch to Kąobawä. It was brought to his house and placed on the ground, wrapped up in leaves. Kąobawä ignored it for a while and then slowly began to unpack it (see Fig. 4-1) while everybody watched— especially the hunters, who were quite proud of the quantity of meat they had obtained: seventeen *basho* monkeys, seven wild turkeys, and three large armadillos. Hunting trips are not usually this successful, but the hunters had fortunately stumbled into a large band of *basho* and had nearly wiped it out.

Kąobawä and his group were anxious to conduct the feast for their visitors and present them with the food, because by so doing the visitors would be obliged to leave for home, thereby ending the drain on the gardens.[2]

The feast was scheduled for the day following the return of the hunters, even though the Karohi-teri had not yet arrived. Kąobawä and his group were so anxious to rid themselves of their ravenous guests by this time that they decided to hold a separate feast for the Karohi-teri on the day following the departure of the Mahekodo-teri. This would involve a considerable amount of extra work, but they were more than willing to

---

[2] I have seen several instances of Yąnomamö groups getting rid of visitors who have joined them semiperma- nently by holding a feast in their honor; when the ceremonial food is presented, the visitors are obliged to leave.

undertake it if it meant getting rid of their first group of visitors, who, by this time, had spent nearly a week eating Kạobawä's produce.

On the morning of the feast three large pieces of bark from the *arapuri* tree were cut and brought to the village. These were made into troughs to contain the boiled, ripe plantain soup. All day long Kạobawä's younger brothers, who had returned from the hunt the day before, labored at cooking the enormous quantity of ripe plantains, pouring each boiling containerful into the trough as it was prepared.[3]

The plantains that Kạobawä had hung in his *shabono* roof a week before were now ripe. The young men who were preparing the soup would cut the bunches of plantains from the roof, split each fruit with their thumb, throw the two halves of the flesh into a cooking pot, and toss the skins onto a pile. They worked at this task from early morning until late afternoon, in addition to boiling a nearly equal quantity of green plantains, which provided the green vegetable food that customarily accompanies the presentation of meat. Yąnomamö etiquette dictates that meat must be accompanied by vegetable food and vice versa.[4] It is an insult, for example, to offer someone meat without simultaneously offering a vegetable food with it. Peeling green plantains is a little more difficult than peeling ripe ones, which are very tough and brittle. The Yąnomamö solve this problem, like they solve so many others, by using their teeth. Each plantain is bitten along its length several times, cracking the peel, which in turn is removed with the fingernails and further application of the dentition. On this particular occasion, two young men peeled, with their thumbs, enough ripe plantains to make approximately 95 gallons of soup, and, with their teeth, a sufficiently large quantity of green plantains to fill a dozen large pack-baskets.

In the morning on the day of the feast, Kạobawä went to the center of the village clearing where all could see him and proceeded to pull weeds. The clearing has to look presentable to the visitors, as it functions as the dancing plaza. As noted before, since Yąnomamö headmen cannot directly order their followers to execute tasks such as these, they usually initiate them and hope that others will follow. By and by, a number of older men joined him, as well as a few women, and when a sufficient number of workers were pulling weeds and hauling them out, Kạobawä quietly retired to his hammock, from which he oversaw the food preparations and calculated the distribution of meat.

Excitement in the village grew conspicuously as the hours passed, and by noon there was a constant din of laughter and chatter, punctuated now and then with a shrill scream from some young man overcome with the thrill of the feast. Occasionally, the visitors would reply to the shouts, setting off a brief contest of screaming between hosts

---

[3]Kạobawä's group has access to aluminum pots now and uses them extensively in food preparations. Most Yąnomamö groups still use crude clay pots, although these are being rapidly replaced by aluminum ware, which is traded inland to the more remote villages.

[4]The three vegetable foods considered to be suitable accompaniments for the meat presentation are: boiled green plantains, boiled *rasha* fruit, and cassava bread. A number of missionaries and a few scientific observers have identified the Yąnomamö feast strongly with the *rasha* fruit (Zerries 1955; de Barandiaran 1966). If it is to be identified with any food, it should be called the "plantain feast," but to identify the feast with a food that sometimes (*rasha*) or invariably (plantains) accompanies it is to overlook the sociopolitical causes of the feast. *Rasha* is so unnecessary to the feast that it was served at only two of six feasts I attended. In short, the Yąnomamö feast is a social and political event, not a harvest ceremony, and occurs independently of the abundance or availability of *rasha* fruit. *Rasha* fruit ripens in February, the peak of the dry season. It is only in the dry season that feasts can be held, because travel is difficult or impossible at other times of the year. The correlation of the ripening of *rasha* and feasting is rather more fortuitous than causal.

and guests that gradually died off as each group busied itself in preparation for the dance.

Shortly after noon a rumor circulated through the village that the visitors had been raiding the gardens at night and stealing plantains. A number of people, particularly older men, were visibly upset by this new information, giving rise to another rumor that there would be a chest-pounding duel to set the matter straight. The guests had already worn their welcome thin by arriving uninvited a week in advance and by eating excessively. Their hosts were becoming angry with them, as it was all too obvious that they were deliberately taxing their hosts' patience; they were intimidating them.

The men of the host group had finished their preparations for the feast; they were all painted in red and black, bearing colorful feathers. They had cleaned the debris from their houses, had finished hauling out the weeds they had picked from the village clearing, and had brought in quantities of food to give their guests. Now, it was time for them to take *ebene,* their hallucinogenic drug. They separated into several groups and began blowing the brownish-green powder up each other's nostrils with 3-foot long hollow tubes. As the drug would be administered, each recipient would reel from the concussion of air, groan, and stagger off to some convenient post to vomit. Within ten minutes of taking the drug, the men would be bleary-eyed and wild, prancing around in front of their houses, stopping occasionally to vomit or to catch their breath. In each group there would be one man particularly adept at chanting to the *hekura,* the mountain demons, and he would soon take over the show, while the others retired to the sidelines in a stupor, green slime dripping from their nostrils. Should there be sick people in the village, the adept chanters—the *shabori*—would cure them by chanting, massaging, sucking, and vomiting out the evil spirit that caused the sickness. Otherwise, they would chant about other things, perhaps sending their *hekura* to enemy villages to eat the souls of children, or enjoining them to prevent their enemies from doing the same. Occasionally, one of the men takes too much of the drug and become violent. On this particular occasion, Shiimima, one of Kąobawä's brothers, grabbed his bow and arrows and ran to the center of the village. This caused a minor sensation for a moment, but one of the men managed to catch and disarm him, hiding his weapons so he could not find them. Things returned to normal again, and the other participants in the drug-taking began chanting to Shiimima to restore him to his senses. The chanting lasted for an hour or so, and the participants, one by one, returned to their houses to clean up their paint jobs; most of them had smeared their careful work by vomiting all over themselves.

While the men were taking their drugs, the women were busy painting and decorating themselves with feathers and red pigment. The visitors, also, were busy at the same tasks, and the excitement of the feast reached fever proportions by mid-afternoon. A few women were still busy finishing trade baskets, while Kąobawä's younger brothers continued with the monotonous cooking of what seemed to them an endless number of plantains.

Finally, an old man from the visiting group entered the village and marched unceremoniously across the clearing while the members of Kąobawä's group cheered him. He was too old to join the dancing, but too respected to wait behind with the women and children while the younger men put on their display. This was evidence that the visitors were about to send in their delegate to accept the feast invitation at Kąobawä's house.

The members of Lower Bisaasi-teri had joined Kąobawä's group for the feast, as they, too, were on friendly terms with the Mahekodo-teri and had benefited from the latter's hospitality after the treacherous feast in 1950. Before Kąobawä's group had separated from the Lower Bisaasi-teri, there had been one headman over the entire composite village. This was a brother to Kąobawä's father; when the groups split, the older man led the faction of Lower Bisaasi-teri, leaving Kąobawä to lead the Upper group. On this particular day, when the two groups had temporarily coalesced for the feast, the older man was conceded the honor of chanting with the visitor's delegate, Asiawä, the son of the Mahekodo-teri headman.

Ten minutes after the old visitor entered the village, Asiawä entered the clearing, touching off an explosion of wild cheering that marked the opening of the dance. He was spectacular in his bright new loin cloth, long red parrot feathers streaming from his armbands, and black monkey-tail headband covered with white buzzard down. He marched dramatically to the center of the village clearing, while all of Kąobawä's followers cheered, and struck the visitor's pose: motionless, head upward, and weapons held vertically next to his face. He stood there two or three minutes so his hosts could admire him. This gesture signified that he had come in peace and was announcing his benevolent intentions by standing where all could see him. If they bore him malice, they had to shoot him then or not at all.[5] He then marched to Kąobawä's house and was met by Kąobawä's father's brother, the temporary leader of the combined host group, and the two men immediately began to chant. This was the formal acceptance of the feast invitation by Asiawä on behalf of his entire group. They chanted for five minutes or so, bouncing up and down from the knees, now face to face, now side to side, but always lively and loud. Suddenly, they stopped, and Asiawä squatted, his back to the sun, while the host's representative retired to his hammock. The cheering died down. Asiawä squatted for several minutes before one of Kąobawä's younger brothers brought a half-gourd full of plantain soup to him and set it on the ground. He ignored it politely for several minutes, staring into the distance, holding his weapons horizontally next to his mouth. Presently, he put his weapons down, picked up the container of soup, and drained it in one draft before setting it back down. As soon as he had set it down, one of Kąobawä's younger brothers brought him a large pack-basket filled with boiled green plantains and smoked armadillo meat. Asiawä stood while the strap of the basket was placed over his head and adjusted across his shoulders so as to not crumple his headdress. Trying to look dramatic, he staggered rapidly out of the village under his burden of food, while the hosts again cheered wildly. This food was eaten by the visitors while they finished their decorating, each receiving a small portion.

Within a half-hour of Asiawä's departure the visitors had completed their decorating and had assembled just outside the entrance to the village. The men, all finely decorated, stood at the front of the gathering, while the women, girls, and young boys, also decorated, but each carrying a load of family possessions, brought up the rear. At the signal of Asiawä's father, the first two dancers burst into the village, separated, and danced around the periphery of the clearing in opposite directions, while Kąobawä's group welcomed them enthusiastically with shouts and shrill screams. Two at a time,

---

[5]I have a number of informants' accounts of visitors being shot down while standing in the clearing to announce their visit. Whenever I accompanied visitors to strange villages for the first time I, too, was obliged to participate in this rite and always had an uneasy feeling about it.

the visiting dancers entered, pranced around the village periphery, wildly showing off their decorations and weapons and then returning to the group. Each dancer had unique decorations and a unique dance step, something personal that he could exhibit. He would burst into the village screaming a memorized phrase, wheel and spin, stop in his tracks, dance in place, throw his weapons down, pick them up again, aim them at the line of hosts with a wild expression on his face, prance ahead a few steps, repeat his performance, and continue on around the village in this manner, while the hosts cheered wildly. When everyone had had an individual turn, the entire group entered, danced single file around the periphery several times, and gathered at the center of the clearing, where they formed a tightly knit group. They stood motionless, except for the heaving of their chests, hold-ing their weapons vertically. After they had stood there a few moments—in a final display of decorations—Kạobawä's followers emerged from their houses and approached the center of the village, each man inviting one or more of the visitors to his house, leading him away from the village center by the arm. As each visitor was led away, his family, watching from the village entrance, unceremoniously joined him at the host's house, bringing the family possessions along. Within a few minutes the dance plaza was deserted and the visitors were resting comfortably in their hosts' hammocks. Even in the ham-mocks, the Yạnomamö visitors are able to put on a silent display of their finery as they lay with their legs crossed, one arm behind their head, staring at the ceiling, waiting for their hosts to feed them ripe plantain soup from the bark troughs—it is almost as if they are strutting from a reclining position.

After the guests had been given their first round of soup, the men of Kạobawä's village assembled outside the entrance and came in to dance around the village for their guests. They, too, had an opportunity to put on a display of their own decorations, after which they retired to entertain the guests.

There were three troughs full of soup in the village. The first one was emptied in the process of bringing numerous gourdsful to the some one hundred visitors (see Fig. 4-2). After they had consumed this, the guests then assembled at the second trough and began eating there. Before this trough was finished, they moved as a group to the third trough and repeated their ceremonial consumption, before returning to their hammocks to rest and regain their appetites. Approximately two hours had passed from the time the first dancers entered the village until the guests retired from the third trough of soup. They had not yet eaten all of the contents—all in all, some 95 gallons of it—but managed to do so by morning.[6]

Shortly after dark the marathon chanting (waiyamou) began—it continued until dawn. At dawn the visitors conducted their trade and were given the baskets of "going-home food": boiled green plantains with smoked meat. The women and children de-parted with the food, leaving the men behind to trade. The visitors made requests through their headman, and Kạobawä would produce the item by enjoining one of the local men to give it. The item would be thrown at the feet of the man who wanted it. He would ignore it for a while and then give it a cursory examination, throwing it back on the ground. His peers would then examine it in greater detail and extol its virtues, while the

_____

[6]During some feasts, the ashes of the dead are mixed with the boiled, ripe plantain soup and eaten by friends and relatives of the deceased. The feast also serves as a preliminary to a raid that involves two or more villages. The sponsor of the raid will entertain his allies in a feast the day before the raiding party departs. See Chapter 5 for a discussion of the raid.

giver would apologize for its defects. If it were a particularly poor item, just the opposite would occur; the giver would cite its not-so-obvious merits, while the recipient would draw attention to the conspicuous shortcomings. In every trade the hosts always feel as though they had been over generous, and the guests, after they depart, complain that they had not received enough. The trade was conducted in an atmosphere of efficiency, with very little argumentation. The hosts had concealed their choicest items and vigorously denied having some goods, and the guests had done likewise—sinking their prize bows in a river before arriving at feast, for example, and bringing an inferior one along in case one of the hosts asked for it during the trading. As this was the first time in some years that the two groups feasted together, there was nothing for either one to repay. Instead, the visitors asked for items *no mraiha*—to be repaid later—and the guests did the same.

Fig. 4–2. Guests drinking boiled ripe plantain soup at a feast; the trough is made from the bark of a large tree, arapuri.

By 8:00 A.M. the going-home food had been presented to the visitors, and the trade had been conducted. Had the visitors been polite, they would have left for home at that time. Instead, they decided to stay and witness the second, smaller, feast that Kąobawä was going to conduct for the Karohi-teri, who had not arrived in time for the major event. This capped the series of insults the visitors had heaped upon Kąobawä's group. The visitors were warned that if they should stay, they would be expected to fight in a chest-pounding duel.

It was obvious now that the visitors were looking for trouble, and Kąobawä's group was obliged to react or be subject to even further intimidation. Hence, the challenge to pound chests. At this point the visitors broke camp and departed, much to the relief and joy of Kąobawä's group. In fact, they were pleased that they had been successful in intimidating their guests into leaving, and the men gloated over this accomplishment the rest of the day. They were convinced that their threats were credible enough to force their potential adversaries to withdraw, presumably because the Mahekodo-teri felt they were inferior in strength.

Kąobawä and his group held another feast for the Karohi-teri that same day, but without the assistance of the Lower Bisaasi-teri who left shortly after the previous feast terminated.

The Chest-pounding Duel

The feast for Karohi-teri was essentially the same as the one for the Mahekodo-teri and Boreta-teri. When the dancing was over and darkness fell, the men began to chant again. The first pair of chanters had not completed their rhythmic presentation when the jungle around the village erupted with hoots and screams, causing all of the people in the village to jump from their hammocks and arm themselves. When the men had found their arrows and were prepared, they began yelling back at the unseen guests, rattling the shafts of their arrows together or against their bows and/or pounding the heads of axes against pieces of firewood or on the ground to make noise. The Boreta-teri and Mahekodo-teri had returned to accept the chest-pounding challenge and entered the village, each man brandishing his axe, club, or bow and arrows. They circled the village once, feinting attack on particular men among the hosts, then grouped at the center of the village clearing. The hosts surrounded them excitedly, dancing with their weapons poised to strike, then entering into the mass of bodies. Heated arguments about food theft and gluttony developed, and the hosts and guests threateningly waved their weapons in each other's faces. Within minutes the large group had bifurcated and the chest-pounding began. The Karohi-teri aided Kąobawä and his followers, whose joint numbers were even further swelled when the Lower Bisaasi-teri rushed to the village after hearing the commotion. There were about sixty adult men on each side in the fight, divided into two arenas, each comprised of hosts and guests. Two men, one from each side, would step into the center of the milling, belligerent crowd of weapon-wielding partisans, urged on by their comrades. One would step up, spread his legs apart, bare his chest, and hold his arms behind his back, daring the other to hit him. The opponent would size him up, adjust the man's chest or arms so as to give himself the greatest advantage when he struck, and then step back to deliver his close-fisted blow. The striker would painstakingly adjust

Fig. 4-3. Chest-pounding duel about to be escalated.

his own distance from his victim by measuring his arm length to the man's chest, taking several dry runs before delivering his blow. He would then wind up like a baseball pitcher, but keeping both feet on the ground, and deliver a tremendous wallop with his fist to the man's left pectoral muscle, putting all of his weight into the blow. The victim's knees would often buckle and he would stagger around a few moments, shaking his head to clear the stars, but remain silent. The blow invariably raised a "frog" on the recipient's pectoral muscle where the striker's knuckles bit into his flesh. After each blow, the comrades of the deliverer would cheer and bounce up and down from the knees, waving and clacking their weapons over their heads. The victim's supporters, meanwhile, would urge their champion on frantically, insisting that he take another blow. If the delivery were made with sufficient force to knock the recipient to the ground, the man who delivered it would throw his arms above his head, roll his eyes back, and prance victoriously in a circle around his victim, growling and screaming, his feet almost a blur from his excited dance. The recipient would stand poised and take as many as four blows before demanding to hit his adversary. He would be permitted to strike his opponent as many times as the latter struck him, provided that the opponent could take it. If not, he would be forced to retire, much to the dismay of his comrades and the delirious joy of their opponents. No fighter could retire after delivering a blow. If he attempted to do so, his adversary would plunge into the crowd and roughly haul him back out, sometimes being aided by the man's own supporters. Only after having received his just dues could he retire. If he had delivered three blows, he had to receive three or else be proven a poor fighter. He could retire with less than three only if he were injured. Then, one of his comrades would replace him and demand to hit the victorious opponent. The injured man's two remaining blows would be canceled, and the man who delivered the victorious blow would have to receive more blows than he delivered. Thus, good fighters are at a disadvantage, since they receive disproportionately more punishment than they deliver. Their only reward is status: they earn the reputation of being fierce.

Some of the younger men in Kạobawä's group were reluctant to participate in the fighting because they were afraid of being injured. This put more strain on the others, who were forced to take extra turns in order to preserve the group's reputation. At one point Kạobawä's men, sore from the punishment they had taken and worried that they would ultimately lose the fight, wanted to escalate the contest to an axe duel (see Fig. 4-3). Kạobawä was vigorously opposed to this, as he knew it would lead to bloodshed. He therefore recruited the younger men into the fighting, as well as a few of the older ones who had done nothing but demand the others to step into the arena, thereby reducing the strain on those who wanted to escalate the level of violence. A few of the younger men retired after a single blow, privately admitting to me later that they pretended to be injured to avoid being forced to fight more. The fighting continued in this fashion for nearly three hours, tempers growing hotter and hotter. Kạobawä and the headman from the other group stood by with their weapons, attempting to keep the fighting innocuous, but not participating in it. Some of the fighters went through several turns of three or four blows each, their pectoral muscles swollen and red from the number of blows each had received. The fight had still not been decided, although Kạobawä's group seemed to be getting the worst of it. They then insisted on escalating the fighting to side slapping, partly because their chests were too sore to continue in that fashion, and partly because their opponents seemed to have an edge on them.

The side slapping duel is nearly identical in form to chest pounding, except that the blow is delivered with an open hand across the flanks of the opponent, between his rib-cage and pelvis bone. It is a little more severe than chest pounding because casualties are more frequent and tempers grow hotter more rapidly when a group's champion falls to the ground, gasping for wind, and faints. The side slapping only lasted fifteen minutes or so; one of the more influential men in Kạobawä's group was knocked unconscious, enraging the others. The fighting continued for just a few minutes after this, but during

Fig. 4–4. Many feasts end in prearranged chest-pounding duels; this permits the allies to display the fact that they are friendly but capable of defending their sovereignty. These two men were pounding each other's chests a few minutes before this photo was taken. Here, they embrace each other intimately, vowing eternal friendship, and ask each other for specific trade goods.

these few minutes the men were rapidly changing the points of their arrows to war tips: curare and lanceolate bamboo. The women and children began to cry, knowing that the situation was getting serious, and they grouped into the farthest corners of their houses near the exits. One by one the men withdrew, returned to their houses, and drew their bows. The visitors pulled back and formed a protective circle around their own women and children, also fitting arrows into their bows and drawing them. The village grew almost silent. The leaders of the respective groups stepped into the no man's land separating the two groups of armed men and began arguing violently, waving axes and clubs at each other. Suddenly, the spokesmen from the visiting group surged toward Kạobawä and his supporters, swinging their axes and clubs wildly at them, forcing them back to the line of men whose bowstrings were drawn taut. Kạobawä and his followers regained their footing and repelled their adversaries at this point, while the women and children from both groups began fleeing from the village, screaming and wailing. It looked as if they were about to release their arrows point-blank at Kąobawä's attackers, but when he and his aides turned them back, the crisis was over. The leaders of the visiting group rejoined the other men, some of whom had picked up glowing brands of firewood, and they backed out of the village, weapons still drawn, their way illuminated by those who were waving the brands.[7]

Kąobawä's group took no further action in this affair and was not invited to feast at Mahekodo-teri. Later in the year, their relationships worsened because of a club fight in yet another village, and for a while both groups threatened to shoot each other on sight. A temporary rapprochement developed after the club fight, when a group of raiders from Kąobawä's group met a group of hunters from Mahekodo-teri while en route to attack the village of one of their enemies. The men from both villages traded with each other and departed on friendly terms, the raiders abandoning their raid and returning to their village lest they be later ambushed on the way home by the Mahekodo-teri. They are presently on trading terms with each other, but their relationship is still somewhat strained and potentially hostile.

In general, feasts are exciting for both the hosts and the guests and contribute to their mutual solidarity. Under normal circumstances, allies that customarily feast with each other do not fight. Nevertheless, even the best allies occasionally agree beforehand to terminate their feast with a chest-pounding duel, thereby demonstrating to each other that they are friends, but capable of maintaining their sovereignty and willing to fight if necessary (Fig. 4–4). Kąobawä's group had a chest-pounding duel with one of its staunchest allies in 1966, as each had heard that the other was spreading rumors that it was cowardly. Of the six feasts I witnessed during the nineteen months I spent with the Yąnomamö, two of them ended in fighting.

Any Yąnomamö feast can potentially end in violence because of the nature of the attitudes the participants hold regarding canons of behavior and obligations to display ferocity.

Still, the feast and its attendant trade serve to reduce the possibility of neighbors fighting with each other at a more serious level of violence, and they contribute to intervillage solidarity and mutual interdependence.

---

[7]At this time, I was crouched in the house behind the line of bowmen, trembling in my boots.

5

Yąnomamö Warfare

Levels of Violence

THE FEAST AND ALLIANCE can and often do fail to establish stable, amicable relationships between sovereign villages. When this happens, the groups may coexist for a period of time without any overt expressions of hostility. This, however, is an unstable situation, and no two villages that are within comfortable walking distance from each other can maintain such a relationship indefinitely: They must become allies, or hostility is likely to develop between them. Indifference leads to ignorance or suspicion, and this soon gives way to accusations of sorcery. Once the relationship is of this sort, a death in one of the villages will be attributed to the malevolent *hekura* sent by shamans in the other village, and raids will eventually take place between them.

Yąnomamö warfare proper is the raid. That is, not all of their feuding and squabbles can be considered as war, although the values associated with war—bellicosity, ferocity, and violence—undoubtedly increase the amount of all kinds of fighting.

War is only one form of violence in a graded series of aggressive activities (Chagnon 1967). Indeed, some of the other forms of fighting, such as the formal chest-pounding duel, may even be considered as the antithesis of war, for it provides an alternative to killing. Duels are formal and are regulated by stringent rules about proper ways to deliver and receive blows. Much of Yąnomamö fighting is kept innocuous by these rules so that the concerned parties do not have to resort to drastic means to resolve their grievances. The three most innocuous forms of violence, chest pounding, side slapping, and club fights, permit the contestants to express their hostilities in such a way that they can continue to remain on relatively peaceful terms with each other after the contest is settled. Thus, Yąnomamö culture calls forth aggressive behavior, but at the same time provides a regulated system in which the expressions of violence can be controlled.

The most innocuous form of fighting is the chest-pounding duel described in the last chapter. These duels usually take place between the members of different villages and are precipitated by such minor affronts as malicious gossip, accusations of cowardice, stinginess with food, or niggardliness in trading.

If such a duel is escalated, it usually develops into a side-slapping contest. Occasionally, the combatants will sue for the use of machetes and axes, but this is rare. If machetes are used, the object of the contest still remains the same: Injure your opponent seriously enough so that he will withdraw from the contest, but try not to draw blood. Hence, opponents strike each other with only the flat of the blade when they resort to machetes.

In some areas the Yąnomamö modify the chest-pounding duel in another way: The opponents hold rocks in their clenched fists and strike their adversaries on the chest with an even more stunning blow. They try not to let the stone itself touch the flesh of the man they are fighting. Even without the use of stones, however, they are able to deliver their blows with such force that some of the participants cough up blood for days after having been in a duel.

Club fights represent the next level of violence. These can take place both within and between villages. Most of the club fights result from arguments over women, but a few of them develop out of disputes associated with food theft. Dikawä, a young man about twenty years old, came home one day and discovered a bunch of eating bananas his father, about fifty-five years old, had hung up in his house, above his hearth, to ripen in the smoke. Dikawä, however, ate a number of them without his father's permission. When his father discovered the theft, he ripped a pole out of his house and began clubbing Dikawä. Dikawä armed himself with a similar club and attacked his father, precipitating a general melee that soon involved most of the men in the village, each taking the side of the father or son, as they saw fit. In brawls such as these, many individuals join in the fighting just to keep the sides even; if a group is badly outnumbered, they will be joined by friends whose sense of fairness stimulates them to take sides, no matter what the issue is. The net result of the above fight was a number of lacerated skulls, bashed fingers, and sore shoulders. The contestants try to hit each other on the top of the head, but when the fight gets out of hand, the participants swing wildly and rarely hit their opponents on the skull. More frequently, the blow lands on the shoulder or arm.

The clubs used in these fights are, ideally, 8 to 10 feet long. They are very wiry, quite heavy, and deliver a tremendous wallop. In general shape and dimensions, they resemble pool cues, but are nearly twice as long. The club is held at the thin end, which is frequently sharpened to a long point in case the fighting escalates to spear thrusting, in which case the club is inverted and used as a pike.

Most duels start between two men, usually after one of them has been caught *en flagrante* trysting with the other's wife. The enraged husband challenges his opponent to strike him on the head with a club. He holds his own club vertically, leans against it and exposes his head for his opponent to strike. After he has sustained a blow on the head, he can then deliver one on the culprit's skull. But as soon as blood starts to flow, almost everybody rips a pole out of the house frame and joins in the fighting, supporting one or the other of the contestants.

Needless to say, the tops of most men's heads are covered with long, ugly scars of which their bearers are immensely proud. Some of them, in fact, keep their head cleanly shaved on top to display these scars, rubbing red pigment on their bare scalps to define them more precisely. Viewed from the top, the skull of an accomplished man of forty years looks like a road map, for it is criss-crossed by as many as twenty large scars (see

Fig. 5–1). Others keep their heads shaved for decorative reasons only, irrespective of the number of scars they bear. Some do not shave their heads at all.

Club fighting is frequent in large villages, primarily because there are more opportunities for men to establish clandestine sexual liaisons without getting caught at it. Most affairs are, however, discovered. The larger the village, the more frequent the club fighting; and as fighting increases, so too does the probability that the village will fission and result in two separate groups. Most village fissioning I investigated resulted from a specific club fight over a woman, a fight that was merely one such incident in a whole series of similar squabbles.

The village of Patanowä-teri split during the last month of my first field trip. One of the young men took the wife of another because she was allegedly being mistreated by him. This resulted in a brutal club fight that involved almost every man in the village. The fight escalated to jabbing with the sharpened ends of the clubs when the husband of the woman in question was speared by his rival and wounded. The headman of the village, a brother of Kaobawä, had been attempting to keep the fighting restricted to clubs. When the husband's rival speared his opponent, the headman went into a rage and speared him in turn, running his own sharpened club completely through the young man's body. He died when they tried to remove the weapon. The wife was then given back to her legitimate husband, who punished her by cutting both her ears off with his machete.

The kinsmen of the dead man were then ordered to leave the village before there was further bloodshed. The aggrieved faction joined the Monou-teri and the Bisaasi-teri because these two groups were at war with their natal village, and they knew that they would have an opportunity to raid their own village to get revenge. The Monou-teri and the two Bisaasi-teri groups accepted these new arrivals; they were kinsmen and would actively prosecute the war against the Patanowä-teri. The hosts, of course, took several women from the refugees, the price a vulnerable group must pay for protection.

Spears are not commonly used by the Yanomanö. A rare form of fighting, however, does involve the use of these weapons. It is a formal contest in the sense that the fight is prearranged and the participants agree beforehand to refrain from using their bows and arrows. Fights such as these take place when the members of two villages are not angry enough with each other to shoot to kill, but are too furious to be able to satisfy their grudges with chest pounding or club fighting.

The spears themselves are about 6 feet long, lightweight, and frequently painted with red and black designs. They are merely peeled saplings sharpened to a long point at the heavy end. Each man makes several of them.

The single spear-throwing incident that took place during my fieldwork started over a woman. Her husband had been very cruel to her, so the woman's brother, the headman of one of the villages north of Kaobawä's area, took her away from him by force. This enraged his entire following, which was considerably smaller than that of the wife's brother. A club fight temporarily settled the dispute, but the smaller of the groups was thoroughly trounced by the followers of the wife's brother. They challenged their adversaries to a spear fight and notified them they were going to return with reinforcements.

The woman over which the dispute began then ran away from her brother and rejoined her husband. But the die was cast and the fight was now a matter of pride, the

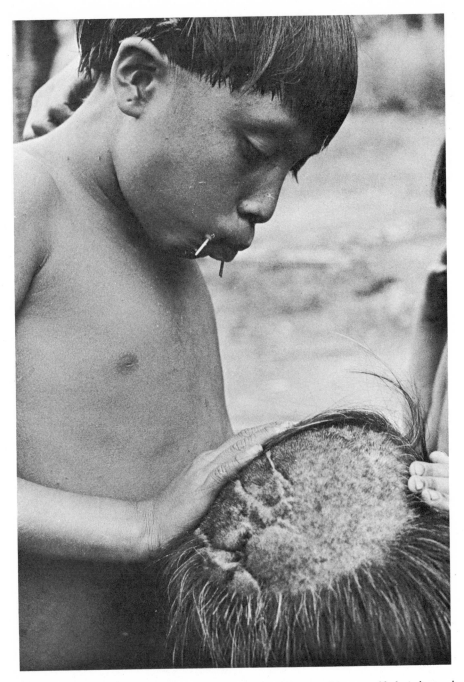

Fig. 5-1. Karöma, one of Kaobawä's daughters, picking lice out of her grandfather's battered head—his scars are from club fights. She wears decorative sticks inserted in the corners of her mouth as a beauty aid. These were inserted at about age five, together with one in the lower lip and another in the nasal septum.

original cause being quite irrelevant. Each of the principals in the dispute busily recruited aid from their allies. Kąobawä's group sent a delegation of young men to the village that took the woman away from the cruel husband.

When the cruel husband's incensed group and their allies arrived, about a week after the challenge, they entered their opponent's village and drove them out in a hail of spears. Many of them were wounded superficially, but one old man, not able to dodge missiles as well as he used to, suffered a bad wound and subsequently died. The victors stole all the hammocks, machetes, and cooking pots they could find and fled. The losers regrouped and gave chase, this time intending to escalate the fight to shooting. Some of them tied pieces of steel to their spears to make them more effective.

They caught up to the victorious group and another spear fight took place. This time tempers grew hot because one man in each of the fighting groups had managed to borrow a shotgun from the missionaries associated with the respective villages; these were repeatedly discharged over the heads of the fighters. The Yąnomamö had deceived the missionaries into loaning them two guns on the pretext of getting fresh game for the mission personnel. One of the shotgun-wielding Indians, standing at the front of his group, was struck by two sharpened spears. At this, he discharged his shotgun into the face of the headman of the other group, terminating the fight. The wounded man nearly died from the blast, but after many months of nursing by the missionaries he managed to recover. He still carries several balls of lead in his face.[1] Thereafter, the two groups were at war and raided each other with the intention of killing.

The Raid and Nomohoni

The raid is the next level in the scale of violence; this is warfare proper. The objective of the raid is to kill one or more of the enemy and flee without being discovered. If, however, the victims of the raid discover their assailants and manage to kill one of them, the campaign is not considered to be a success, no matter how many people the raiders may have killed before sustaining their single loss. Rerebawä told me of a raid he went on several years before I arrived. They managed to kill the headman of the village they raided, abduct his small son, and kill one more man as he fled to the village to recruit help. They were chased, but kept ahead of their pursuers for almost two days. Their pursuers caught up with them after dark on the second day and attacked them while they slept. They killed one man in his hammock, but in so doing, alarmed the others. A skirmish between the two groups developed, and the raiders managed to kill two more of their enemy in this struggle. Still, according to Rerebawä, the raid was not a good one because one of their own men was killed. The son of the slain headman was later shot by Torokoiwä, who presently lives in Monou-teri. The little boy was persecuted and tormented by the other children. Finally, Torokoiwä got sick of seeing this, so he shot the little boy as he was bathing in the stream.

---

[1]The members of two villages in contact with the missions occasionally borrow shotguns from the missionaries. The missionaries are very cautious about loaning the Yąnomamö firearms, knowing that these would be used in the wars. Shotguns are beginning to be rather common in Brazilian Yąnomamö villages, as the Indians there now have opportunities to make contacts with settlers and backwoodsmen and do not have to rely on missionaries for these weapons. This, however, is a recent development. Brazilian Yąnomamö, armed with these shotguns, have raided into Venezuela against villages that have not yet had any contact with outsiders.

Although few raids are initiated solely with the intention of capturing women, this is always a desired side benefit. A few wars, however, are started with the intention of abducting women. I visited a village in Brazil in 1967 that had a critical shortage of women. A group of missionaries had moved into this village a few years earlier and learned of the treachery by which the group managed to obtain a number of their women. One of them gave me this account. The headman of the group organized a raiding party to abduct women from a distant group. They went there and told these people that they had machetes and cooking pots from the foreigners, who prayed to a spirit that gave such items in answer to the prayers. They then volunteered to teach these people how to pray. When the men knelt down and bowed their heads, the raiders attacked them with their machetes and killed them. They captured their women and fled.

Treachery of this kind, the *nomohoni,* is the ultimate form of violence. Kạobawä's group suffered a massacre in 1950, as I have mentioned earlier, but the treachery in this case was in revenge for a murder. Still, their assailants attempted to abduct women after the objectives of their treachery were accomplished. Had it not been for their greed to capture women, the massacre would have been even more complete. Many escaped because the assailants turned their attention to the women.

Generally, however, the desire to abduct women does not lead to the initiation of hostilities between groups that have had no history of mutual raiding in the past. New wars usually develop when charges of sorcery are leveled against the members of a different group. Once raiding has begun between two villages, however, the raiders all hope to acquire women if the circumstances are such that they can flee without being discovered. If they catch a man and his wife at some distance from the village, they will more than likely take the woman after they kill her husband. If, however, the raiders are near the village, they may flee without dragging a captured woman along, as the body of their victim will be discovered quickly and pursuit will be immediate. Hence, they do not take a chance on hindering their flight by dragging a reluctant captive with them. A captured woman is raped by all the men in the raiding party and, later, by the men in the village who wish to do so but did not participate in the raid. She is then given to one of the men as a wife. If the captured woman is related to her captors, she is not raped.

Most wars are merely a prolongation of earlier hostilities, stimulated by revenge motives. The first causes of hostilities are usually sorcery, murders, or club fights over women in which someone is badly injured or killed. Occasionally, food theft involving related villages also precipitates raiding. This was the cause of the first raids between Kạobawä's group and the Patanowä-teri; they split from each other after a series of club fights over women. Each group made a new garden and returned periodically to the old one to collect peach-palm fruit, a crop that continues to produce long after the garden itself has gone to weeds. Someone stole the peach-palm fruit belonging to a man in the other group, resulting in another food theft for revenge, a club fight, and then raiding, but it should be pointed out that the raiding came about only after a long history of disputes between the groups; food theft was merely the catalyst that finally initiated the hostilities.

The Yạnomamö themselves regard fights over women as the primary causes of their wars. I was in one of the more remote villages in 1967, visiting with people I had met on my first field trip. The headman of the village, Säsäwä, coveted my British commando knife and kept begging me to give it to him. He wanted me to tell him all about the knife, its origin, history, and how often it had been exchanged in trades. When I told him that it was used by people of my "group" when they went on raids against their enemies, his interest shifted to our military exploits.

"Who did you raid?" he asked.

"Germany-teri."

"Did you go on the raid?"

"No, but my father did."

"How many of the enemy did he kill?"

"None."

"Did any of your kinsmen get killed by the enemy?"

"No."

"You probably raided because of woman theft, didn't you?"

"No."

At this answer he was visibly disturbed. He chatted for a moment with the others, seeming to doubt my answer.

"Was it because of witchcraft?" he then asked.

"No," I replied again.

"Ah! Someone stole cultivated food from the other!" he exclaimed, citing confidently the only other incident that is deemed serious enough to provoke man to wage war.

Perhaps the best way to illustrate Yąnomamö warfare, its causes, and the techniques of raid is to give a history of the recent military activities of Monou-teri, a small village that split away from Kąobawä's group in the mid-1950s.

A Specific War

The headman of the village, whom I shall call Damowä (since he was recently killed by raiders), was a particularly aggressive man. According to Rerebawä, Damowä was the only fierce man in the entire village, the true *waiteri* (fierce one) of the group.

Damowä had a habit of seducing the wives of other men, a factor that led to frequent feuding in the village and resulted in a number of club fights. Of the numerous affairs he had, two in particular illustrate the nature of possible consequences. His youngest brother was married to an abducted Shamatari girl. Damowä seduced her, thereby enraging his brother. The young man was afraid to vent his anger on the real culprit, his brother, so, instead, he shot his wife with an arrow. He intended only to wound her, but the arrow struck her in a vital spot and she died.

Manasinawä, a man of some fifty-five years at the present time, joined Damowä's group with his wife and young daughter. He fled from his own village in order to take refuge in a group that was raiding his own village, as he wanted to get revenge against them for a wrong they had committed. Damowä, who already had several wives, decided to take Manasinawä's wife from him and add her to his own family. This resulted in the final club fight that led to the separation of Kąobawä's group from the Monou-teri. Manasinawä's wife took the daughter and fled to yet another village. Kąobawä then organized a raid to recover the woman and child when their protectors refused to give them back. The two were taken by force from this group by Kąobawä's raiders. Nobody was killed in the incident. Manasinawä, his wife, and his daughter remained with Kạobawä's group, and he ultimately gave the daughter to Kạobawä for a second wife. Kạobawä still has her.

At this time, the groups, of Damowä and Kạobawä, respectively, were still at war with the Patanowä-teri, from whom they separated some fifteen years earlier. Damowä's group, after separating from Kạobawä's, attempted to make peace with the Patanowä-teri, as they were now vulnerable and could ill afford to remain on hostile terms with them. Damowä's group also made an alliance with the two Shamatari villages, which had given them cooperation when they staged the revenge treacherous feast discussed in the last chapter. For about five years relationships between Damowä's group and the Patanowä-teri were relatively amicable, but as the former's alliances with the Shamatari grew in strength, their relationship to the Patanowä-teri grew cool once again.

The Patanowä-teri then became embroiled in new wars with several villages on the Orinoco River and turned to Kạobawä's group for aid, hoping to patch up their old grievances and remain at peace. The first day I began my fieldwork marked the initiation of complete peace between Kạobawä's group and the Patanowä-teri: They were having a feast together in Bisaasi-teri. Damowä's group, the Monou-teri, were not participating in the feast, but a large number of men came anyway. They discovered a group of seven Patanowä-teri females outside the main village and could not resist the temptation: They forcefully took them back to Monou-teri. Later that day the Patanowä-teri men discovered that the women were missing, so they searched the neighborhood and found the tracks of the Monou-teri men at the site of the abduction, where signs of struggling abounded. The next morning they went to Monou-teri armed with clubs: They were bound to get their women back, but did not care to start another shooting war with the Monou-teri. They took five of the women away from the Monou-teri in a heated struggle, but had to pull back without the remaining two, unless they were willing to shoot to kill: The Monou-teri were determined to keep the other women at all costs.

The significance of this incident is this: The headman of Monou-teri realized that the Patanowä-teri would not risk getting into a shooting war with them since they already had more enemies than they could comfortably handle. Hence, this provided an excellent opportunity for the Monou-teri to abduct women with relatively little chance of getting shot in retaliation.

Damowä, the headman of Monou-teri, was angry because the Patanowä-teri had recovered so many of their women. He then threatened to ambush the Patanowä-teri when they left for home after the feast at Bisaasi-teri was over. The Patanowä-teri, in view of this, cut their stay short and left for home before the feast was over, hoping to avoid trouble with the Monou-teri.

Damowä was not satisfied, however, that he forced the Patanowä-teri to capitulate, leave for home, and not attempt to recover the two remaining women. He decided to raid them. In January of 1966 he and a party of men from Monou-teri raided the Patanowä-teri at the latter's village. They caught Bosibrei climbing a *rasha* tree, a prickly, cultivated palm that must be climbed slowly and with the aid of a pair of moveable stick frames in order to avoid getting pierced by the needle-sharp thorns that protrude from the tree's trunk (see Fig. 2–6). Bosibrei was almost to the top of the tree when the raiders caught him—he made an excellent target silhouetted against the sky. They shot and killed him with one volley of arrows as he reached for the fruits of the palm. One of

Damowä's brothers—who also participated in this raid—was married to one of the victim's daughters.

The Monou-teri had anticipated their raid by clearing a new garden site across the Mavaca River, where they hoped to take refuge after the inevitable revenge raids from Patanowä-teri began. They had hoped to complete their garden before the raids became intense, as the Mavaca River would have provided a natural obstacle to raiders. The Patanowä-teri, however, were infuriated by this killing and raided the Monou-teri immediately. Two of the raiders were Damowä's "brothers."

The raiders caught Damowä outside the new garden searching for honey. This was in the first week of February. He had two of his wives with him and one child. He was looking up a tree when the raiders shot a volley of arrows into his body, at least five of which struck him in the abdomen. He managed to nock one of his own arrows and shoot at the raiders, although he was probably mortally wounded at the time. Then Bishewä, one of the raiders, shot a final arrow at Damowä, piercing his neck below his ear. He fell to the ground and died after being struck by this arrow.

The raiders did not attempt to abduct the women, as they were close to the Monou-teri campsite and they had to cross the Mavaca River to escape. The women ran back to the village to tell the others what happened. Instead of giving chase, as they ought to have done—according to Kąobawä and the others in Bisaasi-teri—the Monou-teri themselves fled into the jungle and hid until darkness, afraid that the raiders might return.

The man who fired the fatal arrow into Damowä's neck was a son of the man the Monou-teri shot in their raid. Two of the men who shot Damowä were his classificatory brothers (members of the same lineage), three were brothers-in-law (including the man who shot the fatal arrow), and one was a man who had been adopted into the Patanowä-teri village as a child, after he and his mother were abducted from a distant Shamatari village.

The Monou-teri burned the corpse of Damowä the next day. They held a mortuary ceremony that week and invited their allies, members of the two Shamatari villages and the two groups of Bisaasi-teri, to participate. Gourds of the dead man's ashes were given to specific men in several of the allied villages, an act calculated to reaffirm solidarity and friendship. Damowä's widows were given to his two eldest surviving brothers.

Kąobawä, a classificatory brother to Damowä, assumed the responsibility of organizing a revenge raid. Damowä's own brothers failed to step forward to assume this responsibility, and for a while there was no leadership whatsoever in Monou-teri. Finally, Orusiwä, the oldest and most competent member of the *Hor* lineage, emerged as the *de facto* village leader, a position he acquired largely by default. He was related to the slain headman as brother-in-law, and their respective descent groups dominated village politics.[2] Hence, leadership in Monou-teri shifted from the *Sha* lineage to the *Hor* lineage.

Kąobawä delayed the revenge raid until April, giving the Monou-teri time to expand their new garden. This date also coincided with the beginning of the rains, thus reducing the possibility of a retaliation until the next dry season and providing the Monou-teri even more time to expand their new garden and abandon the old one.

The Monou-teri were afraid to return to their producing garden, so they divided their time between their newly cleared site, where they worked at cutting timber and

---

[2]See Table 3–1 and Fig. 3–5 of Chapter 3 for the lineage composition of Monou-teri.

burning it, and Kҙobawä's village, where they took occasional rests to regain their energy. They returned to their old site only to collect plantains, which they carried to the new site. Kҙobawä's group then built a new *shabono* and fortified it, anticipating the war they knew would be inevitable. Up to this point, Kҙobawä's group, Upper Bisaasi-teri, maintained two small *shabonos* a few yards apart from each other, but they coalesced into a single, larger group and moved into the new *shabono* when it was completed. The visiting Monou-teri also helped them work on the new structure.

Meanwhile, the Patanowä-teri, knowing that they would be raided by the Monou-teri and their allies, also began clearing a new garden. They selected a site abandoned by Kҙobawä's group many years ago, knowing that the peach-palm trees were still producing there. By this time the Patanowä-teri were in rather desperate straits. Their old enemies, the several groups on the Orinoco River, began raiding them with even greater frequency, as they had learned that the Monou-teri and Bisaasi-teri were again at war with the Patanowä-teri. A few additional villages began raiding the Patanowä-teri to settle old grudges, realizing that the Patanowä-teri had so many enemies that they could not possibly retaliate against all of them.

The Patanowä-teri then began moving from one location to another, hoping to avoid and confuse their enemies. They spent the dry season in turns at their main producing garden, with the Ashadowä-teri, their only ally, and at their new garden. Each group that raided them passed the word to other villages concerning the location of the Patanowä-teri. If they were not at one place, then they had to be at one of the other two. The raids were frequent and took a heavy toll. At least eight people were killed by raiders, and a number of others were wounded. Some of the dead were women and children, a consequence of the fact that the Patanowä-teri themselves sent a heavy volley of arrows into the village of one of their enemies and killed two women. To revenge this, the enemy began deliberately shooting Patanowä-teri women. Females are normally not the target of raiders' arrows. The Patanowä-teri were raided at least twenty-five times while I conducted my fieldwork. They themselves retaliated as frequently as possible, but could not return tit for tat. They managed to drive their main enemies, the Hasaböwä-teri, away from their garden, forcing them to flee across the Orinoco. They concentrated on raiding this group until they had killed most of the *waiteri* (fierce ones). They were so successful at doing this that the Hasaböwä-teri ultimately withdrew from the war. Several of my informants claimed that they did so because their fierce ones were all dead, and nobody was interested in prosecuting the war any further.

When the Hasaböwä-teri withdrew from the raiding, the Patanowä-teri then concentrated on raiding the Monou-teri. Every time the Monou-teri returned to their main site they found the tracks of numerous men who had visited the village, tracks that always came from the direction of Patanowä-teri. Consequently, the Monou-teri moved into Kҙobawä's group for protection, fearing to return to their old site until the jungle was completely inundated by the rains.

Kҙobawä's group resented this somewhat and made no bones about reminding the Monou-teri that they were eating large quantities of food from the gardens. When complaining became intense, the Monou-teri moved into the village of the Lower Bisaasi-teri and lived off their produce until the latter also began to complain. Then they traveled to the Mǫmariböwei-teri and lived with them for a while, returning to Kҙobawä's village when these allies wearied of the visitors. When the hosts, the Lower

Bisaasi-teri, for example, wanted to get rid of the Monou-teri, they would hold a feast in their honor. When the going-home food was presented to them, they had no alternative but to leave. It would have been insulting to remain after the food was presented. In between their moves they returned to their own producing site to collect plantains and carry them to their new garden. They subsisted there off the food they carried with them.

The Monou-teri soon resented being treated like pariahs by their allies and began to regain their courage. Much of this treatment was due to the fact that they failed to chase the raiders when Damowä was slain, displaying cowardice instead of ferocity. Many of the men in the Bisaasi-teri groups resented the Monou-teri for this and were not timid about displaying their disgust. The Monou-teri were a burden, as they rarely helped at expanding Bisaasi-teri's gardens and ate a good deal of the time.

The raid Kąobawä organized to revenge Damowä's death took place late in April. The Shamatari allies—Mǫmaribǫwei-teri and Reyabǫwei-teri—were invited to participate, but they failed to send a contingency. As allies never really trust each other, the raid was delayed because some of the Bisaasi-teri suspected that their allies were waiting for the raiders to leave so that they could descend on the poorly protected women and make off with captives. Finally, a few of them did arrive and the *wayu itou* (warrior line-up) got under way. Still, the Bisaasi-teri feared treachery on the part of their Shamatari friends, so the men of Lower Bisaasi-teri decided to stay home and protect the women left behind by the Monou-teri and Upper Bisaasi-teri raiders. A small feast was held to entertain the visiting Shamatari allies.

On the afternoon of the feast a grass dummy was set up in the village, and the men who were to participate in the raid conducted a mock attack on the dummy, which was supposed to represent the body of a Patanowä-teri man. They painted themselves black, crept slowly around the village with bows and arrows ready, searching for the tracks of the enemy. They converged at one point, spread out, crept toward the dummy, and, at Kąobawä's signal, let fly with a volley of arrows. The Yąnomamö are good archers. None of the arrows missed its mark, and the dummy, looking like a pincushion, toppled ominously to the ground, a dozen or more bamboo-tipped arrows protruding from it. Then the raiders screamed and ran out of the village, simulating their retreat from the enemy. They drifted back into the village, one at a time or in small groups, and retired to their hammocks to wait for darkness.

The village became unusually quiet shortly after dark. Suddenly, the stillness was pierced by an animal-like noise, half-scream and half-growl, as the first raider marched slowly out to the center of the village, clacking his arrows against his bow, growling his individualized fierce noise, usually a mimic of a carnivore: a wasp, or a buzzard. At this signal—not knowing fully what to expect and a little nervous—I crept from my own hammock and went to the center of the village with my tape recorder. The other raiders joined the first man, coming one at a time after short intervals, each clacking his arrows and growling some hideous noise. Kąobawä stood by and made sure the line was straight and faced the direction of the enemy; he would push or pull the individual warriors until they formed a perfectly straight line, joining them after the last one took his place.

The procession to the line-up took about twenty minutes, as about 50 or so men participated (see Fig. 5–2). When the last one was in line, the murmurs among the

Fig. 5–2. Kąobawä's men and their allies lining up (wayu itou) *to raid the Patanowä-teri.*

children and women died down and all was quiet in the village once again. I squatted there, unable to see what was going on, growing more nervous by the moment, half suspecting that the warriors were sneaking up on me to murder me for tape recording a sacred rite. Then the silence was broken when a single man began singing in a deep baritone voice: "I am meat hungry! I am meat hungry! Like the carrion-eating buzzard I hunger for flesh!" When he completed the last line, the rest of the raiders repeated his song, ending in an ear-piercing, high-pitched scream that raised goose bumps all over my arms and scalp. A second chorus, led by the same man, followed the scream. This one referred to meat hunger of the kind characteristic of a particular species of carnivorous wasp. They screamed again, becoming distinctly more enraged. On the third chorus, they referred again to the buzzard's meat hunger, and a few men simultaneously interjected such descriptions of their ferocity as: "I'm so fierce that when I shoot the enemy my arrow will strike with such force that blood will splash all over the material possessions in his household!"

Then the line of warriors broke, and the men gathered into a tight formation, weapons held above their heads. They shouted three times, beginning modestly and increasing their volume until they reached a climax at the end of the third shout: "Whaaaa! Whaaaa! WHAAAA!" They listened as the jungle echoed back their last shout, identified by them as the spirit of the enemy. They noted the direction from which the echo came. On hearing it, they pranced about frantically, hissed and groaned, waving their weapons, until Kąobawä calmed them down, and the shouting was repeated two more times. At the end of the third shout of the third repetition, the formation broke, and the men ran back to the respective houses, each making a noise—"Bubububububu-bubu"—as he ran. When they reached their hammocks, they all simulated vomiting, passing out of their mouths the rotten flesh of the enemy they had symbolically devoured in the line-up.

They retired for the night. Many of them wept and moaned, mourning the loss of their friend and kinsman, Damowä. At dawn the women went to the gardens and gathered large quantities of plantains. These were carried to the raiders, wrapped with their vine hammocks, and deposited outside the village for the men to collect as they marched in single file to war.

The men painted themselves black again (Fig. 5-3). Some even put on bright red loincloths which I had traded to them, as the warrior line-up is a spectacle in which the younger men can show off to the girls. The loincloths were left behind when the men departed. They tinkered with their bows and checked to see if the bowstrings were weak at any spot, sharpened their best arrow points, and waited nervously for Kąobawä to signal for the line-up to begin again. The *wayu itou* was repeated, each man marching to the center of the village and taking his place in line. This time, however, they did not sing the war song. They merely shouted, as they had done the previous night, waited for the echo to return, and marched dramatically out of the village. Their mothers and sisters wept or shouted last minute bits of advice as they left the village: "Don't get yourself shot up!" "You be careful now!"

The men picked up their supplies of food where the women had cached them and left for Patanowä-teri. Kąobawä had been complaining all year of severe pains in his lower back, abdomen, and urinal tract, and was in considerable pain when he walked. Still, he insisted on going on the raid, suspecting that the others would turn back if he did not lead it. The raiders had not been gone five hours when the first one came back, a boastful young man, complaining that he had a sore foot and could not keep up with the others. The next day a few more young men returned, complaining that they had malaria and pains in the stomach. They enjoyed participating in the pomp of the *wayu itou*, for this impressed the women, but were, at heart, cowards.

The raiders travel slowly their first day away from the village. They have heavy burdens of food and try to pace themselves so as to arrive in the enemy's territory just as their food runs out. They also attempt to reach a point in the enemy's neighborhood that will permit them to reach his village at dawn: far enough away so that enemy hunters will not discover their presence, but close enough to the village that they can reach it in an hour or so from their last camp.

The men use fire only when they camp at a considerable distance from the enemy's territory. As they approach their destination, they exercise greater caution. Their final evening is spent shivering in the darkness, since they dare not make a fire to warm themselves. Most of the raiders emphasized this, as sleeping without fire is considered to be both dangerous and uncomfortable. The danger lies in the possibility of jaguar attacks, but even more in the fear that spirits will molest the unprotected raiders. On the last evening the raiding party's fierce ones have difficulties with the younger men; most of them are afraid, cold, and worried about every sort of hazard, and all of them complain of sore feet and belly aches.

The raiders always develop a strategy for attacking the unwary enemy. They usually split into two or more groups and agree to meet later at a predetermined location

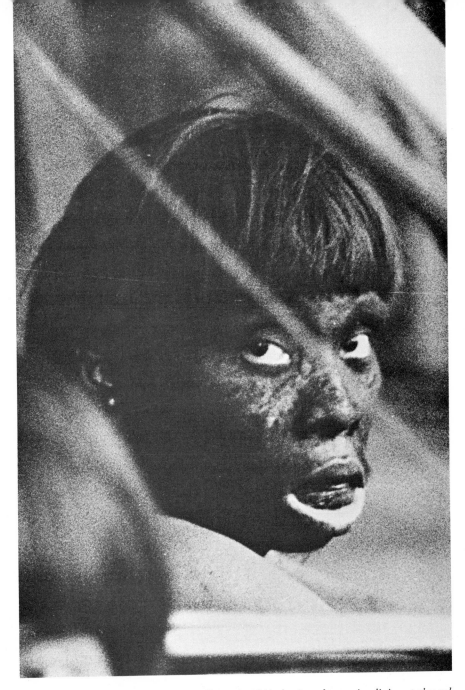

Fig. 5–3. One of Kạobawä's Shamatari allies, painted black, views the warriors lining up through his bowstring. He waits his turn to join them, a wad of tobacco protruding from his mouth.

at some point between their own village and the enemy's. These smaller groups must contain at least four men, six, if possible. This is so because the raiders retreat in a pattern. While the others flee, two men will lie in ambush, shooting any pursuers that might follow. They, in turn, flee, while their comrades lie in ambush to shoot at their pursuers.

If there are novices in the raiding party, the older men will conduct mock raids, showing them how they are to participate. A grass dummy or soft log is frequently employed in this, as was the case in the *wayu itou* held in the village the day before the raiders left. Particularly young men will be positioned in the marching party somewhere in the middle of the single file of raiders so they will not be the first ones to be exposed to danger should the raiders themselves be ambushed. These young men will also be permitted to retreat first. Damowä had a twelve-year-old son when he was killed. This boy, Matarawä, was recruited into the raiding party to give him an opportunity to avenge his father's death. The older men made sure he would be exposed to minimum danger, as this was his first raid.

The separated groups of raiders approach the village at dawn and conceal themselves near the commonly used paths to the source of drinking water. They wait for the enemy to come to them. A good many of the victims of raids are shot while fetching water.

Frequently, the enemy is wary and acts defensively at all times when there is an active war going on. Only large groups of people can leave the village, and these are well armed. Raiders will not attack a large group such as this. When the enemy is found to be this cautious, the raiders have no choice but to retreat or to shoot volleys of arrows blindly into the village, hoping to strike someone at a distance. They retreat after they release their arrows, depending on the gossip of other villages to learn if their arrows did find their marks. Rarely, one of the raiders will attempt to enter the village during the night and kill someone while he sleeps. Damowä's younger brother allegedly accomplished this on one raid, but few men are brave enough to try it. Most of the time the raiders manage to ambush a single individual, kill him, and retreat before they are discovered. This is considered to be the most desirable outcome of the raid.

The women were nervous, frightened, and irritable while the men were away, and they were constantly on the lookout for raiders from other villages. This is always a time to suspect raiders, since allies occasionally turn on their friends when the women are poorly guarded, abducting as many as possible while their husbands are away.

After several days the women were so frustrated and anxious that fights began to break out among them. One woman got angry because another one, her sister and co-wife, left her to tend a small baby. When the mother returned, the angry one picked up a piece of firewood and bashed her on the side of her head with it, knocking her unconscious and causing her ear to bleed profusely.

The raiders had been gone almost a week when Kąobawä and his youngest brother staggered into the village, nearly dead from exhaustion. Kąobawä's pains had gotten so bad that he decided to turn back just before they reached the Patanowä-teri village. He could barely walk by that time and would not have been able to elude pursuers should the enemy have given chase. Shararaiwä, his brother, decided to accompany him back lest he run into a group of Patanowä-teri hunters, or his condition grow even more severe. Shortly after they had dropped out of the raiding party, Shararaiwä stepped on a snake and was bitten. The rains had started, and the snakes were beginning to concentrate on the higher grounds, making walking a hazard. His leg began to swell immediately, and he could not walk. Hence, Kąobawä had to carry him out on his back, despite the fact that he could barely walk himself. Carrying him for nearly two days, he managed to reach the Orinoco River. Here, he intended to make a bark canoe and float the rest of the way back down, but they located a dugout canoe someone had concealed,[3] so they borrowed this and reached home about dark, three days after Shararaiwä had been bitten. He survived the snake bite, but Kạobawä was very exhausted from the trip.

That night an advance party of the raiders returned, chanted briefly with Kạobawä, explaining that they had reached Patanowä-teri, shot and killed one man, and fled. The Patanowä-teri pursued them, got ahead of them at one point, and ambushed them when they passed. They wounded Konoreiwä of Monou-teri, shooting a bamboo-tipped arrow completely through his chest just above his heart.

The next morning the main body of raiders returned to the village, carrying Konoreiwä with them in a litter. They had removed the arrow, but he was very weak and continuously coughed up mouthfuls of blood. They put him in a hammock and tended his fire for him. They asked me to treat his wound.

He lay in his hammock for a week, not eating or drinking all that time—the Yạnomamö have a taboo against taking water when wounded with a bamboo-type arrow, and Konoreiwä was slowly wasting away. Finally, I could stand it no longer and made a batch of lemonade. I called for them to gather around, ceremoniously crushed an aspirin into the lemonade, and explained that this was very powerful medicine. So powerful that it had to be diluted with a large amount of water. I then demanded that he take some, which he gladly did, the others not interfering. By then he was so weak that he could not sit up, so I spoon-fed the liquid to him. A knowing glance passed between us as he gulped down the first spoonful of sweet liquid. He ultimately recovered.

The two men who shot the fatal arrows into the Patanowä-teri were both brothers of the slain Damowä. They were killers and had to purify themselves by going through the *unokaimou* ceremony.

They were given spaces in Kạobawä's *shabono* for their hammocks. The area each man occupied was sealed off from the adjoining houses by palm leaves, and the men had their food brought to them for the week they were confined to this small area. They each used a pair of sticks to scratch their bodies and did not touch the food with their fingers when they ate, again using sticks to transfer the food from the container to their mouths.

At the end of their confinement, the vine hammocks they used while they were on the raid, along with the scratching sticks, were taken out of the village and tied to a particular kind of tree. The hammocks were placed about 6 feet above the ground and separated from each other by about 1 foot. After this was done, the men resumed their normal activities.

Kạobawä felt that he had satisfied his obligation to avenge Damowä's death. The Monou-teri, however, wanted to prosecute the war further and continue raiding. It was at this point that Paruriwä of Kạobawä's group began to emerge as one of the more prominent men in the village. He stepped forward and actively prosecuted the war against the Patanowä-teri, encouraged by the esteem in which the Monou-teri held him. Still, he was not enthusiastic enough for the Monou-teri. On one raid he subsequently led, he elected to turn back and go home when the Patanowä-teri were not found at their main garden. The Monou-teri insisted that the party should continue on until they

---

[3] The canoe was hidden in the brush by Kạobawä's son-in-law, who lives in a village up the Orinoco. He had come to Bisaasi-teri that day to visit and hid his canoe so that the Bisaasi-teri would not borrow it.

Fig. 5–4. Blowing drugs (ebene) *on the pulverized bones of Damowä, slain Monou-teri headman.*

located the enemy, but Paruriwä refused to go any further. When he turned back, so did the entire party.

The Monou-teri and Bisaasi-teri raided against the Patanowä-teri six times while I lived with them, and each time the preparations for the raid closely followed the description given above. The Monou-teri returned to their producing site only when the jungle was inundated; only at that time could they exist without the support of their allies. The remainder of the year they had to take refuge with members of allied villages or expose themselves to the risk of being attacked by superior forces by remaining in their own producing garden.

The Monou-teri also raided the Patanowä-teri without aid from their allies. One of the raids was conducted near the end of the rainy season, and I was staying in their village at the time the raid was held.

A special ceremony took place the day before the raid. The gourds containing the ashes of the slain Damowä were put on the ground in front of his brother's house.

Everyone in the village gathered around the ashes and wept aloud. The bamboo quiver of the dead man was brought to the gourds, smashed, the points taken out, and the quiver itself burned. While this was going on, the mourners were in a state of frenzy, pulling at their hair and striking themselves, screaming and wailing. One of his brothers took a snuff tube and blew some of the drug into the gourds containing the ashes (see Fig. 5-4). The tube was then cut in half, one of the dead man's arrow points being used to measure the point at which the snuff tube was cut. I was never able to determine whether the arrow points taken from the quiver were possessions of the dead man or were, in fact, the points removed from his body. There were ten of them, and my informants were too touchy about the matter to be questioned in detail: I received affirmative nods to both questions. In any event, the ten bamboo points were distributed to the raiders, who fondled them and examined them carefully. Each man brought one with him on the raid that followed this ceremony. The severed snuff tube and the gourds of ashes were wrapped in leaves and put back in the thatch of the brother's house.

That night I think I became emotionally close to the Yąnomamö for the first time. I remained in my hammock and gave up collecting genealogies. As darkness fell Damowä's brothers began weeping in their hammocks. I lay there and listened, not bothering to tape record it or photograph it or write notes. One of the others asked me why I was not making a nuisance of myself as usual, and I told him that my innermost being (*buhii*) was cold—that is, I was sad. This was whispered around the village, and as each person heard it, he looked over at me. The children who inevitably accumulate around my hammock were told by their elders to go home and not bother me anymore. I was *hushuo*, in a state of emotional disequilibrium, and had finally begun to act like a human being as far as they were concerned.

The next day the raiders lined up, shouted in the direction of the Patanowä-teri, heard the echo come back, and left the village to collect their provisions and hammocks. I allowed them to talk me into taking the entire raiding party up the Mavaca River in my canoe. There, they could find high ground and reach the Patanowä-teri without having to cross the numerous swamps that lay between the two villages. There were only ten men in the raiding party, the smallest the war party can get and still have maximum effectiveness. As we traveled up the river, the younger men began complaining. One had sore feet, and two or three others claimed to have malaria. They wanted to turn back because I had forgotten to bring my malaria pills with me as I had promised. Hukoshikuwä (Fig. 5-5), a brother of the slain headman, silenced their complaints with an angry lecture on cowardice. I let them all out at the mouth of a stream they intended to follow. They unloaded their seemingly enormous supply of plantains and politely waited for me to leave. I sat among them and chatted, thinking that they were doing essential tasks as they fiddled with arrows and retied their provisions. Finally, one of them hinted that I should be leaving because I had a long trip and might not get home before dark. It was then that I discovered they were dallying, trying to be polite to me. They all thanked me for taking them upstream in my canoe, the only time Yąnomamö ever expressed gratitude to me, and I got in my canoe to leave. Hukoshikuwä came down to untie my rope for me and shove me off the bank. He watched, silently, as my canoe got caught up in the current and drifted away. He looked frightened, reluctant, anxious, but determined. After I had gotten my motor started and was under way, I looked back to see him turn, pick up his plantains and weapons, and disappear into the jungle. Even

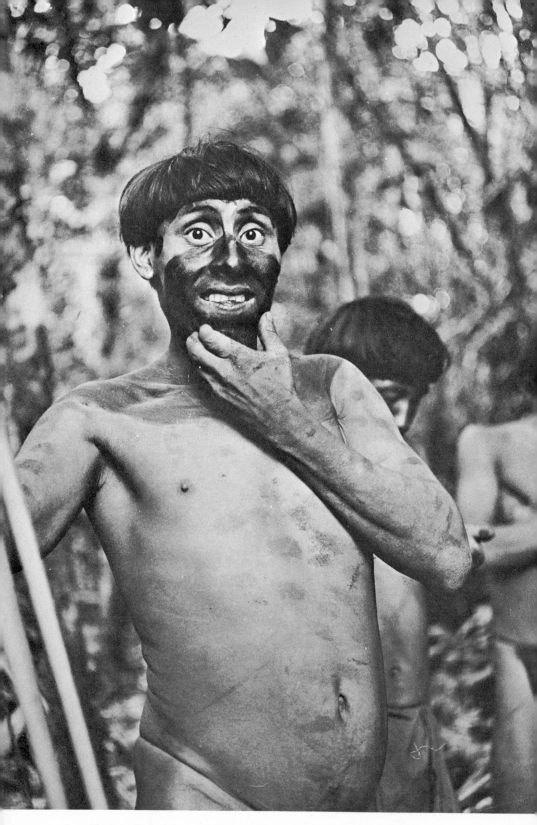

Fig. 5-5. Hukoshikuwä leading a raiding party against the Patanowä-teri.

he was not enthusiastic about going on the raid, despite the fact that he lectured the younger members of the raiding party about their overt reluctance and cowardice. He was older, however, and had to display the ferocity that adult men are supposed to show. In short, although Hukoshikuwä probably had very little desire as an individual to participate in the raiding, he was obliged to do so by the pressures of the entire system. He could ill afford to remain neutral, as his very own kinsmen–even Kạobawä–implied by word and action that it was disgusting for him not to avenge the death of his brother; and some of his kinsmen in other villages openly accused him of cowardice for not chasing the raiders when they shot Damowä. Again, his erstwhile allies, when they complained about having to feed him and his relatives, were blunt and discourteous. The Shamatari allies even managed to demand a number of women from Hukoshikuwä's group in payment for girls they had given them earlier, when the Monou-teri were superordinate in the alliance pecking order. In short, if Hukoshikuwä failed to put on a show of ferocity and vindictiveness, it would not be long before his friends in allied villages would be taking even greater liberties and demanding more women. Thus, the system worked against him and demanded that he be fierce. Since his own group was small, it had to protect its sovereignty even more rigorously, or be absorbed by a greedy ally whose protection would be tendered at the price of women.

Hukoshikuwä and his raiders did not locate the Patanowä-teri on this raid, although they searched for over a week. They knew it would be difficult to find them in the rainy season, largely because they would have to take many detours around impassable swamps. It was with this in mind that they brought their larger-than-usual supply of plantains.

The war was still being conducted, but on a lesser scale, when I returned to Monou-teri a year later. They had managed to kill two Patanowä-teri and abduct two women. The Patanowä-teri only killed one Monou-teri, the headman. Hence, the Monou-teri, at least for the time being, came out ahead. The Patanowä-teri will not cease raiding them until they kill at least one more Monou-teri, but then the Monou-teri will be obliged to avenge this death when it occurs.[4]

There will probably be a respite to the raiding because the Patanowä-teri group fissioned and subsequently lost a significant fraction of their numbers. The Monou-teri have completed their move to the new garden and now live there. If the raiding stops, they will be able to live alternatively between their two gardens at any season. Otherwise, they can only occupy their old site in the peak of the wet season. Having two gardens makes them more independent of their allies, and they can again be aggressive in their political dealings with them. Since they have exchanged women with one of their Shamatari allies and are now living only a half-day's journey from them, they most likely will bind their political fate to the fate of this ally. Their relationships to the two Bisaasi-teri groups, on the other hand, will probably grow cool. Already, the Monou-teri have taken sides with their Shamatari allies in club fights against the Upper Bisaasi-teri, and they still resent the fact that the Lower Bisaasi-teri forcefully took one of the abducted Patanowä-teri women away from them. Despite the fact that the Monou-teri share a common history and common blood with the two Bisaasi-teri groups, they are now entering into a political situation that frequently leads such related groups to mutual hostilities.

---

[4] The Bisaasi-teri were still trying to avenge Damowä's death in 1975 and were actively raiding the Patanowa-teri but had, by then, acquired shotguns and were using them in the raids.

6

The Beginning of Western Acculturation

Introduction

THOSE OF US who live in industrialized societies look on change and progress as being "good" and "desirable." Our entire system of values and goals is constituted in such a way that we strive to make changes, improve and tinker with rules and technology, and reward those who are skillful at it. "Progress" for its own sake is beneficial by definition. The Yąnomamö are now entering a new and potentially hazardous time in their history, for our kind of culture is confronting them and urging, in the name of "progress," that they give up their way of life and adopt some rural form of ours. The agents of progress among the Yąnomamö are mostly missionaries—Salesian Catholics and several independent groups of Protestant Evangelists—whose presence among the Yąnomamö is permitted by Venezuelan and Brazilian law. Incorporation of the Yąnomamö into the national culture has been left almost entirely in the hands of the missionaries, who have been and continue to remain free to use whatever means or techniques they have to accomplish this objective. While the explicit goal of all the missionaries is the conversion of the Yąnomamö to Christianity and the salvation of their souls, a few far-sighted individuals in both groups have independently realized that they likewise have an obligation to prepare the Yąnomamö in other ways for their inevitable absorption into Western culture—teaching them to speak the Spanish or Portuguese language, reading, writing and counting, introducing domesticated animals that can later serve as predictable sources of protein, market principles, the use of money, scales of economic values, and so on. Other missionaries are more narrowly dedicated to saving souls at any cost, and are insensitive to the point of being inhumane in the techniques they use to bring salvation to the Yąnomamö.

It is inevitable that the Yąnomamö, and all tribal peoples, will be absorbed by the national cultures in whose territories they coincidentally reside. The process of acculturation is nearly as old as culture itself: all dominant cultures impinge on and transform their less-dominant neighbors. There are, however, enlightened and humane ways of accomplishing this . . . and there are insensitive and inhumane ways. Knowing that acculturation is inevitable, I must conclude that it is essential that a rational and sympathetic policy of acculturation be developed for the Yąnomamö, for the process of change has already begun at a number of mission villages, and it is off to a poor start. Such a policy will require the cooperation of missionaries, government officials, and field-experienced, informed anthropologists. It is yet to be developed.

This raises a dilemma for me. Anthropologists who have worked in "traditional" or "tribal" cultures are often frustrated and saddened by the vectors of change that transform the peoples they have grown to admire during their studies, especially when the changes diminish the freedom and dignity of those peoples. Many anthropologists are, in fact, alarmed by any change and would prefer to see native cultures persist indefinitely while the rest of the maddening world mires itself deeper and deeper into the technological, ecological, and political morass that is one certain artifact of cultural evolution and "progress." It is an open question whether particular anthropologists are attracted to primitive cultures because such cultures seemingly represent a more rational, more comprehensible means for coping with the external world . . . that is to say, a more human way. It is jokingly said that psychiatrists become what they are to better understand their own personal problems, and I suspect that some anthropologists, by analogy, are attracted to their craft for equally personal reasons. A few of my colleagues have even good-naturedly suggested to me that my own intensive involvement with the Yąnomamö is not without reason, for they suspect that I might fit as well in Yąnomamö culture as I do in my own!

But any similarity between an anthropologist and the people with whom he or she has spent a significant portion of his or her life is probably due more to association and learning than to initial equivalencies of personality. Anthropology as a science differs radically from, let us say, chemistry or genetics. Our subject matter is made essentially of the same kind of stuff as the observer—the "subject matter" itself has hopes, fears, desires, and emotions. It is easy to identify with people and become intimate with them; a chemist or geneticist cannot have much empathy for carbon or the genes that determine eye color.

My long association with the Yąnomamö, my intimate friendships among them, and my awareness of the values in their culture account for my sense of frustration and alarm when I reflect on the changes that are taking place in the mission posts and the means by which some of the changes have been effected. Some of them are wrong, in my estimation, perhaps even cruel. Others are ineffective and harmless. Still others are amusing and downright funny.

Acculturation is a subject that has all but become a major subdiscipline within anthropology. Perhaps the most appropriate way to end this case study would be to cast the process into academic terms and adopt a strictly formal, pedagogical stance as I discuss what is now happening to the Yąnomamö. I should like, however, to communicate something about the human dimension of the process, to relate a few incidents and anecdotes that reveal more than a neutral description can expose. What the Yąnomamö must now endure has happened to countless other tribesmen. Perhaps if more citizens of the twentieth century and industrialized culture knew, from the tribesman's point of view, what acculturation means, we might have more compassion and sympathy for the traumas they must endure as they are required to make, usually unwillingly, their transformation. Hopefully such knowledge will be used to a good end, and rational policies of directed change will be forged.

In addition, by looking at the means and methods of the changes that are being made in Yᶏnomamöland through their eyes we can gain insights into the nature of our own culture. Very often the things that we ourselves take to be normal, progressive, and desirable look very different when viewed through a tribal lens. Sometimes they appear to be merely humorous. At other times they appear to be hideous.

————

Yᶏnomamö Glimpses of Us

Rerebawä looked frail and dwarfed in my trousers and shirt as we sat in the blistering sun on the savannah of Esmeralda waiting for the Venezuelan Air Force cargo plane to appear out of the cloudy north. The *piums*—tiny, biting black gnats—were out in astronomical numbers; their annoying bites left miniscule blood clots, that itched for a day and then turned black. The *piums* liked the larger rivers and savanna areas, and I speculated about the distribution of the Yᶏnomamö villages—inland, on tiny streams, away from this annoying *plaga*. I pitied those groups that had started moving out to the Orinoco River to make contact with foreigners—to obtain the highly desirable steel tools that they brought with them. Life without clothing for them was unbearable in the dry season, and they would come to the mission stations to work for days at hard labor to earn a tattered garment that some charity had sent into the missions gratis. The Yᶏnomamö always looked so pathetic in European hand-me-downs, especially after wearing them for several months and not washing them. They would be crusted with filth and rancid, and their skins would begin to have boils and sores all over them.

I was in a gloomy mood, reflecting on the changes that I noticed were taking place among the Yᶏnomamö. Each year I returned to them there were more missionaries, new mission posts, and now alarming numbers of tourists were beginning to arrive. I did not like what I was seeing and it was no longer possible to ignore the problems that acculturation would bring the Yᶏnomamö. My personal relationships with the Yᶏnomamö had deepened and grown more intimate every year. As I observed what some mission activities and the tourists were doing to the Yᶏnomamö, my attitude hardened.

Rerebawä had indicated to me several times in the past few years that he would like to see Caracas and how the Caraca-teri lived, especially the Caracateriyoma: "Perhaps I could abduct a few when nobody is looking and drag them back to Bisaasi-teri in the plane!" he would tease mischievously. "But they eat only cows and bread and sugar and would run away from you if you brought them only monkeys and *yei* fruits!" I teased back. "You have warts on your forehead!" he insulted me good-naturedly, and jabbed me in the ribs to make me laugh, for he knew I was ticklish. "You'd better be careful in Caraca-teri," I warned, "almost all the men run around with large guns like shotguns and they will ask you for your 'decorated leaves' they call 'papers' and if you don't have any, they will take you away . . . and me with you!" He puffed his chest out and said: "Huh! I'll just grab a large club and insult them and then we'll see who takes who away!" He adjusted the wad of chewing tobacco he always carried in his lip. "Will we bump into the upper layer when we fly to Caraca-teri?", he asked anxiously, I chuckled to myself. Rerebawä had spent many months with me during my annual returns to his people and he was quite cosmopolitan by Yᶏnomamö standards, but nevertheless a firm believer in the Yᶏnomamö notion of the cosmos—a series of rigid bowl-like layers, one over the other, separated by only a few hundred feet or yards. "No, the *Hedu kä misi* layer is too high for the plane to reach." I responded, choosing to confirm his beliefs about the cosmic layers rather than rouse his anxiety further by denying their existence. This would be his first plane ride and his first glimpse of the civilization that lay beyond Ya̧nomamöland, and I wanted him to enjoy his experience.

It was always difficult for me to impress the Ya̧nomamö with the size of the world beyond their villages and tropical forest, including Rerebawä. I recall being teased by my companions on one of my inland trips as we sat around the campfire before retiring to our hammocks for the evening. They were bantering me about how numerous the Ya̧nomamö were and how few foreigners there were by comparison. Rerebawä was among them, and just as vociferous. I stood up to underscore my argument, pointing dramatically to the north, northeast, east, reciting names of cities as they came indiscriminately to my mind: "Over there lie the New York-teri, the Boston-teri, the Washington-teri, the Miami-teri; and over there the London-teri, the Paris-teri, and Madrid-teri, and Berlin-teri. . ." and on, around the globe. They chuckled confidently, and one of them rose. "Over there lie the Shibariwä-teri, the Yabroba-teri, the Wabutawä-teri, the Yeisi-teri, the Auwei-teri and over there the Niyaiyoba-teri, the Maiyo-teri, the Boreta-teri, the Ihirubö-teri . . ." and on around the cardinal points of the compass. I protested, arguing that ". . . Caraca-teri is huge! There are many people there and you are just a few by comparison!" Their response would be, inevitably, "But have you seen the new Patanowä-teri *shabono* or Mishimishi-maböwei-teri *shabono?* They stretch in a great arc, like this . . ." and an arm would slowly describe the vast arc while the others listened intently, clicking their tongues to exaggerate the size. Caracas, to them, was just another large *shabono,* with a large, thatched roof, and I knew that the only way to convince them otherwise was to bring one of them there to see it with his own eyes.

Perhaps if Rerebawä saw the scope and magnitude of the culture that was moving inexorably to assimilate his own he would be more prepared to understand and deal with it when it eventually came. Would the same thing happen to Ya̧nomamö culture that happened to so many North American Indian societies? Would the Ya̧nomamö be reduced biologically and culturally to a mere shadow of the proud and free people I had grown to know and admire during 12 years of research among them? My personal dilemma was that I hoped that the Ya̧nomamö would be permitted to remain sovereign and unchanged, but my sense of history and understanding of culture contact told me that change was inevitable.

Storm clouds were piling up over Duida, the massive, abrupt cliff that rose 10,000 feet up from the small savanna at Esmeralda, and I hoped the plane would arrive soon, for in an hour the clouds would obscure the landing strip and it might be weeks or months before another flight would be scheduled to Esmeralda. A free lift out to Caracas with Rerebawä today would be very convenient, for I could spend five days with him working in comfort on myth translations and return with my bush-pilot, who was coming in with my medical colleagues. There would be space for us in the plane.

"Avion! Avion!" shouted the Makiritare Indians who idly waited for the plane to arrive, for it always brought cargo for them. Rerebawä was on his feet in an instant, his hand over his brow, peering intently into the cloud-blackened northern sky. *"Kihamö kä a! A ösöwä he barohowä!"* he jabbered excitedly, and I agreed that indeed it was visible and very high. He raced over to his possessions, a small cluster of tightly bound cloth bags made from the remains of a shirt I had given him last year. "Hold on! It will not get here for a while yet. It has to circle the landing area and chase the Makiritare cows off the savanna." He sat down, clutching his bags and grinning. I hadn't noticed his bags until now, and asked him what he had in them. "Just some 'things'," he responded nonchalantly. "What kind of 'things'?" I asked suspiciously. He untied the knot and opened the larger bag: it was full of grey wood ashes, about a quart of them. Before I could ask him why in the world he was bringing ashes to Caracas, he had opened the other bag: it was full of tightly bound cured tobacco leaves. I clicked my tongue approvingly and he wrapped them back up. The ashes were to mix with the chewing tobacco, and I recall that he had asked me earlier if the Caraca-teri made fires on the floor of their houses to cook by. He was way ahead of me.

The gigantic transport plane—a C-123 designed for paratroop drops and hauling heavy cargo—lumbered to a dusty stop and the Makiritare descended on it to unload the cargo. The crew was in a hurry, for they had caught the edge of the storm and wanted to be airborne as soon as possible. They were reluctant to fly over Amazonas, a vast jungle with no radio communications or emergency landing strips, in a tropical storm.

Within an hour the plane was unloaded and the crew motioning for any passengers who wanted a lift to get aboard. We stepped into the giant, empty belly of the plane and I strapped Rerebawä into his safety harness. He had grown very quiet and was now obviously worried . . . if we weren't going to crash into the upper layer, why is it necessary to tie ourselves into the seats? The plane lumbered to the end of the savanna, turned, and screeched to a halt. The pilot tested the motors, and the roar was deafening: Rerebawä's knuckles were white as he clutched the edge of his seat. The plane lurched forward and gathered speed, bouncing unpredictably over the irregularities of the unimproved dirt landing strip. Then the nose tipped upward sharply and we were airborne.

It was one of the worst flights I ever had, for we hit the storm soon after we gained cruising altitude. The plane jerked and twisted violently, dipping first one wing and then, suddenly, the other. Gusts of wind bounced us around, and jarring losses of altitude would leave us breathless, pinning us against our safety harnesses and then, as the frail plane fought back upwards, forcing us into our canvas seats. We could hear the ominous beating of rain on the fuselage above the roar of the motors. In an hour we were over the llanos and the flight had become more calm, but the noise was still deafening as the two motors labored incessantly. I unsnapped my harness and walked around the plane, but I was unsuccessful in persuading Rerebawä to untie himself or look out one of the fogged-up portholes. He just sat there, staring blankly at the opposite side of the plane, his tobacco buried deeply between his lower lip and teeth, clutching his seat. He relaxed a bit when I told him that we were approaching our landing strip at Maracay, and whispered cautiously that he was very cold. I assured him that I, too, was cold but that it would be warm when we landed. He rolled his eyes back and nodded his understanding.

The tires squealed and gave off a puff of blue smoke as we touched the concrete runway, taxied in, and coasted to a stop in front of the gigantic hanger that Rerebawä immediately recognized as the "den" of the creature in which we were riding. The crew opened the tiny side doors of the plane, and a blast of hot, dry air burst in. Our ears continued to ring, even though the deafening engines had stopped. We climbed out and stood on the concrete pad that stretched as far as our eyes could see, disappearing in the shimmering heatwaves near the horizon. Rerebawä touched it carefully and asked me how we found so much flat stone to make such a huge trail. Before I could answer that question, a dozen more, equally startling, came from his dry lips. One of the crew asked me if I wanted a lift up to the headquarters, from which we could call a taxi to take us to Caracas, some 35 miles away. I accepted, and told Rerebawä that we were going to have a ride in a "car." "What is a 'car'?" he asked suspiciously, remembering his airplane trip. I pointed to the white Ford parked a short way off. "Why don't you get into it and wait for me there while I unload our things?" I suggested. He headed slowly for the car and I gathered our things from the plane. When I stepped out of the plane, he was standing by the car, examining it carefully, glancing periodically at me, then at the car. "Get into it!" I shouted, "I'll be right there!" I watched him walk slowly around the car, scratch his head, and look up at me with a puzzled expression. "Don't be afraid!" I shouted as I walked toward him. "Get in it!" He adjusted the tobacco in his mouth, took a half-step toward the car, and dived through the open window on the passenger's side, his feet and legs hanging curiously out the gaping hole in the side! I had forgotten to tell him about doors, and realized how much I had taken things for granted, and how incredibly bizarre much of our culture would be to the Yanomamö.

The next week proved to be both sobering and outrageously funny at times as Rerebawä discovered what Caraca-teri and its customs and ways were like, and how much he would have to report to his co-villagers. The staggering size of the buildings reaching to the sky, built of stone laid upon stone, elevators, people staying up all night, the bright lights of the automobiles coming at an incredible speed at you during night travel, looking like the piercing eyes of the *bore* spirits, the ridiculous shoes that women wore with high heels and how they would cause you to trip if you tried to walk through the jungle in them, and the marvels of flush toilets and running water. He was astounded at how clean the floors were in the houses, was afraid to climb suspended stairs for fear they would collapse and could not drink enough orange soda pop, or get over the fact that a machine would dispense it when you put a coin in and pushed a button. "How could you invite these things to a feast?" He queried. "They certainly are generous and give their 'goods' away, but they expect to be reciprocated on the spot!"

He enjoyed himself in Caracas but was happy to return to his village, and spoke grandiloquently to his peers about the size of Caraca-teri. "Is it bigger than Patanowä-teri's *shabono?*" they asked him skeptically, and he looked at me, somewhat embarrassed, and knew that he could not explain it to them. We both knew that they would not be able to conceive of what Rerebawä had seen. His arm stretched out and he described a large arc, slowly, saying with the greatest of exaggeration his language permitted: "it stretches from here to . . . way over . . . there!" And they clicked their tongues, for it was bigger than they imagined.

In a few days Rerebawä had ceased discussing Caracas and his exciting trip there. He was busily and happily going about his normal Yanomamö activities as if nothing extraordinary had happened. I marvelled at his resiliency and was relieved that the experience in Caracas had not diminished his enthusiastic view of his own culture as being inherently superior to and dominant over the ways of the *nabä*—the rest of the world that fell short of full humanness, the Non-Yanomamö.

Rerebawä's almost nonchalant reaction to Caracas puzzled me, but it likewise reminded me of a similar reaction that Hioduwä, the headman of Iyäwei-teri, had after he had been taken to Rome to meet the Pope. Padre Luis Cocco, the Salesian priest at that village (Cocco 1972), had spent 15 years attempting to introduce Western ideas and ways into Hįoduwä's village. A kind and resourceful man, Padre Cocco went to ingenious lengths to expose the Yąnomamö to aspects of our culture that would impress them and, hopefully, encourage them to become more like us. Thus, when the opportunity arose to have an audience with the Pope in 1971, he arranged to bring Hįoduwä with him. Hįoduwä later told me that he treated the Pope very courteously, called him affectionately "Shoriwä," and presented him with a particularly beautiful Guacamaya parrot. What impressed him more than meeting the Pope, for he could not comprehend the awesomeness and pomp of the circumstances, was seeing the Roman ruins, which he perceptively described as the ". . . old abandoned villages of their ancestors." He thought that it was quite appropriate for the present Romans to hold the deeds and crumbling ruins of their "mythical" ancestors in awe, as a testimony perhaps that the past is connected to the present in an intimate, concrete way—as it is in Yąnomamö myth where present, past, and future are unchanging and indistinguishable.

Hįoduwä, by comparison to Rerebawä and Kąobawä, was indeed a worldly, cosmopolitan man. If any Yąnomamö should be preadapted to coping with our kind of culture, it should be him. His group has been in constant contact with the outside world since 1955 or so, and, because of the mission there, has served as some sort of Amazonian center for visitors, tourists, scientists, government officials, and benefactors of the Salesian missionaries working in Yąnomamö territory.

Hįoduwä had also been to Caracas on a number of occasions and had frequently accompanied the mission boat down to the territorial capital, Puerto Ayacucho. Padre Cocco had hoped to teach Hįoduwä enough about boatsmanship, outboard motors, and the ways of the Venezuelan settlers he would meet downstream so that he could eventually make the long trip himself . . . to sell plantains to the merchants of Puerto Ayacucho for a handsome profit. The Venezuelans who carried supplies upstream to the mission always bought plantains from the Yąnomamö for ridiculously low prices and sold them for up to 800 percent profit, and Padre Cocco thought it would be fair and reasonable if the Yąnomamö themselves made this profit. Thus, he sent Hįoduwä up and down the Orinoco on the mission boat several times to familiarize him with the customs and procedures before he felt he was ready for his solo entrepreneurial venture.

Padre Cocco had arranged everything in advance to make sure that Hįoduwä would be met by mission personnel at Puerto Ayacucho who would help him sell the plantains for a reasonable price. He loaned him the large mission launch, a giant dugout canoe that had been planked up on the gunwales to increase its carrying capacity. He also loaned him a large, new outboard motor and provided him with enough gasoline to make the voyage. Hįoduwä cut and loaded the approximately 300 plantain *racimas* he and his kinsmen had produced for the venture and set out on his three-day trip to Puerto Ayacucho. If things had gone well, he would have earned a profit of about $500 for the load of plantains. However, things did not go well, for Yąnomamö trading customs dominated the trip. To make a long story short, Hįoduwä visited a number of Venezuelan families on the lower Orinoco and they "asked" him for plantains as gifts. He also had motor trouble and a kind Venezuelan "traded" an old but still functioning tiny outboard motor to him for Padre Cocco's new, large but temporarily malfunctioning motor. As he passed by the National Guard post at San Fernando de Apure, he was a bit intimidated by the gun-toting soldiers, so he made them a handsome gift of more of his plantains to assure their friendship. By the time he reached Puerto Ayacucho, he had only 100 or so *racimas* of plantains left. His mission friends helped him sell these for a good price, but then he went shopping with the cash by himself—and the wily storekeepers quickly relieved him of that burden. He managed to acquire a few machetes, a dozen straw hats, a few trinkets, and several small transistor radios. He was happy as a lark, contented with his transaction. When he left Puerto Ayacucho for the five-day return trip, a clever settler correctly pointed out that his tiny motor was not able to push his very large boat very fast and that it would take him many days to reach his destination. Hioduwä agreed with him. The man, as it turned out, had a much smaller canoe and was willing to trade it for the clumsier boat. He would even throw in his dog as part of the bargain. Well, the boat *was* heavy and the dog *was* handsome, so the bargain was struck. Hioduwä returned triumphantly to the mission with his straw hats, transistor radios, trinkets, and dog—and matter of factly explained to a chagrined Padre Cocco what had happened to his new motor and mission launch.

While this might be an amusing anecdote, there are some very grave implications in it for the future of the Yąnomamö as they are placed under increasing pressure from the national culture to change their tribal ways and become incorporated into the nation state as civilized citizens. For if Hioduwä had such difficulty after years of sympathetic preparation by Padre Cocco, then it should be clear that premature exposure to national culture will be difficult for the Yąnomamö who have had much less preparation. And while the pressures are now focused on only those few mission posts that presently exist in their land, the consequences of directed change will radically affect the entire tribe—even the most remote and presently uncontacted villages.

The Beginning of Tourism and Change

Before discussing some of the implications of this emerging problem, let me briefly comment on my research since the publication of the first edition of this book, for the Yąnomamö are, in 1977, in a much different situation than they were in 1964, when I first visited them. On several of my many returns to the Yąnomamö since 1967 I had mentioned to Rerebawä and Kąobawä that the people in "my village" have heard of them and have grown very fond of them, indicating so through the "decorated leaves" (letters) they send to me. That always pleased them immensely, and they wanted to know if the females thought them attractive, why some people thought that Rerebawä should clear a garden in Kąobawä's area, or why my people thought they should stop raiding the Patanowä-teri ("But they don't know what a bunch of nasty critters they are!"). I also told them about our own wars and what some of my people think of theirs. They find us abominable for dropping napalm on women and children, or stupid for fighting over land—and that we should think more about the merits of wife stealing. Their perspective on war is both amusing and penetrating, and they clearly would enjoy reading Darwin on "sexual selection" rather than Marx on "means of production," and as academics would make some interesting observations about a number of theoretical debates in the contemporary anthropological literature—to a number of which their own behavior contributed! I explained one of the controversies to them, one having to do with my ongoing disagreement with Professor Marvin Harris (Harris 1975; Chagnon 1975) about the relevance of protein abundance in the genesis of their warfare, and they laughed: "Yaro yamakö buhii makuwi, suwä käbä yamakö buhii baröwo!" ("Even though we like meat, we like women a whole lot more!")

I have now spent more time among the Yąnomamö after I wrote *The Fierce People* than I did initially to collect the information that went into that book. My return trips each year made me increasingly aware of the gradual impact that our culture was having on the Yąnomamö, for each year saw the arrival of new missionaries and more visitors, the clearing of airstrips from the jungle, and the increased ease with which curious tourists or adventurers could visit Yąnomamöland. With these increased contacts came new dangers to the Yąnomamö, particularly health risks. In 1967, while participating with my medical colleagues in a biomedical study of selected Yąnomamö villages, we collected blood samples that clearly showed how vulnerable and isolated the Yąnomamö were: they had not yet been exposed to measles. Thus, in 1968, when we returned again to extend this study, we brought 3000 measles vaccines with us to initiate an innoculation program in the areas we visited. Unfortunately, the very week we arrived an epidemic of measles broke out at a number of mission posts and began spreading to the more remote villages as the frightened Yąnomamö tried to flee from the dreaded epidemic. We worked frantically for the next month trying to vaccinate a barrier around the epidemic, ultimately succeeding after visiting many villages and being reinforced, toward the end of our efforts, by additional amounts of vaccine flown into us by the Venezuelan government and through the efforts of a group of French researchers and the local missionaries. Still, a large number of Yąnomamö died in the epidemic in some regions—villages that were remote and difficult to reach (Neel et al 1970).[1]

The health problems that are beginning to emerge among the Yąnomamö are far more serious in the remoter villages than they are at the mission stations, for at least at the missions there are radios with which assistance from Caracas can be solicited in emergencies, or stores of antibiotics and other medical supplies to treat the more common and more frequent illnesses. And most of the local missionaries are patient and good people who are sensitive to the medical problems that arise within their groups, working indefatiguably at times to nurse the children and adults through a lingering malady that no shaman on earth

---

[1]Many of my colleagues and students ask me what the Atomic Energy Commission had to do with some of my research support during my study of the Yąnomamö. The medical scientists with whom I collaborated at the University of Michigan's Department of Human Genetics had, after World War II, held positions in the Atomic Bomb Casualty Commission, a medical-genetics group whose responsibility it was to treat the survivors of the nuclear bombings at Hiroshima and Nagasaki. After they returned to their regular academic lives at various universities and medical schools across the United States, they continued some of their genetics studies, for the effects of radiation can show up several generations after the initial exposure. When I joined Michigan's Department of Human Genetics in 1966 to participate in a multidisciplinary study of South American Indians, some of the studies of irradiated Japanese families was still in progress. By then, however, members of the department were turning to more academic projects, such as the study of non-Japanese populations and especially marriage and reproduction in these populations. The biomedical studies on the Yąnomamö Indians they made were, for a while, subsumed into their Atomic Energy Commission contract and justified in the sense that both the Japanese and the Yąnomamö reproduce according to cultural rules. As the Yąnomamö work became more conspicuous and expanded, it was difficult to continue that justification and, in time, we obtained National Science Foundation money to continue that work. See Neel et al, 1971, for references to some of the results of that research. As a result of this research, the Yąnomamö are biomedically one of the most thoroughly studied tribes in the world.

could cure, but, on the other hand, no *hekura* from a distant village could have caused. Beyond the village help dwindles rapidly, for the Yąnomamö cannot communicate their problems in time, since the distances they must travel on foot to reach help are enormous.

The increased contact at mission posts has complicated the health problems dramatically. With airstrips, visitors can reach the area with tremendous ease and innocently carry with them the latest version of infections that our own population can live with relatively comfortably, for our biological systems have sustained similar abuses time and time again and we have, or can develop, ready cures for most of them. A Yąnomamö visitor to the same post, eagerly searching for a machete, just as innocently carries a new bug back inland to his fellow villagers, and by the time they realize they are sick, they are too weak or too isolated to get help. One remote village I had been studying for five years had never seen a foreigner other than me in their entire history. When I last visited them in 1972, they numbered 179 people. I did not return to them for three years; in 1975 when I went inland to update my census on them, I found that they had suffered a 40 percent mortality the previous year and there were virtually no children below the age of ten years. The only thing that had changed during my three-year absence was the initiation of contact with the foreigners downstream, whom they had begun visiting regularly to obtain machetes. Rerebawä, in reflecting on what was happening, commented introspectively: "When I was a boy we did not have epidemics like this. It did not begin until foreigners started coming here." I believe he was close to the truth.

There are only a dozen or so Yąnomamö villages in which missionaries have permanent posts in Brazil and Venezuela. This seems trifling in view of the fact that there are perhaps as many as 150 villages of Yąnomamö in total. However, the impact of mission contact is increasing every year. In 1964, when there were somewhat fewer posts, the missionaries generally concentrated their efforts in local areas and only sporadically visited the neighboring Yąnomamö groups. With time, and with increased competition between Catholic and Protestant missionaries, active and ambitious visiting programs have taken form and the missionaries aggressively try to visit more and more remote villages. There were vast areas of uncontacted Yąnomamö in 1964. In 1976 these areas had shrunk to just a few pockets of isolated villages, and their existence and location are enviously viewed by both mission groups as challenges . . . lest the competition gets there first and establishes a settlement. The Protestant groups have their own air support and have established posts in the very heartland of the uncontacted areas in the past few years. They send their young men deep into the jungle on foot, with Yąnomamö guides from "saved" villages as evangelical helpers. Once near a remote village, they clear an airstrip with the help of the local and soon-to-be-saved Yąnomamö. Shortly thereafter, a family moves in and establishes a post. In time, the location of the airstrip becomes known to others, especially to wealthy Venezuelans who own their own private airplanes and who enjoy spending weekends or longer vacations in exotic places, observing naked Indians, collecting curios and mission anecdotes. Soon there are so many regular visitors to these remote posts that the missionaries have to build special houses to accomodate their regular but unpredictable guests, if for no other reason than to have some privacy for their family life. The few enterprising bush pilots who are skillful or daring enough to fly in this area soon find out about the strip and exploit the situation extensively, ever willing to take planeloads of prosperous tourists into the remote villages for a handsome fee. Such visiting begins, innocently and often against the wishes of the local missionaries, but soon reaches grotesque proportions. Complaints, however, are averted by the substantial cash gifts that the tourists generally leave to "support" the mission work.

The Catholic missions likewise find themselves involved in catering to increasing numbers of visitors, sometimes unwillingly but sometimes by deliberate design and choice. One Salesian priest in particular actively promoted and cultivated tourism to his mission for several years. The mission had been established by others and lay dormant for a number of years, stagnating in the lethargy of its disinterested sequence of occupants until about 1970. When I visited it in 1969 there was only one official there—a lay brother, who was assisted by two Brazilian men. Shortly thereafter an ambitious Spanish priest was assigned to the post. In 1971 the Venezuelan government (CODESUR—Conquest of the South— project) cleared a large airstrip there and the priest embarked on a vigorous campaign to promote tourism and civilization with a passion that would have embarassed the Con- quistadores. A tour agent in Caracas soon had a fleet of sleek speedboats there and the priest kept him supplied with ample quantities of gasoline. He also built a number of guest houses to accomodate the visitors and soon the mission was a booming tourist center. Direct flights from Munich and other European cities were advertised in 1973, stopping briefly in Caracas for a changeover to a small twin-engine craft that would fly them directly to the Yąnomamö village of Mahekodo-teri on the Upper Orinoco, and into the Stone Age. This dimension of his scheme, however, was opposed by some of his ecclesiastical colleagues and superiors, and discouraged . . . with only partial success. Large numbers of tourists, many from Europe, visited there. In 1975 when I passed through his mission there were at least 40 Brazilians living there, engaged in some sort of support activity ranging from machine shop maintenance to lumbering and hunting. Their hunting techniques, I should add, are as devastating as they are illegal by Venezuelan law—hunting by night with large flashlights from motorized canoes and fishing with seine nets. Apart from feeding themselves and their families, they kept the mission's kerosene-operated freezer full of fresh game and fish for the hordes of tourists that came every year. I might add that Yąnomamö hunting techniques do not lead to overexploitation of the fauna, but the use of shotguns, night hunting with torches and motorized canoes and seining fish produces, in a short time, a severe impact on the balance of nature. I remember the incredible herds of Capybara, wild pigs, flocks of ducks and river otters that abounded in the upper Mavaca River from 1968 through 1971, when I was the only Westerner who ascended it. After the mission personnel and Venezuelan or Brazilian employees thereof began hunting it, it turned into a near desert. Now, not a single otter can be seen along its entire course, and many other species of common game animals are almost nonexistent. The impact of this intensity of hunting on the local game supply—and the Yąnomamö diet—will eventually be catastrophic.

Tourism still continues at the above mentioned mission village, although it is entirely illegal. This particular priest justified his scheme by referring to the objectives of the Venezuelan Indian Commission—to acculturate the Indian populations as rapidly as possible, and his method, he argued, would accomplish that goal. The more the Indians were exposed to outsiders, the more rapidly they would learn Western ways and emulate them. The Yąnomamö, I might add, appeared to disagree with him: they abandoned their village and moved across the Orinoco to have some peace and respite from the tourists.

The introduction of shotguns by missionaries and those who work for them is also a major and serious issue. Several missionaries, both Catholic and Protestant, have told me that they like to give trade goods such as shotguns and flashlights, for it made the Indians dependent on them for batteries and ammunition . . . and the Indians would therefore be less likely to move away once they became accustomed to these items. The shotguns, however, are inevitably used in raids and they kill. The problem is more severe in Brazil than it is in Venezuela, for shotguns are very cheap there by comparison.

One missionary I met related, sadly, an incident in which several men from the village raided a distant group with their newly acquired shotguns and killed several people, including a few women and children. She was still giving shot and powder to the men "for hunting purposes," which I found incredible. When I asked her why she continued to dispense shot and powder, she explained: "Well, we only gave one shotgun to the men. A Brazilian trader came up and gave the other guns to them. We don't know for sure if the gun we gave them actually killed anyone on that raid and we are not going to ask, because we know we would have to take the gun away. If we do that, the Indians will probably move away from the mission and all our investment will be lost." Other missionaries I have spoken to about the known military use of shotguns by men in their villages likewise continue to give ammunition to the offenders, preferring to discount my information as "just another of those Yąnomamö 'rumors.'" One Yąnomamö man I know has killed at least three people with his shotgun, and the missionaries continue to provide him with shot and powder. Kumaiewä, the bearded man in the film The Feast, had his head blown off with a shotgun shortly after we completed the film (Asch and Chagnon 1970). Some of the raids in which shotguns have been used were conducted only because the raiders had a new, superior weapon and wanted to try it out—the possession of the gun caused wars where none previously existed. When I asked Rerebawä why a particular village, in possession of shotguns, raided an especially distant village with whom it had no previous contact, he replied: "The headman there is fierce. He now has a shotgun. When you give a fierce man a shotgun, he becomes ever fiercer and wants to kill without cause."

There are many good and reasonable missionaries who are genuinely concerned about the Yąnomamö as human beings and who are patient enough to realize that conversion to Christianity is still a long way off and can only be effected through a gradual process of change. And, there are many sympathetic Venezuelans who recognize the difficulties and dangers of abrupt and capricious acculturation practices that a minority of local missionaries occasionally practice. It would be both reasonable and humane if the civil authorities and missionaries established guidelines and policies based on sound information and developed an acculturation program that would at least attempt to preserve and enhance particular Yąnomamö beliefs and conceptions that might optimize their ability to cope with the larger national society. One particularly important step would be the "assignment" of family names according to Yąnomamö notions of descent and affinity. Patrilineal descent is an indiginous notion that could be used to bolster solidarity and a sense of oneness among the Yąnomamö. For example, all the descendants of a man acknowledge their agnatic relatedness irrespective of their village of residence. However, one must have detailed genealogical information to identify such lineal descent groups, and the work required to obtain this information is difficult, time-consuming and, at times, unpleasant. At present the missionaries are arbitrarily inventing Christian family names for the Yąnomamö in such a way that members of the same sibship or agnatic group end up with completely different surnames. Eventually this will create artificial distinctions and promote dissension within culturally significant groups; it would be much more practical and beneficial to bestow the same family name on the entire agnatic group. Genealogical information of the kind discussed in this book could be used for a practical purpose, and it would be very desirable to have local missionaries follow Yąnomamö notions of descent when they create the names that become official.

A sound program of acculturation can only be developed with professional anthro-pological counsel and input. At present there are no Venezuelan anthropologists with first-hand experience among the Yąnomamö who could participate in the development of such a program. While many Venezuelan anthropologists are genuinely alarmed about the status of Venezuelan tribes and their future, and argue that something beneficial must be done for them, thus far none of their students have risen to the challenge of committing themselves to a long-term study of and involvement with Yąnomamö culture. This is an alarming situation, since it is imperative that a Venezuelan anthropologist represent these people to the national authorities and speak on their behalf with the authority that only long-term field knowledge can provide. It is all the more serious in view of the increased difficulty that foreign anthropologists have in obtaining research permits.[2]

As a foreigner, and especially as a North American foreigner, in Venezuela, I could not speak out publicly and criticize some of the harsher and questionable mission policies I witnessed . . . unless I was willing to risk the possibility that I would not be granted a research permit to continue my fieldwork. On the one occasion I took a public stand by signing my name to a relatively moderate document that expressed concern about what was happening to many of the native peoples of Venezuela, I was passionately accused by many Venezuelans of "meddling" in the internal affairs of their government. (Many of the signatories were Venezuelan anthropologists.) One of my graduate students, who was awaiting official word about his permission to initiate fieldwork in a newly contacted tribe of hitherto unknown Indians (Hoti, Yowana, Yuwana) just north of the Yąnomamö, was summarily denied a permit to work there—but a group of American Evangelists was simultaneously allowed to move in. One doesn't need a degree in logic to realize that the price of dissent is the jeopardizing of research privileges.

While I could not freely express my opinion in the Venezuelan press or before my Venezuelan colleagues, things were different in the jungle where local policies and events took place before my eyes and where there were fewer official restraints to my reactions. In some cases I could speak to and reason with local missionaries about their particular methods and policies. Some of them were willing to consider my views and at least listened politely. In rare cases the missionaries even asked my opinion and carried on a dialogue with me. I cherish the memory of these discussions and the people who initiated them, for enlightened reason and not dogma appeared to mean something to them. In most cases

---

[2] In 1976 the Ministry of Justice of Venezuela, through which anthropological research permits must be obtained, announced that new permits for foreign anthropologists would be denied for an indefinite period of time. I went to Caracas to discuss the new policy with the representatives of this ministry and to request permits for myself and two of my advanced graduate students. At the same time, I discussed a collaborative project with several of my Venezuelan colleagues, a project in which two Venezuelan students would participate in a one-year field study among the Yąnomamö. The permits for myself and my students were contingent on the acceptability of my proposed collaboration with my Venezuelan colleagues. Unfortunately, they found the proposal unacceptable.

reason and dialogue were not possible, for the missionaries were incapable of viewing the differences between "good" and "bad" in anything other than narrow biblical or theological terms, and could not appreciate the argument that the wanton destruction of a culture, if not its human bearers, was morally "bad" by some standards. Evangelism was by definition "good" in their terms if only a single soul was saved, and any price was worth paying to accomplish that end and any method legitimate. I once put a hypothetical question to a Protestant missionary as follows: Would you risk exposing 200 Yąnomamö to some infectious disease if you thought you could save one of them from Hell—and the other 199 died from the disease? His answer was unequivocal and firm: Yes. A Catholic priest once commented to me, "I believe the Yąnomamö are subhuman—they act like animals and lack the essential faculties of being human."

I had largely ignored the policies and motives of the missionaries during my first 15 months of field research, partially because they were not too obvious where I was working, partly because I wished to avoid confrontations with them, and partly because there were so many uncontacted Yąnomamö villages to study where these problems did not exist. There was a Salesian (Catholic) mission across the river from Kąobawä's village all during my initial research, but there were no Yąnomamö there. It was easy to ignore them at that time for they had no impact on the Yąnomamö. All of the Indians were on the south side of the Orinoco, where the Protestants had established two families to conduct their work among the Bisaasi-teri, who were then divided into two villages, "upper" and "lower." Indeed, during the first three months I lived among the Yąnomamö there were no missionaries whatsoever present, for one Protestant family was downstream recovering from malaria and the other was just returning from the United States after a year's absence from Venezuela. By the end of my fieldwork that year I was spending a good deal of my time in the more remote villages, which deflected my attention from local missionary activity in Bisaasi-teri.

When I left the field in 1966 that was what the missionary picture was like. In 1967 when I returned again to Bisaasi-teri, Kąobawä's village was only half the size it had been the year before. The Salesian priest across the river had taken advantage of the fact that a fission was developing in Kąobawä's village and that Paruriwä (Hontonawä), Kąobawä's brother-in-law, was emerging as a strong leader in the dissident faction: he lured Paruriwä and his group across the river with generous gifts of outboard motors, shotguns, and other desirable trade commodities. I saw Paruriwä in 1967 when I stopped to greet the priest; he was proudly bearing a presumptuous Spanish title, beating his chest with his fist, urging me to pay attention: "Me Capitan! Me Capitan! Me Capitan!" He swaggered off after I acknowledged that I understood that he was a leader now, carelessly shouldering a rusty 16-gauge shotgun, barking commands to his followers in the three or four Spanish words he had learned during the year, a shadow of the man I had last seen, dwarfed in the raggy and tattered pants that marked his new status and guaranteed in that status by *his* monopoly on the priest's trade goods.

I was depressed when I saw this and reflected on what lay behind the missionary attempts to make the Yąnomamö more worthy in God's eyes. I had returned to study the Shamatari groups south of Kąobawä's village and was glad that I had made that decision, for I knew that if I worked in Bisaasi-teri I would ultimately come into conflict with the missionaries and would, as they put it, "interfere in their work."

First Contacts with the Shamatari

I nevertheless made Kạobawä's village my base of operations that year and in the succeeding years as my Shamatari work progressed.[3] Kạobawä and Rerebawä were always happy to see me return, and I always went out of my way to spend as much time with them as I could to maintain our long friendship. They were always disappointed that I went off to the Shamatari for long visits because, as they put it, they ". . . wanted to possess me for themselves and not share me with others," a sentiment that applied less and less to my material possessions as it did to my person. Rerebawä often accompanied me on my Shamatari trips and was well informed about the magnitude of my generosity to the Shamatari.

My Shamatari trips inland were always punctuated with a return to and a rest for a few days at Kạobawä's village.

While I used Kạobawä's village only as my base of operations during these recent field trips, I nevertheless spent many enjoyable hours with Rerebawä, who accompanied me on many of my trips into the headwaters of the Mavaca River and to the Shamatari villages in that area. Over the years I watched Rerebawä mature from a boisterous, cocky 20-year-old youth that had married into Kạobawä's village to a measured, respected, and politically astute man of two and thirty, one of the leaders in the village and a valued confidant of Kạobawä. Yes, he finally did clear his own garden there and settled in as one of the politically important men of the group, and became the proud father of five healthy, mischievous and charming children, the oldest daughter of which he has already promised in marriage to a young man from a Shamatari village.

Rerebawä did not, however, accompany me in 1968 on the occasion of my first attempt to contact the mysterious, if not notorious, Shamatari to the south: Sibarariwä's village.[4] Kạobawä's village had been at war with Sibarariwä for many years, and Rerebawä, as a very young man, had participated in the raiding when members of his natal village allied with Kạobawä's group on some of the incursions. He was afraid that they might recognize him and shoot him. My initial contact, therefore, found me in the hands of two very young guides—the only two I could persuade to make what they were sure was a dangerous and risky journey. One of these "men" was a boy of about 12 years old, a lad named Karina. He had grown up in Sibarariwä's village, for his mother had been abducted by that group when he was a baby. In 1967 he moved back to his natal village, Mömariböwei-teri, where he was something of a stranger. He was not afraid to guide me to Sibarariwä's village for he knew all the residents very well. My second guide was an 18-year-old youth named Bäkotawä, who came along in the conviction that he was a "Patanowa-teri," and not a "Bisaasi-teri," or at least that is what he planned to tell Sibarariwä's people (if Karina would vouch for his story) and therefore a neutral party. Neither Kạobawä nor Rerebawä wanted me to go on the trip, for they were genuinely afraid that the Shamatari would do me harm. They tried to dissuade me from making the

---

[3] My French colleague Jacques Lizot began studying the Yạnomamö in 1968. He generously permitted me to use his small hut for my base camp, since he, too, had made Bisaasi-teri his own base of operations in 1971. Lizot's excellent field research has resulted in a major contribution to Yạnomamö ethnography and ethnology, especially his 1971a, 1971b, 1971c, 1973, 1975, and 1976 works.

[4] This village, on the maps in the first edition, was called Möwaraoba-teri.

trip by all manner of terrifying stories of Shamatari treachery and, when that failed, by recourse to the terrible threats to my life that the *Raharas* would pose, for the Mavaca River was thought to be teeming with these fabulous serpents who were large enough to devour humans by the canoefull. There was also an element of enlightened self-interest in their attempts to discourage me from going to that village, for they knew that any subsequent visits would lead to a distribution of gifts of steel tools that might otherwise be given to them or to members of their village. Still, the objectives of my field project required a detailed genealogical picture and census base from which to interpret the history, warfare, and settlement pattern of the cluster of Shamatari villages, and I was stubbornly determined to reach Sibarariwä's village.

I succeeded in finding and contacting Sibarariwä's people, who received me rather courteously—and irately chastised me for not having come sooner. They knew more about me before I contacted them than I imagined (Chagnon 1974). The first contact, however, was not without its problems, for one of my guides, Bäkotawä, panicked as we got closer and closer to the near fabulous village and insisted on returning to where I had beached my canoe. He insisted on waiting there for me while I pushed on with my stalwart 12-year-old guide. Bäkotawä did not stop at the canoe when he reached it, but promptly put it into the water and fled the three or four days downstream to safety even before I had found Sibarariwä's group. He thus abandoned me to my fate, certain that the Shamatari would shoot me on the spot. Several days later, when the Shamatari escorted me down to the Mavaca River to collect the gifts I had left for them at my canoe, I discovered to my horror that the gifts were gone—as well as the canoe. I ultimately had to chop down a large tree and hollow it out into a crude dugout to make the return trip to Bisaasi-teri, a boat so crude and unseaworthy that Karina and I spent as much time in the river as we did in the craft, for we swamped countless times trying to make it back. Despite the dangers to himself, Rerebawä was the only Yąnomamö who demanded to go up the Mavaca to look for me among the Shamatari. I met him and the others on the lower Mavaca—I had nearly made it home in my crude boat when I ran into the three valiant souls who decided that I had gotten into a jam: a missionary, a Makiritare Indian, and Rerebawä (Chagnon 1974).

Thus began my several most recent years of field research, much of which was spent in Sibarariwä's village—Mishimishimaböwei-teri, the subject of my 1974 book *Studying the Yąnomamö*. The Shamatari were somewhat more difficult to live with than Kąobawä's people, for their villages were extremely large and the leaders there were under correspondingly greater compulsion to keep order with awesome firmness. By the time I had contacted Sibarariwä's group, other younger men were emerging as political powers and challenging his authority. Möawä, an aggressive and somewhat sullen man of 35 years, had emerged as the true headman, and Sibarariwä, his father's brother, had fissioned away from him with the smaller half of the village as his followers. Möawä's group contained 280 people, one of the largest Yąnomamö villages I had ever lived in, while Sibarariwä's splinter group was over 125. They had fissioned just a year or so before I contacted them, and their prefission size was well over 400 people, staggeringly large by Yąnomamö standards.

My research among the Shamatari was one of the most exciting and rewarding periods of my professional and personal life. There was great danger, for as my personal relationship with Möawä developed, it grew more tense, and in the end he almost killed me with his ax. Beyond his village lay other more remote villages whence his own had sprung. I recall vividly the long trek through the gloomy forest to contact Börösöwä's village, and how Boraböwä and his brothers tried to do me in while I slept fitfully, suffering from some unknown allergy, and the safe passage that Wishahewä gave me out of the area. And beyond this village lay Tananowä's, and I periodically reflect on what might have happened to me had I reached that group. I turned back from that trip when Rerebawä told me that Tananowä, whom I had never met, vowed to kill me if I ever came to his village, for he concluded that I was practicing harmful magic against him. He, along with some of my Patanowä-teri friends, had made an effigy of me on the occasion of a raid they initiated against the Bisaasi-teri and ceremoniously shot it full of arrows. I had become a named enemy and target of their raid. But, I have described these incidents in more detail in another book on field methods (Chagnon 1974) and plan to elaborate them further in another publication. Suffice it to say that the danger contrasted with and intensified the pleasure of my happier experiences among the Shamatari, my friendship with Dedeheiwä (Chagnon 1973b, *Magical Death*), and the enormous amount of valuable new information I collected there, information that will contribute to a greater understanding of population dynamics and political processes in an expanding horticultural tribe and, hopefully, to a greater understanding of the role of warfare in the history of our species.

My Adventure with *Ebene:* A "Religious Experience"

On one of my annual return trips I became deeply involved with Kąobawä's relationship to the Protestant missionaries. A new missionary family had moved into his village to maintain the "field station" for a period of about a year while the resident local missionary returned to the United States on a "furlough." Missionaries, I might add, utilize a good many paramilitary phrases in their work—they regard themselves as "Commandos for Christ," "wage war on the Devil" and take "furloughs" from "active duty." I did not know this particular missionary very well, for he was usually living in Yąnomamö villages in a region that fell outside the area of my field study. However, I knew that "Pete," as I will call him here, was more prone to conduct his evangelical objectives through recourse to fire and brimstone techniques than most of the more patient, younger Protestant missionaries I had met, often flying into tirades whenever the Yąnomamö would "revert" to chewing tobacco (". . . the work of the Devil . . ."), taking extra wives, or, most annoyingly, insufflating their hallucinogens and chanting to their *hekura* spirits. Pete particularly disliked the village shamans, and made extraordinary attempts to discredit them, for they constituted a serious threat to his attempts at convincing the others that there was only one true spirit and that a belief in many spirits was evil.

At first, the Yąnomamö very diplomatically, but with considerable inconvenience to themselves, accommodated his peculiarities by moving off into the jungle a few miles to conduct their daily religious activities. This kept the trade goods flowing into the village. On the surface and verbally they behaved as though they had ". . . accepted Dios" and ". . . thrown their hekura away," for they were ". . . filthy spirits." The inconvenience, however, became too much, and eventually the shamanism and hallucinogens moved back into the village. The noisy chanting and curing ceremonies would bring an overheated Pete running into the village, screaming and yelling recriminations at the bewildered participants, embarrassing them and intimidating them. Most important, it frightened them for Pete was not beyond showing them paintings of Yąnomamö-like people being driven off a cliff into a fiery chasm below as punishment by "Dios" for evil doings, such as shamanism. The Yąnomamö do not understand the difference between a painting and a photograph, and Pete knew this.

I tried to ignore this as much as possible, for it angered me; I knew that it would lead to bitter arguments with the missionaries and perhaps, ultimately, to trouble with the Venezuelan officials. In general, with most of the missionaries, the problem was not too serious, for most of them were relatively patient with the Yąnomamö and employed more inconspicuous and subtle methods, and a few of them were downright humane—given their ultimate goal of destroying Yąnomamö religion.

Kąobawä himself had recently taken up the use of hallucinogenic drugs and participated in the daily rituals—something he had not done during my first stay in his village. It puzzled me at first, but it ultimately made sense when I began to understand the extent to which the Protestant missionaries were intimidating and threatening his village's religious activities. It seems clear to me now that his use of hallucinogens was a calculated act to lay his prestige as a leader behind the efforts of the village curers, giving them confidence and informing the missionaries that he, as the headman, approved of what they were doing.

It was a hot afternoon, threatening to rain, and the mugginess was almost unbearable. I was working on Shamatari genealogical notes in my hut when Kąobawä and Rerebawä appeared at the door, urgently demanding to speak to me about "God-teri": The Protestant missionaries are all called "Diosi-urihi-teri"—those from the Village of God. I let them in and could immediately see that they were very upset and were sincerely turning to me for help. For the first time I realized that I had ignored a moral question and I felt ashamed for having done so. They were beginning to question the relative potency of their spirits versus the one from God-teri. They were also very angry with the missionary, for he had just burst into the village and broke up their chanting, denouncing them violently, and "threatening" them. I asked Kąobawä what he meant when he said "threaten." He held up two fingers and explained: "He told us that if we didn't stop chanting to the *hekura,* Dios would destroy us all with fire in this many *rasha* seasons!" I was almost sick with anger and resentment. He and Rerebawä went on to explain that Pete did this regularly, and it was beginning to anger them. They asked me, quite sincerely, if I believed that Dios would destroy them with fire if they chanted to the *hekura* and I told them No. I interfered in the "work" of the missionary thereby, but I felt, somehow, morally better for having done so. I did not stop there. I stripped down to my bathing trunks and said "Let's all go chant to the *hekura!"*

We walked into the village and word soon spread that Shaki was going to chant to his *hekura* and his *shoabe* and *shoriwä* were going to instruct him. I had lived among the Yąnomamö long enough by then that I knew quite a bit about the *hekura,* their particular songs and how to attract them into the great cosmos that resides in the breast of all shamans, where the *hekura* are given their intoxicating magical beverage, *braki aiamo uku,* and in turn, became as one with their human receptacle, flying through the air, visiting distant places, going to the edge of the universe where the layer becomes "rotten" and other *hekura* are suspended from trees, attacking enemies and devouring the *möamo* portion of their souls, inflicting sickness and death on them, or curing their loved ones.

We walked silently over to Kąobawä's house, for that is where the daily religious activities were to begin. "Let me decorate you, my dear brother!" said Rerebawä softly, and

I knelt on the ground while all my friends generously made their special feathers and decorations available to me so that I might become more beautiful and therefore more worthy to the *hekura*. Rerebawä took his *nara* pigment out and began painting my face and, after that, my chest. Kąobawä gave me a *wisha* tail for my head; Koaseedema loaned me his turkey scalp armbands; Makuwä gave me his special *werehi* feathers; Wąkewä gave me *ara* tail feathers. Other men began decorating themselves also. The village was quiet, but a happy excitement seemed to pervade the muggy air: everyone knew that some sort of confrontation between me and the missionary was inevitable, and they were looking forward to it.

Rerebawä took out his *ebene* tube and ran a stick through it to clean it out. His father-in-law, the most prominent shaman in the village, took out a package of *hisiomö* powder and made it available to us. We cleaned off an area in front of Kąobawä's hammock, for that is where we planned to parade and dance as we called to the *hekura*. "Bei!" said Rerebawä, and I knelt forward to receive the end of his filled ebene tube into my nostrils. I

Rerebawä blows hisiomö *powder into my nostrils in preparation for chanting to the* hekura.

closed my eyes, knowing that it would be painful, and he filled his chest with air and blew the magical green powder deep into my head in a long, powerful breath. I coughed and retched almost immediately, rubbing the back of my head violently to relieve the pain. "Bei!" he said again, and pushed the tube toward me. I took another blast, and felt the green mucus gush out of my other nostril as he blew again. More pain, more retching, and still another blast, and another. The pain seemed to diminish each time, and I squatted on my haunches, waiting for the *hisiomö* to take effect. Others began to take the drug around me, and I gradually lost interest in them as my knees grew rubbery and my peripheral vision faded. "Ai!" I said, and Rerebawä gave me more. "Ai" I said again, and he smiled: "You've had enough for now," and pointed his tube toward someone else. I was beginning to feel light and felt as though I was filled with a strange power. Songs that I had heard the Shamans from a dozen villages sing began to whirr through my mind and almost involuntarily my lips began to move, and I stood up and looked to Mavaca mountain and began singing. Blips of light and spots flashed before me, and I began the methodical prancing that I had witnessed a thousand times. My arms seemed light and began moving almost of their own accord, rhythmically up and down at my sides, and I called to Ferefereriwä and Periboriwä, hot and meat hungry *hekura,* and asked them to come into my chest and dwell within me. I felt great power and confidence, and sang louder and louder, and pranced and danced in evermore complex patterns. I took up Makuwä's arrows, manipulating them as I had seen Dedeheiwä and other shamans manipulate them, striking out magical blows, searching the horizon for *hekura,* singing and singing and singing. Others joined me and still others hid the machetes and bows, for I announced that *Rahakanariwä* dwelled within my chest and directed my actions, and all know that he caused men to be violent. We pranced together and communed with the spirits and shared something between us that was as undefinable as it was fundamentally human, a freedom to create with our minds the mystical universe that began with the beginning of time, something that seemed to be lodged in the back of imagination, something hidden and remote from consciousness, and I knew intimately why the shamans went daily through the pain of taking their drugs, for the experience was exhilirating and stimulating. But the freedom to give complete reign to the imagination was the most startling and pleasurable part, to shed my cultural shackles and fetters, to cease being a North American animal up to a point and be Yąnomamö or the part of me that I and all others have in common with Yąnomamö. Wild things passed through my mind. I thought of Levi-Strauss' argument about the wisdom of looking for the nature of human logic and thought in primitive culture because it was not contaminated with layers of accumulated precepts and intellectual entanglements—and felt it was a marvelous idea. I could hear the initial strains of Richard Strauss' *Also Sprach Zarathustra.* I didn't care what the missionary, or the startled German visitor thought about me as he clicked off photos of the mad anthropologist going native. As my high reached ecstatic proportions, I remember Kaobawä and the others groaning as I broke the arrows over my head and pranced wildly with the shambles and splinters clutched tightly in my fists, striking the ground and enjoying the soft rain that had now begun to fall.

The village became suddenly silent, and through the haze I could see a stubby figure running into the village, screaming and shouting that the *hekura* were "filthy" and that Dios would "punish" us. And through the haze the stubby figure suddenly recognized the noisiest and most active sinner: it was the anthropologist. He gawked in astonishment at me and I grinned. My arm tropismatically described a smooth, effortless arc upward in his direction, and I noticed that it had the bird finger conspicuously and rigidly raised at him, and I felt the fire in my own eyes as I lined him up on it. Pious men do not curse . . . at least in their own language. He returned my signal with a Yąnomamö equivalent—a bared eyeball, exposed by pulling the lower eyelid down—and left in disgust. The others resumed their chanting, confident that if I didn't think Dios would destroy *me* in fire for chanting to the *hekura,* they shouldn't be too concerned either, for was I not myself a refugee from Diosi-urihi-teri, and therefore knowledgeable about the machinations of Dios and the limitations on his power to destroy men with fire?

As the effect of the drug gradually wore off and the fatigue of my wild prancing began to be noticeable, I staggered over to Kąobawä's house and collapsed into one of the empty hammocks. Rerebawä's younger children happily surrounded me and looked at me with large, admiring eyes, gently stroking my arms and legs, inquiring whether I had seen the *hekura,* but not waiting for or expecting an answer. I wondered, in a shadowy daze, why

Christian missionaries differed so strongly on simple issues, such as the putative "evil" or "innocence" of hallucinogenic snuff. Padre Cocco made no attempt to discourage it and felt that it was not only relatively harmless, but had some positive features—it gave the Yąnomamö hope when they concluded that they had been "bewitched" by enemies, a sickness that the nuns could not cure with penicillin or mercurochrome. Most of the Protestants, on the other hand, were passionately opposed to it and tried to abolish its use. I thought also about the expansion of our own culture and how politics and religion reinforced each other, as they had since the inception of the state; how the expansion of political authority often followed the proselytizing attempts of religious functionaries; how the destruction of cultures by dominant groups was expressed as moral or theological necessity; and how the sword accompanied or rapidly followed the Bible.

The Protestants, mostly American Evangelists, and the Catholics, mostly Italian or Spanish Salesians, differed radically. Indeed, the Protestants did not even regard the Catholics as Christians, for they "worshipped" idols and appeared not to oppose basic evils, such as drink, drugs, and polygamy. I recalled, with some amusement, an incident that Padre Cocco related to me. He had purchased a large quantity of manioc flour from a Makiritare Indian, within whose tribe both Catholic and Protestant missionaries had worked. He asked the man if he were a Protestant. The man answered: "No, Padre. I'm a Catholic. I smoke, I drink, and I have three wives."

Where the Protestants impatiently attack the whole culture and try to bring salvation to all, including adults, the Catholics are more patient and focus on the children, partially accounting for Pete's reaction to hallucinogens and shamanism and Padre Cocco's rather humane attitude about drug use. (See Asch and Chagnon 1974, and Chagnon and Asch 1974 for a comparison, through documentary films, of the different strategies and philosophies of Catholic and Protestant missionaries among the Yąnomamö Indians). As early as 1967 I was aware that the Salesians had taken a few Yąnomamö youths downstream to their elementary school near Puerto Ayacucho, and that a few boys had been sent to Caracas to their trade school. I was disturbed when I learned about this, mainly because of the health hazards this raised, but in 1972/1973 I was alarmed to learn that the Salesians established a boarding school for Yąnomamö children as young as 6 or 7 years at La Esmeralda, and began taking children from many different villages away from their families and sending them to this school for months at a time. While the school was near the Yąnomamö tribal territory, it nevertheless was almost inaccessible to the parents in many villages whose children were taken away. The parents were "compensated" for their temporary losses by well-calculated gifts, but in time they wanted desperately to have their children returned to them . . . but were denied. This, I feel, is a terrible price to ask a Yąnomamö family to pay to insure incorporation into the nation, but an effective and ancient practice used by other dominant cultures to subdue, modify, and incorporate obdurate ethnic minorities who differ in custom and who remain independent of the nation at large: "The Inca kings also disposed that the heirs of lords of vassals should be brought up at court and reside there until they inherited their estates so that they should be well indoctrinated and accustomed to the mentality and ways of the Incas, holding friendly converse with them so that later, on account of this familiar intercourse, they would love them and serve them with real affection. . . . The Inca kings sought thus to oblige their vassals to be loyal to them out of gratitude, or if they should prove so ungrateful that they did not appreciate what was done for them, at least their evil desires might be checked by

Children from Kạobawä's village are learning to write.

the knowledge that their sons and heirs were at the capital as hostages and gages of their own fidelity" (Garcilaso 1966:404–405). The Yąnomamö children will, of course, pass a significant and critical portion of their childhood in a foreign cultural environment and acquire a knowledge of its ways and expectations, and unknowingly forfeit a significant fraction of their own cultural heritage. I suspect that the emotional shock of living away from parents in such an exotic and insensitive environment will lead to serious developmental and emotional problems, crises of identity and personality disturbances that could be avoided. As a parent and a human being, I would question the morality of a state or organization that would remove or permit the removal of my children from me in order to indoctrinate them into beliefs that, by state definition, are superior to and more desirable than my own. I was sympathetic when Kạobawä told me, in 1975, that he would never again let the missionaries take his son, Ariwari, away from him and make him live in Esmeralda.[5]

The adult Yąnomamö in villages where the Salesian missions are active, either because they have a mission post there or because they now visit regularly, are generally ignored insofar as intensive acculturation attempts are concerned. As one of the priests once mentioned, the effective incorporation and acculturation of the Yąnomamö is still a generation off—the children are the key. Thus, the adults are relatively free to do what they

---

[5] Kạobawä and his people began clearing a new garden near their old site at Barawä in 1974 and were living there in 1975/1976 when I last visited them. Whether this will be a permanent move away from the mission posts at the mouth of the Mavaca River remains to be seen. In any event, he expressed great discontent about the location of his village near the mission posts, and the move was made in order to minimize the influence that the growing community of foreigners (non-Yąnomamö) exercised over daily life in his village.

please, but encouraged to adopt some of the mechanical habits of Westerners, such as the use of clothing to cover up thought-provoking sex organs and standards of personal hygiene—where, when, and how to blow one's nose and what to do with the mucus when strangers from Caracas are around—and a system of etiquette that is congenial to visitors. Yąnomamö etiquette, I should add, is rather sophisticated in many respects and quite down to earth—and somewhat difficult to modify. A visitor to one mission awoke early one morning, stepped out of the house and ran into a Yąnomamö gentleman who was headed off to the jungle with his bow and arrows. The Western visitor was favorably impressed with the Yąnomamö man's decorum and politeness, for as the man passed by, he smiled at the visitor and said cheerfully: "Ya shii!" The visitor, reciprocally, returned the greeting, whereupon the Yąnomamö again smiled and said: "Habo. Ya baröwo." When he reported his exchange of social amenities to the missionary, he was a bit distraught at the translation: "I'm on my way to defecate," Response: "I have to defecate (also)." Reply: "Come along, then; I'll lead the way."

Mission posts are, for both Catholic and Protestant missionaries alike, something of showpieces of what their efforts have yielded in civilizing the Indians. Clothing becomes an important concern, for missionaries are unhappy about obvious proclamations that nakedness reveals regarding the extent to which the Indians have not assumed a changed attitude about Western cultural amenities. Among the Yąnomamö, clothing serves two different functions. First, it serves a very important protective function—it effectively prevents the Yąnomamö from being pestered constantly by the biting gnats and mosquitoes, both of which are very noisome at certain times of the year along the major rivers. One must remember that the Yąnomamö traditionally avoid larger rivers and have only moved to them in the very recent past because of the allure of exotic trade goods, such as steel tools, fishhooks, fishline, matches, aluminum cooking pots, and other desirable items. No Yąnomamö would tolerate the discomfort of living near the bug-infested rivers unless there were powerful incentives, such as trade goods, to attract them there. The second function of clothing at the mission posts is essentially ideological from the missionaries' viewpoint: nakedness is assumed to be objectionable to Westerners. A sign of progress in the missions is the degree to which the "naked savages" visibly show their enlightenment by covering their private, and essentially sinful, parts. The Yąnomamö probably didn't realize that the naked body gives people sexy thoughts and evil ideas until Christianity covered it up on the argument that the nude body was sexy and thought-provoking. It conveniently crippled the patient and then provided the crutch. But nakedness to the Yąnomamö is a natural condition and many of the older people gladly accept the clothing given by the missionaries for the protective function it serves, but fail to see the "moral" dimension of the institution. I was amused one day as I passed through a mission village and stopped off to greet the priest and the nuns who lived there. As we were chatting, a Yąnomamö man and his wife strolled from the garden after their afternoon's work, he in a floppy hat and oversized khaki shirt and pants, she in her gingham smock. They came over to say hello, but their presence embarassed the priest and nuns—he had cut the crotch out of his trousers because he apparently found the zipper cumbersome, and she had cut the bosom out of her smock so she could nurse her baby more conveniently. They stood there, grinning innocently and chatting happily—only their faces, their feet, and most of their sex organs visible. The baggy clothing seemed like a large frame around that which was not covered and to which the eye should be naturally attracted.

The younger people, especially young men, eagerly seek loincloths and rapidly acquire an attitude that a piece of cloth over the genitals is prestigious. More valuable than loincloths are bathing trunks or old underwear. These items are used as decorations at first, but later become almost "necessities," and any young man without either considers himself unfortunate and, the more accustomed he has become to them, embarrassed. I recall with some astonishment making first contact with the village of Mishimishimaböwei-teri (described in Chapter 1 of Chagnon 1974) and finding a young man in the village wearing a tattered pair of jockey undershorts! The villagers had never seen a non-Yąnomamö before my visit, but a pair of undies had managed to make it into the village via the trading network that also brought the broken and battered steel tools they acquired.

This is not to say that the Yąnomamö have no beliefs of their own about propriety and decorum insofar as genitalia are concerned. Indeed, once you understand their standards, it is quite clear that an untied penis is an outrage to society at large, and if a man's string accidentally becomes "undone" in public, he hastily ceases what he is doing—even if he is in a chest-pounding duel (see the scene in *Yąnomamö: A Multidisciplinary Study*, Neel, Asch, and Chagnon 1971)—and ties his penis back up. A young girl, on the other hand, is very careful to cross her legs when squatting or getting up so as to minimize the chances of men seeing her vagina. This sense of propriety about exposure, genitalia, and sex is immortalized in one of their quite hilarious myths about the adventures of the Twin Heroes: Omawä shows his brother Yoasiwä how to copulate properly and silently without making the foul, repulsive "Soka! Soka! Soka!" noise as the penis rhythmically enters the vagina and is withdrawn before the next thrust (Chagnon, in preparation). The quickest way to break up any Yąnomamö village with side-splitting laughter is to ask them if anyone makes the "Soka! Soka! Soka!" noise. The association of clothing with propriety and nakedness with "sexy ideas," however, is new and foreign to them. Rerebawä and Kąobawä, for example, even urge me to bring them nylon bathing trunks each year now, and both consider themselves somewhat undressed without them.

Balancing the Image of Fierceness

The Yąnomamö, largely through the extensive circulation of the first edition of this book and a number of other publications by me, have become established in the anthropological literature as the prime example of a warlike, aggressive people. I would like to end this chapter with a few comments on their warfare and, hopefully, to correct some misunderstandings and false impressions that have crept into some of the literature that contains summaries of their culture based, allegedly, on my descriptions of it.

First of all, the Yąnomamö do not spend all or even a major fraction of their waking hours making war on neighbors or abusing their wives. Second, warfare among the Yąnomamö varies from region to region and from time to time: it is extremely intense in some areas at particular times, and almost nonexistent in other areas. Even the most "warlike" villages have long periods of relative peace during which time daily life is tranquil and happy, especially when a large group can fission into smaller, more cohesive villages within which the obligations and strictures of kinship and marriage are able to organize and guide the workaday activities of tribal life. On the other hand, even the least warlike villages suddenly find themselves embroiled in an active war, or the peace of the temporarily tranquil is shattered by an unexpected raid. Third, the Yąnomamö, as a tribe, are *not* aberrant or unusual in having sovereignty and the warfare that sovereignty implies or entails. What is unusual about the Yąnomamö is the fact that they have managed to survive into the twentieth century in relative isolation and independence. If the world's tribal cultures had been described before the destructive forces of colonialism had all but eradicated them, we would have a much more realistic picture of the extent to which warfare operated in such cultures and the Yąnomamö would appear as relatively normal tribesmen. Finally, it is not true, as a few of my colleagues believe, that the Yąnomamö were described at a particularly "turbulent" period of their history . . . as if to say that had I visited them 15 years earlier or later they would have been just the average peaceful tribe, the likes of which have populated our textbooks for decades. Warfare among the Yąnomamö—or any sovereign tribal people—is an expectable form of political behavior and no more requires special explanations than do religion or economy. The quality of life that I witnessed when I lived among the Yąnomamö is not something that is readily found in our anthropological textbooks or journal articles. Yet it is a quality that should be documented and understood, for it can help us understand a large fraction of our own history and behavior. I decided, when I first went to live among the Yąnomamö in 1964, that their warfare was the most important single topic that demanded ethnological attention, for primitive warfare was a topic that had received very little attention from the profession, largely because the emergence of a mature anthropological discipline came long after most tribesmen had been pacified. The important fact is that very few anthropologists have had the opportunity to live with and study native peoples while warfare was a significant fact of life among them.

A meaningful description of Yąnomamö, or any other, warfare necessarily requires the presentation of facts and information that many of us would prefer not to consider. Infanticide, personal ferocity, clubfights, and raids are all part of the phenomenon and have to be described and explained, no matter how unpleasant they might appear to us. Viewed, however, against the violence and militancy found in other cultures—including, or perhaps *especially,* our own, the Yąnomamö, to paraphrase Mark Twain, stand rather closer to the Angels than to the Devil. I have attempted, largely through the numerous ethnographic films I have made with my filmmaking colleague, Timothy Asch, to balance the "hyper-fierce" image that is emerging as the exclusive characteristic of the Yąnomamö.[6] Now that my period of active field research among the Yąnomamö is drawing to an end, I will have greater opportunity to write more complete descriptions of their culture and bring out more indelibly the amiable dimensions of that culture. However, there is enough of an overall context in the first edition of *The Fierce People* so that most of its readers have escaped with the correct impression that the Yąnomamö, as both individuals and as a population, exhibit a range of behavior that is found in other human societies, including humor, wit, happiness, and satisfaction with the good life.

The Yąnomamö are now threatened as a culture and as a population. I fervently hope

---

[6]The large number of films presently available for purchase or rental are listed in a separate bibliography at the end of the book, along with information describing how to order the films.

that those who assume the responsibility for assimilating them into national culture treat them with the dignity they deserve and fully understand and appreciate what it is they are changing and the comparative value of what they provide in return. I also hope that my Brazilian and Venezuelan colleagues understand that there are still some very noble people in the remaining isolated and uncontacted Yąnomamö villages who are able to, as Dedeheiwä once proudly told me, teach foreigners something about being human. They are, as one of my anthropology teachers aptly phrased it, our contemporary ancestors.

Glossary

AFFINES: Relatives by marriage. These can also include blood relatives when, for example, a man marries his mother's brother's daughter. The word "cognate" is used to describe those blood relatives who are related by marriage. Cognates also include kinsmen who have a common ancestor.

AGNATES: Persons who trace their relationships to each other through males. This is distinct from cognatic kinship, where the relationship may be traced through either males or females.

BANANA, WILD: A distant relative to the common banana, but producing a fruit pod that is very different from the banana. The pod contains seeds that taste like maize. It is the only American member of the Musaceae family. Plantains and bananas now cultivated by the Yąnomamö were probably introduced to the Americas after Columbus.

BIFURCATING MERGING: A term used to describe the widespread type of kinship system in which an individual's paternal relatives are distinguished (bifurcated) from maternal relatives in the terminology. Furthermore, a single term is used in reference to, for example, father and father's brother; that is, they are merged terminologically into the same kinship category. The Yąnomamö have the most commonly found variant of this type, the Iroquois system. *See* Iroquois kinship terms.

BILATERAL CROSS-COUSINS: In practical terms, an individual's mother's brother's children *together with* his father's sister's children. Unilateral cross-cousins are mother's brother's children *or* father's sister's children, but not both. These two terms are frequently ued in discussions of types of marriage rules found in primitive societies. Mother's brother's daughter is a *uni*lateral cross-cousin; properly speaking, she is a *matri*lateral cross-cousin. In Yąnomamö (Iroquois) kinship this person is simultaneously father's sister's daughter. Some societies have rules forbidding marriage with the latter type of cousin, that is, they have a *uni*lateral cross-cousin marriage rule. *See* Cross-cousins.

COGNATES: Individuals who are related to each other through either males or females. *See* Affines, Agnates.

CORPORATION: A group of people sharing some estate, having definite rights with respect to each other and to the estate, and able to demonstrate their membership to that group by citing a recognized rule concerning recruitment.

CROSS-COUSINS: The children of a man and his sister are cross-cousins to each other. The children of a man and his brother are *parallel* cousins to each other. Similarly, the children of a woman and her sister are parallel cousins.

DEMOGRAPHY: The study of populations with the intention of gathering certain kinds of vital statistics, such as birth rate, death rate, and family size.

DEMONSTRATED KINSHIP: Tracing relationships to kinsmen by citing the putative biological links. *See* Lineage.

IROQUOIS KINSHIP TERMS: Classifying both kinds of cross-cousins (matrilateral and patrilateral) into the same kinship category and distinguishing them from brothers and sisters and parallel cousins. In most Iroquois systems the parallel cousins are called by the same terms that are used for brothers and sisters.

LEVIRATE: A rule enjoining a man to marry the widow of his dead brother.

LINEAGE: A kinship group comprised of people who trace relationships to each other through either males or females, but not both. If the relationship is traced through males, as among the Yąnomamö, the group so defined is a *patri*lineage. The distinctive feature of the lineage is that the relationships are demonstrated by citing genealogical links. In a clan, relationships are merely *stipulated* by citing the fact that the two individuals in question belong to the same named kinship group. In short, a clan is a *named lineage* the members of which do not remember or do not care how they are related to each other biologically. *See* Demonstrated kinship.

LOCAL DESCENT GROUP: Among the Yąnomamö, a group of people who are related to each other patrilineally, who live in the same village, and one of whose major functions is to arrange marriages for the younger members of the group. It is usually the older males of the group who arrange the marriages.

MACHETE: A broad-bladed, long knife commonly used throughout South America for cutting brush. The closest English equivalent is the cutlass.

MATRILATERAL: Tracing relationships on the mother's side.

PARALLEL COUSINS: Cousins who are decended from two brothers or from two sisters.

PATRILATERAL: Tracing relationships on the father's side.

PLANTAIN: A member of the banana family. The fruit looks like the common banana, but is considerably larger. When ripe, the fruit resembles the common banana in taste, but differs in that its texture is crude and stringy. Plantains are usually eaten cooked. Green plantains resemble raw potatoes in taste, even after cooking. Plantains appear to have been introduced to the Americas after the arrival of Europeans, but they spread with such rapidity that many early travelers described them as being native crops. (*See* References, Reynolds, 1927.)

SIBLINGS: One's brothers and sisters.

SORORAL POLYGYNY: A type of marriage in which a man marries two or more women who are related to each other as sisters.

TEKNONYMY: The practice of addressing an individual by the name of one of his children rather than by his own personal name. A kinship term is used in combination with the child's name, such as *father* of so-and-so.

References Cited and Additional Readings

ARENDS, TULIO, *et al.*, 1967, "Intratribal Genetic Differentiation among the Yanomama Indians of Southern Venezuela," *Proceedings of the National Academy of Science,* 57:1252–1259.

ASCH, TIMOTHY, and NAPOLEON A. CHAGNON, 1970, *The Feast* (16mm film). National Audiovisual Center, Washington, D.C.

————, 1974, *New Tribes Mission* (16mm film). Documentary Educational Resources, Somerville, Mass.

BARANDIARAN, DE, DANIEL, 1966. "La fiesta del Pijiguao entre los Indios Waikas," *El Farol,* 219:8–15.

BECHER, HANS, 1960, *Die Surára und Pakidái: Zwei Yanonámi-Stämme in Nordwest-Brasilien,* Vol. 26, Hamburg: Mitteilungen aus dem Museum für Völkerkunde.

BIOCCA, ETTORE, 1970, *Yanomama: The Narrative of a White Girl Kidnapped by Amazonian Indians.* New York: E. P. Dutton & Co. (available in paperback).

BOHANNAN, LAURA, 1964, *Return to Laughter.* New York: Doubleday & Company, Inc.

CHAGNON, NAPOLEON A., 1966, *Yąnomamö Warfare, Social Organization and Marriage Alliances,* doctoral dissertation, University of Michigan.

————, 1967, "Yąnomamö—The Fierce People," *Natural History,* 76:22–31.

————, 1968a, "The Feast," *Natural History,* 76:34–41.

————, 1968b, "Yąnomamö Social Organization and Warfare." In *War, the Anthropology of Armed Conflict and Aggression,* ed. by Morton Fried, Marvin Harris, and Robert Murphy. Garden City, N.Y.: Natural History Press, pp. 109–159.

————, 1968c, "The Culture-Ecology of Shifting (Pioneering) Cultivation Among the Yąnomamö Indians," *Proceedings VIII International Congress of Anthropological and Ethnological Sciences,* Tokyo. 3:249–255.

————, 1970, Review: Yanomama, by Ettore Biocca. *Washington Post, Book World,* IV; no. 6.

————, 1972, "Social Causes for Population Fissioning: Tribal Social Organization and Genetic Microdifferentiation." In *The Structure of Human Populations,* ed. by G. A. Harrison and A. J. Boyce. Oxford: Clarendon Press, pp. 252–282.

————, 1973a, "Yąnomamö. In *Primitive Worlds.* Washington, D.C.: National Geographic Society Special Publication Series, pp. 141–183.

————, 1973b, *Magical Death* (16mm film). Pennsylvania State University, Psychological Cinema Register, University Park, Pa.

————, 1974, *Studying the Yąnomamö.* New York: Holt, Rinehart and Winston (Studies In Anthropological Method Series).

————, 1975, Response to Marvin Harris "Protein Theory of Warfare," *Psychology Today,* 8(12):6–7.

————, 1976a, "Genealogy, Solidarity, and Relatedness: Limits to Local Group Size and Patterns of Fissioning in an Expanding Population" *Yearbook of Physical Anthropology,* 1975, 19:95–110. American Association of Physical Anthropologists. Washington, D.C.

————, 1976b, "Fission in an Amazonian Tribe," *Sciences,* 16(1):14–18.

————, 1976c, "Yanomamö: The True People," *National Geographic Magazine,* 149(8):211–223.

————, (in preparation) *Yąnomamö Myths.*

————, and Timothy Asch, 1974, *Ocamo Is my Town* (16mm Film) Documentary Educational Resources, Somerville, Mass.

————, P. LEQUESNE, and J. COOK, 1970, "Algunos Aspectos de Uso de Drogas, Comercio y Domesticacion de Plantas entre los Indigenas Yąnomamö de Venezuela y Brasil," *Acta Científica Venezolano,* 21:186–193.

————, ————, and ————, 1971, "Yąnomamö Hallucinogens: Anthropological, Botanical, and Chemical Findings," *Current Anthropology,* 12:72–74.

————, J. V., NEEL, L. R. WEITKAMP, H. GERSHOWITZ, and M. AYRES, 1970, "The Influence of Cultural Factors on the Demography and Pattern of Gene Flow from the Makiritare to the Yąnomamö Indians," *American Journal Physical Anthropology,* 32:339–349.

COCCO, LUIS, 1972, *Iyëwei-teri: Quince anos entre los Yanomamos.* Caracas: Libreria Editorial Salesiana.

COULT, ALLAN D., and A. E. HAMMEL, 1963, "A Corrected Model for Patrilateral Cross-cousin Marriage," *Southwestern Journal of Anthropology,* 19:287–296.

FORTES, MEYER, 1959, "Descent, Filiation and Affinity: A Rejoinder to Dr. Leach," *Man,* 59(309):193–197 and (331):206–212.·

FRIED, MORTON, 1957, "The Classification of Corporate Unilineal Descent Groups," *Journal of the Royal Anthropological Institute of Great Britain and Ireland,* 87:1–29.

GARCILASO DE LA VEGA, 1966, *Royal Commentaries of the Inca, Part One.* Austin: University of Texas Press. (Originally published in 1609 and 1616/7).

GERSHOWITZ, H., M. LAYRISSE, Z. LAYRISSE, J. V. NEEL, C. BREWER, N. CHAGNON, and M. AYRES, 1970, "Gene Frequencies and Microdifferentiation Among the Makiritare Indians. I. Eleven Blood Group Systems and the ABH-Le Secretor Traits: A Note on Rh Gene Frequency Determinations." *American Journal Human Genetics,* 22:515–525.

HARRIS, MARVIN, 1974, *Cows, Pigs, Wars and Witches.* New York: Random House, Inc.

LEACH, EDMUND R., 1961, "The Structural Implications of Matrilateral Cross-cousin Marriage," reprinted in *Rethinking Anthropology.* London: The Athlone Press.

————, 1957, "Aspects of Bridewealth and Marriage Stability among the Kachin and Lakher," *Man,* 57(59):50–55.

————, 1965, Letter, *Man,* 65(12):25.

LÉVI-STRAUSS, CLAUDE, 1963, *Structural Anthropology.* New York: Basic Books, Inc.

LIZOT, JACQUES, 1971a, "Aspects économiques et sociaux du changement culturel chez les Yanomami," *L'Homme,* 11(1):32–51.

————, 1971b, "Remarques sur le vocabulaire de parenté Yanomami," *L'Homme,* 11(2):25–38.

————, 1971c, "Société ou économie? Quelques thèmes à propos d'une communauté d'Amérindiens," *Journal de la Société des Américanistes,* 60:136–175.

————, 1975, *El Hombre de la Pantorrilla Preñada.* Monografia no. 21. Caracas: Fundacion la Salle de Ciencias Naturales.

————, 1976, *Le Cercle de Feux.* Paris: Editions du Seuil.

MALINOWSKI, BRONISLAW, 1922, *Argonauts of the Western Pacific.* London: Routledge & Kegan Paul, Ltd.

————, 1926, *Crime and Custom in Savage Society.* London: Routledge & Kegan Paul, Ltd.

————, 1967, *A Dairy in the Strict Sense of the Term.* New York: Harcourt Brace Jovanovich, Inc.

MAUSS, MARCEL, 1954, *The Gift.* New York: The Free Press.

MAYBURY-LEWIS, DAVID, 1960, "The Analysis of Dual Organizations: A Methodological Critique," *Bijdragen tot de Taal-, Land- en Volkenkunde,* 116:17–44.

————, 1965a, "Prescriptive Marriage Systems," *Southwestern Journal of Anthropology,* 21:207–230.

————, 1965b, *The Savage and the Innocent.* London: Evans Bros.

————, 1967, *Akwë-Shavante Society.* Oxford: Clarendon Press.

MEGGITT, MERVYN J., 1962, *Desert People: A Study of the Walbiri Aborigines of Central Australia.* Sydney: Angus and Robertson.

MURDOCK, GEORGE P., 1949, *Social Structure.* New York: The Macmillan Company.

NEEDHAM, RODNEY, 1962a, *Structure and Sentiment.* Chicago: University of Chicago Press.

————, 1962b, "Genealogy and Category in Wikmunkan Society," *Ethnology,* 1:223–264.

————, 1963, "Some Disputed Points in the Study of Prescriptive Alliance," *Southwestern Journal of Anthropology,* 19:186–207.

NEEL, JAMES V., 1970, "Lessons from a 'Primitive' People," *Science,* 170:815–822.

————, W. R. CENTERWALL, N. A., CHAGNON, and H. L. CASEY, 1970. "Notes on the Effect of Measles and Measles Vaccine in a Virgin-Soil Population of South American Indians," *American Journal Epidemiology,* 91:418–429.

————, and NAPOLEON A. CHAGNON, 1968, "The Demography of Two Tribes of Primitive, Relatively Unacculturated American Indians," *Proceedings of the National Academy of Science,* 59:680–689.

————, T. ARENDS, C. BREWER, N. CHAGNON, H. GERSHOWITZ, M. LAYRISSE, Z. LAYRISSE, J. MACCLUER, E. MIGIAZZA, W. OLIVER, F. SALZANO, R. SPIELMAN, R. WARD, and L. WEITKAMP, 1972, "Studies on the Yanomama Indians." *Proceedings of the 4th International Congress of Human Genetics,* Paris, 1971, pp. 96–111.

————, TIMOTHY ASCH, and NAPOLEON A. CHAGNON, 1971; *Yanomamo: A Multidisciplinary Study.* (16mm film). National Audiovisual Center, Washington, D.C.

NIMUENDAJÚ, CURT, and ROBERT LOWIE, 1927, "The Dual Organization of the Ramko' kamekra (Canella) of Southern Brazil," *American Anthropologist,* 39:565–582.

OLIVER, DOUGLAS, 1955, *A Solomon Island Society.* Cambridge, Mass.: Harvard University Press.

RADCLIFFE-BROWN, A. R., 1965, "Patrilineal and Matrilineal Succession," reprinted in *Structure and Function in Primitive Society.* New York: The Free Press.

RAMOS, ALCIDA, 1974, "How the Sanuma Acquire their Names," *Ethnology,* 13(2):171–185.

REYNOLDS, PHILIP KEEP, 1927, *The Banana: Its History, Cultivation and Place among Staple Foods.* Boston: Houghton Mifflin Company.

TAYLOR, KENNETH, 1974, *Sanuma Fauna: Prohibitions and Classifications.* Monografia No. 18, Caracas: Fundacion La Salle de Ciencias Naturales.

TURNBULL, COLIN M., 1966, "Report from Africa: A People Apart," *Natural History,* 75:8–14.

ZERRIES, OTTO, 1955, "Das Lashafest der Waika-Indianer," *Die Umschau in Wissenshaft und Technik,* 55:662–665.

————, 1964, *Waika: Die Kulturgeschichtliche Stellung der Waika-Indianer des Oberen Orinoco im Rahmen der Völkerkunde Südamerikas.* Munich: Klaus Renner Verlag.

Ethnographic Films
on the Yąnomamö

During the several years of my field research among the Yąnomamö I filmed selected activities that, I felt, could not be adequately documented by the more traditional means of note-taking and written descriptions. It became apparent that a more thorough filming effort would be necessary to document Yąnomamö culture and behavior than what I could accomplish by myself. Thus in 1968 I invited an anthropological filmmaker, Timothy Asch, to join me in the field and participate in this aspect of my field research. The collaborative effort during that season resulted in two films: *The Feast* and *Yanomama: A Multidisciplinary Study,* the latter film incorporating some of the footage that I had taken in previous years. In 1971 Asch and I received a grant from the National Science Foundation to extend our film study. A sound man, Craig Johnson, joined us in the project. We shot approximately 80,000 feet of synchronous-sound film in 1971 in the village of Mishimishimaböwei-teri, a remote Shamatari village that had become the focus of my more recent field investigations (see Chagnon 1974). We have thus far completed approximately 20 documentary films out of that material. They are listed below. In addition, we are planning to produce a number of new films at Documentary Educational Resources (D.E.R.) out of the materials that remain, films that will cover a range of topics that varies from mythology to ecology. We anticipate that the new films will be distributed through D.E.R., along with a comparable series of films on the Bushmen of the Kalahari Desert in southern Africa. In this connection many of the sequences Asch and I filmed during our 1971 work were planned in such a way as to complement the large body of Bushmen footage taken by John Marshall during his intensive film study of the Bushmen. While the Yąnomamö and Bushmen are very different kinds of people, they share many common problems and experiences. A number of John Marshall's newer Bushmen films provide excellent comparative ethnographic material when shown in conjunction with Yąnomamö films. Current catalogs of Yąnomamö, Bushmen, and other ethnographic films can be obtained directly from D.E.R. In addition to D.E.R., the Psychological Cinema Register (P.C.R.) of the Pennsylvania State University distributes most of the Yąnomamö films thus far completed. Catalogs of their listings can be obtained by writing to P.C.R. The addresses and telephone numbers of both distributors are:

(1) Documentary Educational Resources
    24 Dane St.
    Somerville, Mass. 02143
    Telephone: [617] 666–1750

(2) Psychological Cinema Register
    Audio-Visual Services
    17 Willard Building
    The Pennsylvania State University
    University Park, Pa. 16802
    Telephone: [814] 865–6315

All films are 16mm, in color and with optical sound track.

The Feast,[1] 1970, 29 min. This film focuses on the alliance practices of the Yąnomamö and documents the emergence of a specific alliance during the context of a feast held in the village of Patanowä-teri in 1968.

Yanomama: A Multidisciplinary Study,[1] 1971, 43 min. This film describes the nature of multidisciplinary field research by a team of human biologists, geneticists, serologists, dentists, and
anthropologists. It includes an ethnographic vignette of Yąnomamö culture and is very useful
in showing how many scientific disciplines can collaborate in the study of human populations
and culture.

Magical Death, 1973, 28 min. This film depicts the interrelationship of religion, politics, and the use
of hallucinogenic snuff in shamanism. It focuses on a specific two-day incident in the village of
Mishimishimaböwei-teri during which all the prominent shamans of the group collectively
demonstrated their good will toward visitors from Bisaasi-teri by practicing harmful magic
against enemies of the latter.

A Man Called Bee: Studying the Yąnomamö, 1974, 40 min. This film illustrates the methods of field
research used by Chagnon during 48 months of fieldwork among the Yąnomamö, emphasizing
investigations of genealogy, settlement pattern, politics, demography and mythology.

Ocamo Is My Town, 1974, 23 min. This film describes the attitudes, accomplishments and objectives of
a Salesian missionary who has spent fourteen years in a Yąnomamö village. Skeptical about the
possibility of immediate success in Christianizing the Yąnomamö, the priest emphasizes the
importance of his attempts to introduce practical measures that will help soften the impact of
civilization when it eventually comes to this village.

Arrow Game, 1974, 7 min. This film depicts Yąnomamö boys learning to shoot accurately under
duress and to dodge arrows shot in return. Man-sized arrows with the points removed are used
in this somewhat hazardous game, which terminates when one of the boys is hit in the face with
an arrow—damaging his ego more than his face.

Weeding the Garden, 1974, 14 min. Even the most prestigious members of the village must engage in
all the economic activities. Dedeheiwä, the most respected shaman in the village, weeds his
garden, interrupted periodically by his wife and children, who tenderly groom him while he
rests.

A Father Washes His Children, 1974, 13 min. Dedeheiwä, respected shaman and political leader, takes
his younger children to the river and bathes them. His wife remains in the village and recovers
from a minor sickness.

Firewood, 1974, 10 min. Yąnomamö women spend several hours each day collecting firewood and
maintaining the family fire. The irksomeness of chopping and carrying firewood is shown as a
woman strenuously brings home the daily kindling. Her older son quietly babysits for his infant
brother while the mother works.

A Man and His Wife Make a Hammock, 1974, 9 min. Yąnomamö hammocks are manufactured on a
pole frame consisting of two upright poles between which the spun cotton threads are plaited.
A strong headman, Möawä, quietly works on the hammock while one of his wives and infant
daughter rest in their hammock and quietly chat with him.

Children's Magical Death, 1974, 8 min. A group of young boys between the ages of 4 and 10 years
imitate the shamans as they blow wood ashes into each other's nostrils through hollow reeds.
Their amusing pantomime clearly reveals how socialized they have become by observing the
elders. This film should be used in conjunction with *Magical Death.*

Climbing the Peach Palm, 1974, 9 min. Fruits from the cultivated peach palm tree can only be
harvested by climbing the spiny trunk. The Yąnomamö have invented an ingeneous device—a
climbing frame—for this purpose. Young men carefully ascend the thorny tree with this
vine-and-pole frame, lowering the bunches of fruit with long vines.

New Tribes Mission, 1974, 12 min. Dedicated members of the New Tribes Mission, an Evangelical
Protestant missionary group, explain their reasons for attempting to bring Christianity to the
Yąnomamö and why the Yąnomamö must stop worshipping their "false demons."

The Ax Fight, 1975, 30 min. A fight erupts in Mishimishimaböwei-teri, involving clubs, machetes,
and axes. The structure of kinship and marriage ties is revealed by the participants as they take
particular sides in the fighting. Slow-motion replay and freeze-frame editing make this film
useful as a methodological tool in both ethnographic and ethno-cinematographic studies.

---

[1] Available for rental only through D.E.R. and P.C.R. Sale distribution through the National Audiovisual
Center, Washington, D.C.

Tapir Distribution, 1975, 12 min. The distribution of meat, particularly large game animals, reveals within-group alliance patterns based on kinship and marriage ties. The village headman presents his kill to his brothers-in-law, who ceremoniously redistribute the meat and cooked vegetables to household heads within the village. After the ceremonial distribution the women move in to distribute the scant remains, followed by the village dogs.

Tug of War, 1975, 9 min. The more playful and amicable aspects of daily life are illustrated by this film, which portrays a group of women and children in a tug-of-war during a rainstorm.

Bride Service, 1975, 10 min. A young man returns from hunting and collecting with a large wild turkey and a heavy basket of wild fruits. Through his father, he presents the food to his father-in-law. A 10-year-old girl is sent to fetch the food. She is embarassed and self-conscious, complicating her own situation by collapsing under the weight of the load amidst the laughter of village onlookers.

The Yąnomamö Myth of Naro as Told by Kąobawä, 1975, 22 min. The intimate relationship among Man, Spirit, and Animal is revealed in the amusing and complicated myth of Opossum (Naro), who invents harmful magic to treacherously slay his brother and acquire the latter's two beautiful wives. Kąobawä's dramatic and intimate presentation of the story brings out his acting and narrative skills. English voice-over narration.

The Yąnomamö Myth of Naro as Told by Dedeheiwä, 1975, 22 min. The same myth that is described above is told by Dedeheiwä, an accomplished and reknown shaman who lives in a remote village far to the south of Kąobawä's village. This film provides an excellent contrast for students interested in comparative mythology. English voice-over narration.

Moonblood: A Yąnomamö Creation Myth as told by Dedeheiwä, 1975, 14 min. The origin of Man (Yąnomamö) is revealed in the myth of Peribo (Moon), who, in Ancestral times, descended to earth and ate the ashes of the deceased Ancestors. Moon is shot in the belly by one of the Ancestors, his blood spilling to earth and transforming into fierce people. English voice-over narration.

Jaguar: A Yąnomamö Twin-Cycle Myth, 1976, 22 Min. The Ancestor, Jaguar, nearly devours all of humanity. All that remains is Curare-Woman, who is too "bitter" to eat, and her pregnant daughter, hidden in the roof. Jaquar discovers the daughter and eats her, but Curare-Woman saves the unborn Twins, Omawä and Yoasiwä, who miraculously grow to adulthood and exact their revenge on Jaguar. English subtitles.

Index

Language, 47n; and kinship behavior, 86; pronunciation, 1n
Leach, E. R., 56, 59–61, 68n, 71, 157
Levirate, 64
Lineage, 55, 56, 65–68
Lowie, R., 57n

Magic, black, 49, 123, and children, 85–86; plants for, 37–39; white, 28, plants for, 37
Makiritare Indians, 3–4, 38n, 70n
Malinowski, B., 4n, 57n
Marriage, 54–72; actual cases, 60; arrangement of, 69; bilateral cross-cousin, 55; and demography, 74–76; discrepancies in pattern, 72–81; ideal pattern, 55; matrilateral cross-cousin, 63; patrilateral cross-cousin, 63; and politics, 76–80; prescriptive, 56–57; taboos, 57; types of, 73
Mauss, M. 102n
Maybury-Lewis, D., 4n, 57n
Missionaries, 138, 150–151; Catholic vs. Protestant, 147–149, 153–161
Mobility, 39; and gardens, 35; migration history, 43
Moiety system, 57, 58, 65–66, 71
Murdock, G. P., 55
Mythology, 45–48

Name taboo, 10, 11
Needham, R., 56, 57, 61n
Neel, J. V., 75n, 157, 185
Nimuendajú, C., 57n
Noble savage concept, 3–4
Nomohoni (treachery), 122–124
Noreshi, 48–50
Number system, 74

Omauwä, mythic figure, 46–47

Part-village, 72n
Periboriwä, mythic figure, 47–48
Personal hygiene, 6
Personality traits, 9
Physical environment, 18–39
Plantains, 33, 34–35
Polygyny, 75
Population, 1
Pottery, 20–21, 100–101
Prescriptive marriage rule, 56–57, 73
Prestige, 10
Puberty, female, 69, 85; male, 85

Quivers, arrow, 22

Radcliffe-Brown, A. R., 69
Raiding, 118, 122–124; preparation and execution, 128–132; revenge, 103
Religion, 44–53; and culture contact, 153–162
Rerebawä, 16–17; in 1976, 151; as outsider, 93; as

source for genealogies, 11–12; trip to Caracas, 140–144

Sense of humor, 11
Settlement pattern, 40–44; and alliances, 101
Sexual behavior, extramarital, 40; of shaman novice, 52; taboos concerning pregnant or nursing woman, 75
Shabono (permanent house), 25–26
Shaman, role of, 28, 45, 49, 52–53, 85
Shamatari village, 151–153
Shotguns, 122, 148–149
Sickness, 49; and culture contact, 146–147; and taboos, 133
Side slapping duel, 115, 119
Snake-bite, 20, 132–133
Social life, daily, 81–88
Social structure, 54–72; dual organization of, 57, 58, 65–66, 71
Sociopolitical environment, 39–44
Sorcery (see Magic, black)
Sororal polygyny, 63
Soul, 48–50; of child, 85–86; and sickness, 49
Spears, 120–122
Status, and activities, 92–96; and fierceness, 115
Steel tools, 33–34, 78

Technology, 20–21; hammocks, 37; specialization in, 100–101
Teknonymy, 85
Tobacco, 37, 89–90
Tourism, 147–148
Trading, 111–112; and alliances, 99–102; functional ignorance concerning, 102
Travel, 19–20
Trough, 24
Turnbull, C., 4

Village, 26, 27; fissioning, 40–44, 70–72; ideal pattern of, 34; palisade, 29; size, and alliances, 39–40; size, and marriage types, 73

Waikas, 38
Warfare, example of, 124–137; internal fighting, 40–41; levels of violence, 118–122; misunderstanding about, 162–163; tactics, 40, 41
Weaning, 74
Weapons, 21–23, 119–122
Wet season, 20, 35
Women, abduction of, 41, 123; brothers as protectors, 69, 83; and division of labor, 81–84; and duels, 119–120; origin of, 48; as political currency, 77, 98–99; as property, 69; treatment by husbands, 82–83; world view of, 83

Zerries, O., 21n, 108n